Supply Chain in the Pharmaceutical Industry

Supply Chain in the Pharmaceutical Industry

Strategic Influences and Supply Chain Responses

ROB WHEWELL

Routledge
Taylor & Francis Group

LONDON AND NEW YORK

First published in paperback 2024

First published 2010 by Gower Publishing

Published 2016 by Routledge
4 Park Square, Milton Park, Abingdon, Oxon OX14 4RN

and by Routledge
605 Third Avenue, New York, NY 10158

Routledge is an imprint of the Taylor & Francis Group, an informa business

Publisher's Note
The publisher has gone to great lengths to ensure the quality of this reprint but points out that some imperfections in the original copies may be apparent.

British Library Cataloguing in Publication Data
Whewell, Rob.
  Supply chain in the pharmaceutical industry : strategic
influences and supply chain responses.
  1. Pharmaceutical industry--Management. 2. Business
logistics.
  I. Title
  338.4'76151-dc22

Library of Congress Cataloging-in-Publication Data
Whewell, Rob.
  Supply chain in the pharmaceutical industry : strategic influences and supply chain responses / by Rob Whewell.
    p. cm.
  Includes bibliographical references and index.
  ISBN 978-0-566-08695-3 (hardcover)
  1. Pharmaceutical industry--Materials management. 2. Pharmaceutical industry--Costs. 3. Pharmaceutical industry--Customer services. 4. Business logistics. 5. Medical supplies. 6. Drugs. I. Title.
  [DNLM: 1. Economics, Pharmaceutical. 2. Technology, Pharmaceutical--economics. 3. Cost Control. QV 736 W569s 2009]
  HD9665.5.W48 2009
  615.1068'7--dc22

                                                                                2009010407

ISBN 13: 978-0-566-08695-3 (hbk)
ISBN 13: 978-1-03-283777-2 (pbk)
ISBN 13: 978-1-315-61133-4 (ebk)

DOI: 10.4324/9781315611334

Contents

List of Figures

List of Tables

1

The Role of Technology in the Supply Chain

Technological progress has been crucial to, and is the reason for, major advances in healthcare; it is often when multiple technologies are juxtaposed that the most dramatic, breakthrough results are achieved. These interactions mean that the processes through which healthcare is delivered are complex, requiring careful design and management. The shape that healthcare processes take has a crucial impact not only on the quality of the resulting service provision but also on the way in which suppliers of healthcare products will need to operate to make the most of their opportunities.

In this initial chapter we identify some of the advances in technology that have either directly or indirectly resulted in a step change in the healthcare environment, as well as the availability or the capability to provide and deliver improved services.

Historical Review

Throughout history the development and application of technology has enabled progress in healthcare provision. The major technology platforms that have advanced healthcare may be grouped under four main headings:

1. Environmental improvements.

2. Pharmaceuticals and chemicals.

3. Diagnostic technologies.

4. Medical devices.

All of these categories have been essential to the continuation of progress in healthcare provision. They are interrelated. Treatment of an infection with advanced antibiotics is likely to be fruitless if the patient returns home to living conditions that are unsanitary.

Without proper diagnostic tools, choice of appropriate therapy is an art, not a science. Improvements in the devices and techniques used to administer drugs and healthcare improvements have arguably been as important as improvements in the drugs or devices themselves. Devices such as dentures, prosthetic limbs, dialysis equipment and contact lenses have had a profound impact on the lifestyle and well-being of patients.

Environmental Improvements

Technology has enhanced healthcare by improving environmental and social conditions in such a way as to prevent disease from occurring or spreading. Civil engineering has played a much more central role in improving health than might be suspected at first sight. General housing and living conditions support and complement any treatment that patients receive in hospital or at clinics. While living in unsanitary conditions, not only is the patient likely to relapse, but also the infection is highly likely to spread. It is generally accepted that, with regret for the loss of life, the Great Fire of London in 1666 could be considered a long-term benefit from the point of view that it destroyed the slum dwellings that had formerly incubated the plague.

These, sadly, are not just historical occurrences. The biggest threat to the human population of New Orleans after the devastating floods of September 2005 caused by hurricane Katrina was infected water. Water supplies were contaminated with oil from damaged refineries, sewage from treatment plants and the rotting corpses of animals and humans floating for days in the putrid floodwaters. Similarly in Pakistan after the massive earthquake that made millions homeless later in the same year and laid waste to tens of villages and hundreds of homes, the immediate concerns for relief agencies were to deliver shelter, in the form of tents, fresh water, by way of portable desalination equipment; and chlorination materials, food supplies and basic medicines.

The following are examples of technologies that have played a key role in health improvement over the years:

• In the home, improved drainage systems and appliances such as lavatories, in particular the U-bend trap, have allowed much higher levels of hygiene to be attained with relatively little effort. In the clinical setting sophisticated air conditioning and the emergence of High Efficiency Particulate Air Filters (HEPA) allow medical procedures to take place in a sterile environment. In this context we should note, however, that technology is not sufficient on its own; it must be used in the context of appropriate processes.

• The prevalence of methicillin-resistant *Staphylococcus aureus* (MRSA) in hospitals shows that even in environments equipped with the latest technologies, infection can spread if basic cleanliness is not maintained. Education in basic hygiene is considered to be the main variable parameter here. Washing hands properly with soap (for example after using the toilet), washing or disposing of contaminated clothing or bedding, and sterilising equipment prior to use are all basic and essential factors. The World Health Organization (WHO) believes that growing levels of drug resistance threaten to erode medical advances of recent decades. In the USA, nosocomial MRSA infection rates have nearly doubled to over 60 per cent since around 2000. Unless antibiotic resistance problems are detected as they emerge, and actions are taken to contain them, the world could be faced with previously treatable diseases becoming untreatable. According to the United States Food and Drug Administration (FDA) 'about 70 percent of bacteria that cause infections in hospitals are resistant to at least one of the drugs most commonly used to treat infections'.

• The engineering of the water supply has been critical to reducing infection. In the nineteenth century, cholera outbreaks were common in cities such as London until it was realised that they were triggered by contamination of the water supply with sewage. The technology that was needed to prevent this contamination was relatively straightforward once the cause was understood. The development of the flush toilet and of sewage systems played a large part (see Panel 1 and Figure 1.1).

PANEL 1: THE DEVELOPMENT OF THE FLUSH TOILET IN BRITAIN

It seems to be a myth that credits Thomas Crapper with the invention of the modern toilet, although an entrepreneurial plumber of that name did play a part in commercialising one nineteenth-century predecessor of the technology we know today, incorporating a siphon-based flushing mechanism.

The remains of several ancient civilisations, including Minoan, Roman and Indus, show evidence of flushing toilets. The technology was, however, lost (at least in the west) and for centuries prior to the rediscovery of the flush toilet the prevailing methods of waste disposal were chamber pots emptied into cesspits, earth closets or 'water closets' containing a seat over a cesspit.

All these methods required manual intervention to remove the accumulated waste and therefore posed a health hazard to residents if not frequently cleared, and regularly to those who had to clear it! Care would also be required to ensure that upon removal it did not contaminate the local drinking-water supply. Only when the waste could be emptied into a sewer were these problems significantly reduced. Until the nineteenth century, gutters and rivers tended to serve as sewers – hardly an improvement on the cesspit system from the health point of view. Even where there was a cesspit, in early nineteenth-century England it could have been shared by dozens of people and would have frequently overflowed into the surrounding streets. During the cholera epidemics that were common in London at that time, sewage tended to pile up in the streets. This created a vicious circle of infection.

By the eighteenth century more hygienic alternatives had started to appear, though they were not in widespread use. Earlier, Queen Elizabeth I's godson, Sir John Harington, is credited with inventing a predecessor of today's flush toilet with a valve and a manually initiated water flow. Alexander Cummings devised a valve-based flushing mechanism called the S-trap, which used water in the bend to prevent the return of air from the sewer. Contemporaneously Samuel Prosser took out patents for a 'plunger closet'. This plunger had two actions: it got rid of waste and also sealed the outflow. Joseph Bramah patented a 'crank valve', another method of sealing the base of the toilet, and also a valve-based flushing mechanism.

One problem that took some time to solve was the need to produce enough water pressure and flow to clean the bowl. This was not easy to solve with valves alone. In the early nineteenth century a solution emerged based on a cistern placed above the bowl together with a siphon that delivered the full contents of the cistern in a single, forceful flow. In 1819 Albert Giblin patented such a siphon-based mechanism and it was this technology that in the 1880s found its way into Thomas Crapper's products, some of which were adopted in Queen Victoria's homes.

Another breakthrough came with Thomas Twyford, a ceramics expert who in 1885 constructed a one-piece, trapless toilet made of china, using a flushing mechanism designed by J.G. Jennings. It was this invention that made the technology more generally affordable. Public health was revolutionised by the combination of flushing toilets and the development of efficient sewage systems in major UK towns, starting with that engineered in London by Joseph Bazalgette in the mid-nineteenth century.

A flurry of activity in the second half of the nineteenth century led to the emergence of toilets similar to those in use today. Later improvements to the siphon mechanism allowed the cistern to be placed just above the bowl instead of several feet up the wall. More recent research in this area has focused on the development of motorised toilets to reduce the amount of water used, or to facilitate the disposal problem by liquefying waste matter.

These developments in Britain were paralleled in the US, although the solution to the flushing problem that emerged in North America was a different one, based on 'flapper valves'. While flush toilets and sewage systems are now the rule in industrialised countries, they are still far from ubiquitous in the developing world.

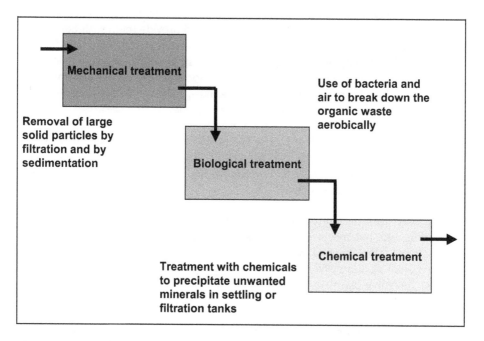

Figure 1.1   Diagrammatic illustration of the sewage treatment process

- The treatment of natural water supplies from rivers and lakes is also crucial to the delivery of a safe, clean, domestic water supply. Water treatment plants make it possible to do more than simply purify the water. For example, after it was identified that people in areas with high natural levels of fluoride in the water supply had fewer dental problems, adding fluoride to the water supply in other areas seemed like a natural consequence. Fluoridation does, however, have its opponents, with some people seeing it as an invasion of their rights and as mass medication without consent.

In addition to technological initiatives targeting specific aspects of health there have also been broader schemes to improve the overall living environment of given groups of people. One example is the model village movement (see Panel 2). Municipal slum clearance projects, for example in Glasgow or the East End of London, can be viewed as attempts to achieve artificially – and in a much more caring and managed way – a similar effect to that of the Great Fire of London outlined previously.

PANEL 2: MODEL VILLAGES

In the nineteenth century the UK saw a range of philanthropic projects that aimed to take workers out of unsatisfactory housing and provide them with healthier accommodation in planned housing developments known as 'model villages'. These were carefully laid out in locations where the air and water were believed to be healthy, though usually conveniently located for the philanthropists' factories. The villages usually included amenities such as laundries and leisure facilities. The consumption of alcohol was sometimes discouraged.

An early example was Saltaire, built by Titus Salt, a Yorkshire textile magnate. Better known perhaps are the villages created by the Quaker chocolate manufacturers Joseph Rowntree and George Cadbury: New Earswick near York and Bournville near Birmingham.

How successful these initiatives were in promoting physical health is not well documented, but recent evidence suggests that well-designed model villages may improve psychosocial well-being. Recent research by the Joseph Rowntree Foundation at Bournville suggested that it is still regarded as one of the UK's most agreeable places to live. An unusually mixed demography, as well as the physical characteristics of the spot, appears to create social cohesion.

Source: 'Neighbourhoods that work – findings' <www.jrf.org.uk/sites/files/jrf/733.pdf>.

Pharmaceuticals and Chemicals

The most obvious area in which technology has enhanced healthcare provision is through the development of pharmaceuticals, vaccines, bio-pharmaceuticals and chemicals to treat and prevent disease. This technology, coupled with the environmental improvements discussed in the next section, has allowed us to develop effective responses to infections against which we were hitherto powerless.

- One of the earliest breakthroughs was the emergence of antisepsis, and vaccines also appeared relatively early on the scene (see Panels 3 and 4).

PANEL 3: LISTER AND ANTISEPSIS

Joseph Lister (1827–1912) was a British doctor who discovered the link between hygiene and post-operative health. In the nineteenth century almost half of patients undergoing major surgery died from sepsis of the wound, referred to as 'ward fever'. Earlier work, including Pasteur's, suggested to Lister that post-operative sepsis arose from the colonisation of the wound by micro-organisms.

It was during the 1860s, while working as a professor of surgery at Glasgow University and as a surgeon at Glasgow Infirmary, that Lister began to experiment by dressing wounds with carbolic acid, which had been shown to inhibit the spread of disease in cattle. Carbolic was also sprayed into the air during surgery.

Hospitals found that post-operative mortality was reduced by these initiatives from 50 per cent or more to below 15 per cent. In recognition of his insight, Lister was appointed Professor of Clinical Surgery at King's College London. Initial scepticism from his colleagues was overcome by the discovery of bacteria in the 1880s.

To strike a personal note, the author has, over the past 15 years, undergone four surgical procedures; a laminectomy, arthrotomy and meniscectomy, an arthroscopic decompression of the shoulder and repair of an umbilical hernia! Given the odds prior to Lister, he would have probably expired. He is, however, very much alive and confident of the hygiene practices, clinical procedures and professionalism and skill of the practitioners that enable these life-improving operations.

PANEL 4: JENNER AND VACCINATION

In the eighteenth century 10–20 per cent of the population would be expected to die of smallpox. In his work as a doctor in Gloucestershire, Edward Jenner (1749–1823) became aware of a widespread belief that milkmaids who had suffered from cowpox, a relatively minor disease, were immune to the much more serious infection, smallpox.

Jenner formulated a theory that cowpox infection was protective, and tested it by injecting an eight-year-old boy with pus from a milkmaid infected with cowpox. After a short bout of illness, he proved to be resistant to smallpox. Jenner had to repeat the experiment several more times before his findings were accepted by the scientific establishment and the community as a whole. It is now understood that vaccines impact on the immune system to develop relevant antibodies.

As vaccination became better understood it ousted the dangerous practice of 'variolation' (infecting oneself with a mild form of smallpox in the hope of preventing a more serious infection). In 1853 the British government, having already prohibited variolation, made vaccination compulsory, albeit in the face of initial public opposition. In modern vaccines the infecting agents are cultured, modified to render them harmless yet still able to stimulate antibodies that provide protection.

During the twentieth century WHO succeeded in eradicating smallpox through the effective use of carefully managed vaccination programmes.

- It has since been possible to eliminate or greatly reduce the incidence of serious diseases such as smallpox, diphtheria and tuberculosis through the use of vaccines in immunisation. A step change represented by the introduction of a vaccine results in a completely different healthcare environment. A whole class of treatments can become redundant, and a whole new class created. Consider, for example, recent work that has successfully produced a vaccine against cervical cancer. If the products prove to be effective, a whole class of healthcare activity will be eliminated and the fear of succumbing to this dreadful disease will be alleviated – good for patients, but not necessarily good for payers for current healthcare provision. This is a theme that will recur throughout this book.

- A conspicuous example of a class of pharmaceutical products that have brought about another transformation is provided by antibiotics (see Panel 5). When penicillin became widely available many childhood diseases and common infections arising from injury or surgery became controllable almost overnight.

- More recent technological milestones include the advent of anti-rejection or immune-suppressant drugs. Pioneered with kidney transplants of the 1960s and 1970s, these drugs illustrate the transformational power of technology: they have made it possible to introduce a host of treatments and procedures that could not be considered before, so creating a completely new healthcare landscape. The most recent tissue engineering technology has enhanced this by allowing the patient's own cells to be used to grow replacement parts.

- Anti-virals, a class of drugs developed in the 1980s and 1990s, allow previously rampant diseases such as HIV to be controlled, though not as yet eradicated. Is it in the interest, we may well ask, of the shareholders of a provider of chronic, long-term treatment for a disease to advocate the development of a miracle cure? And at what price would such a cure be valued? These are important decisions taken within the pharmaceutical industry that have a major ethical dimension.

- Treatments that are currently enjoying a rapid growth include anti-hypertensive, anti-coagulants and cholesterol-reducing drugs, which are important to the current drive for improved cardio-vascular care, both preventative and therapeutic.

- The advent of successive generations of antidepressants, controversial though their use may be, has altered the face of mental healthcare irreversibly, with brand names such as Valium and Prozac becoming part of everyday language.

Some of these technologies have brought about step changes in healthcare, while others, such as antisepsis, have resulted in change through incremental improvements. In many cases other types of technology, particularly environmental improvements, have complemented pharmaceutical discoveries. Indeed the growing prevalence of MRSA mentioned above demonstrates that technology must not be considered in isolation from good hygiene and basic common sense. Taking legal action to recover damages from a food manufacturer because you eat too much, get fat and subsequently develop a range of cardiovascular and related diseases is merely proof that common sense is an oxymoron! The root cause of this healthcare problem would be treatable by education, not technology. Education is the obligation of governments.

PANEL 5: ANTIBIOTICS

The first person to benefit from antibiotics is reputed to have been Ann Sheafe Miller, the wife of a member of staff at Yale University. When in 1942 Miller was close to death, her fever of 107 degrees – which had failed to respond to alternative treatments – was rapidly brought under control with a dose of penicillin from the university's laboratories. She lived to be 90.

Diagnostic Technologies

The development of diagnostic technologies is a prerequisite to identifying, and hence treating, disease. The invention of the stethoscope by the French doctor René Laennec in 1816 is a technology that is particularly valuable because it enables doctors to listen to someone's heart and lungs and so identify any alterations from 'normal'. The advent of more sophisticated diagnostic technologies has transformed our approach to healthcare in many areas.

- Once the flow of blood was understood and described by William Harvey in the early seventeenth century it became possible to develop technology to measure its flow, consistency and pressure. This would lead the way to exploring the relationships between hypertension on the one hand and the range of cardiovascular diseases on the other.

- Visualisation or imaging technologies are also valuable diagnostic tools. X-rays have improved many aspects of healthcare by accurately identifying the cause of symptoms in bones and joints. More recently, magnetic resonance imaging (MRI) has transformed many diagnostic situations by allowing the interior of the body, including soft tissue, to be mapped non-invasively without the use of ionising radiation.

- Blood analysers have had a transformative effect in several areas. Monitoring oxygen levels during an operation reduces the risk to the patient. Blood sugar monitors are becoming increasingly important as the problem of diabetes escalates; fortunately, technological improvements mean that patients with diabetes can monitor their own blood sugar levels continually, so achieving better control compared to when they would have had to go to hospital for such tests.

- On a related theme, blood tests to detect tropins have greatly improved the diagnosis and detection of heart attacks. This detection then enables more appropriate treatment to be provided. It has been common for patients in the USA to be put into cardiac emergency care, only for it to emerge that they were suffering from indigestion rather than a heart attack. Mistakes such as these could result in lawsuits for trauma arising from unnecessary treatment. Since the presence of tropins is a reliable marker for a heart attack, it is now relatively easy to distinguish between heart attacks and other conditions, so that timely and appropriate treatment can be provided. It is interesting to note here that the organisation and regulation of healthcare has been changed in the UK to reflect the importance of these diagnostic techniques to the effective provision of healthcare. The Medicines and Healthcare products Regulatory Agency (MHRA) was established to bring regulations regarding medical devices and diagnostic testing such as tropins, which are integral to the effective treatment of heart attacks, under the same authority as that used to license and provide medicines that will be used to treat the condition.

Medical Devices

The final class of technology we shall consider in this historical review consists of devices used to enhance medical procedures, including prosthetics and replacements for body parts. There are many instances where medical devices have helped to change the face of healthcare.

DRUG DELIVERY DEVICES

Drug delivery devices have had a marked impact on treatment. Something as basic as the introduction of 'microfine' needles has made it possible to deliver drugs to previously inaccessible parts of the body, such as the brain. They also make injections relatively painless, so that, for example, self-administration of insulin by people with diabetes has become less traumatic. Implantable delivery devices and those that deliver drugs through the skin, eliminating the need for injections, are likely to become more important as they will increase patients' willingness to comply with prescribed regimens.

DEVICES THAT ASSIST EXAMINATION AND MONITORING

Other important procedures such as endoscopy have transformed both diagnosis and treatment. Even complex surgery can often now be performed in day surgeries, thereby reducing health service costs and disruption to patients' lives (as well as reducing the risk of contracting infections during hospital stays). Remote monitoring of patients using, for example, external and internal cameras and measuring equipment opens up a range of possibilities: from kerbside treatment of accident victims by non-specialists supervised remotely over the Internet by experts, to sending reminders, advice and support to patients with chronic illnesses in their homes. For patients with diabetes regular monitoring of blood glucose levels and determining the most effective treatment at any given time are major factors in controlling the disease. Patients can now monitor their own glucose levels using simple equipment and, with modern telecommunications, gain advice on correct dosages and treatment.

PROSTHETICS

Great advances have been made in the design and construction of artificial joints, so that hip or knee replacements have become relatively routine procedures compared with the major operations required in the 1980s and 1990s.

NEW MATERIALS

Metals and plastics have led to changes which, while simple, are certainly not trivial in their impact. Titanium, a metal that does not corrode, can be used to reconstruct fractured bones, including even catastrophically damaged skulls associated with war wounds. The introduction of dissolving sutures, made from a variety of synthetic materials, means that the removal of sutures is largely unnecessary.

SYNTHETIC DEVICES

The development of artificial organs and implantable devices that assist bodily functions is a field that has benefited from research in high-tech areas such as NASA's space programme. Pacemakers, first used in the 1950s, are now implanted at the rate of over half a million a year worldwide. They are so commonplace that travellers are now routinely checked for them before passing through airport security scanning equipment. Indeed, artificial hearts are becoming a reality and are expected to extend the life of patients who might otherwise die while waiting for 'traditional' heart transplants.

How the Four Technological Strands Interact

Powerful as the technologies discussed above are individually, they can have the most impact when combined. This can be seen by considering how pharmaceutical and environmental improvements have worked together to reduce mortality from infectious diseases. In the Middle Ages diseases such as plague and smallpox had catastrophic effects on individuals and populations, since they could neither be treated effectively nor their spread checked. As recently as the nineteenth century, outbreaks of cholera and diphtheria could decimate the urban poor; cholera epidemics in 1831, 1848, 1853 and 1865 were estimated to have killed between 14,000 and 58,000 people on each occasion. Even a simple cut could be fatal. Similarly many childhood diseases now viewed as trivial were a sentence of death. Together with improvements to sanitation, pharmaceutical developments have now moved us into a more enlightened environment where life expectancy has increased substantially and where babies born with infections or contracting them shortly after birth are no longer condemned to a premature death.

Another example of synergy between different technologies is provided by tuberculosis: inoculations such as BCG for prevention, lung X-rays for diagnosis and antibiotics to treat those already affected. Together these have allowed us to tackle this once intractable problem head-on. Recent research shows that one dose of BCG vaccine protects an individual for up to 60 years and reduces the risk of infection by about 50 per cent. One study found that TB mortality was reduced by over 80 per cent by the use of the vaccine.[1]

Finally, the ability to diagnose hypertension (high blood pressure), coupled with the advent of antihypertensive and anticoagulant drugs, has enabled health services such as the UK's to adopt a far more proactive approach to heart disease whereby doctors are set targets for reducing the average blood pressure of the patient population. Measuring key indicators such as blood pressure or cholesterol is a routine part of a visit to a doctor, and patients with signs of hypertension are offered prescribed drugs or assistance with lifestyle changes.

Organisational Challenges

A single technology on its own can rarely solve healthcare problems; it must be used with other appropriate techniques. In addition, technologies must be applied within the context of appropriate organisational frameworks and processes. We have already identified the reorganisation of the governance of medical devices and medicines agencies. In the past separate agencies made it difficult for hospitals to introduce routine blood sample analysis as a diagnostic aid; problems were improved by creating the Medicines and Healthcare products Regulatory Agency (MHRA), with responsibility for both medicines and devices with a focus on the provision of appropriate multidimensional treatment protocols.

The problem of infections such as MRSA within hospitals provides a less happy illustration of the importance of process. While technologies undoubtedly exist to reduce if not eliminate such infections, the processes and management controls to apply them effectively are not yet fully in place. The issues that today's healthcare processes have to address are the same ones that have challenged providers of healthcare throughout history. In designing appropriate processes it is helpful to keep in mind certain fundamental questions:

- What is technically and clinically possible?

- What is the standard of service that is expected?

---

1   Borgdorff, M.W., Floyd, K. and Broekmans, J.F. (2002), Interventions to reduce tuberculosis mortality and transmission in low- and middle-income countries, *Bulletin of the World Health Organization* (online) 80:3, 217–27.

- How can this service best be provided?

- What is the cost of providing this service, and who pays?

- What restrictions or approvals are appropriate to regulate providers, suppliers and supplies?

These are issues for policy-makers to resolve. In the rest of this book we shall consider what implications their choices have for the design and management of the supply chain.

2

Managing Supply Chain Technology

In order to create a healthcare environment that will meet the public need there will need to be a vision, or collective view, of what is required both now and into the future. This vision will set the conditions and framework within which supplying organisations can develop and define their services. Any transforming change of requirement, alteration of the vision or challenge from changing circumstances, new diseases, demographics or disruptive technologies will test the supply chain processes and framework. It is necessary, therefore, for all supplying organisations to understand the vision of the market, drivers for change in the environment, the technology landscape, and to exploit ideas and opportunities that emerge to provide better products and services more and more efficiently. In this chapter we will consider how a vision can be generated, and how supplying organisations will need to respond for their businesses to be sustainable in that environment. This is one offering of a route to develop a solution to the problems of supply chain issues in healthcare, or any other sector.

What are we Trying to Manage?

As we saw in Chapter 1, technology has a significant influence on the ability to provide and deliver healthcare services. It can improve the healthcare environment and change the way healthcare is delivered, making delivery better, faster, cheaper and more accessible to an ever-greater population.

However, use of any technology will inevitably raise operational issues if it is to be applied appropriately and managed effectively to deliver the desired result. An obvious and simple example of this is the use of inhalation devices in the treatment of asthma. These devices are brilliantly and expertly engineered, and the drugs they contain are purified and processed to an exacting degree to ensure that the particle size is appropriate for bioavailability within the lung when inhaled. All of this comes to nought, however, if the patient is not carefully instructed in the use of the device. Coordination of breath and product delivery is crucial to ensure that the drug is delivered into the optimum sites within the lungs. In this chapter we will consider four different dimensions in which technology has to be managed:

- building a vision for the future;

- understanding the technology roadmap;

- creating a favourable commercial environment;

- developing the skills, capability and infrastructure required to support the technology.

At this stage we are discussing technology in its widest sense. Technology can be defined as 'the study and application of the scientific and industrial arts'. Here we consider its application to the field of healthcare, especially in the area of 'pre-competitive' technology. Pre-competitive technology is work where companies are willing to share and provide equal access to the results. Such research activity typically has a high cost, or a high risk of failure, such that individual companies are unwilling to fund and undertake the research. Other criteria that help to illustrate this can be identified with an example such as the field of 'tissue engineering' – where now real products are available commercially, at one point there were:

- benefit opportunities for all competitors;

- competitors willing to support on a collaborative basis with results shared;

- basic obstacles that prevented a technology from being used in commercial applications;

- unknown characteristics of the cell materials;

- no processes, techniques, tools, information and data that enabled the development of future products and services;

- no experts who knew how to do it;

- no real definitions, industry standards or test procedures as no precedents existed.

The management of technology at this level is likely to be the responsibility of government agencies such as the National Institutes of Health (NIH) in the USA, the UK's Medical Research Council (MRC), charitable trusts such as the Wellcome Trust, universities and other academic institutions.

This discussion may seem far away from the operational delivery of healthcare products and services through an effective supply chain. The new generation of high-technology products that are being developed will have special needs and characteristics. The supply chain processes and techniques required to deliver them to patients will require careful design. The better the understanding of the product and its use, the more effective will be the supply chain design and delivery, and the more compliant the patients who will benefit more fully from the treatments.

As product concepts are identified from pre-competitive research, so patents will be generated to protect ideas, and industrialisation and commercialisation processes will be initiated. The field of tissue engineering is an excellent example of this, as can be seen by the development of patents in this area since about 1990 (Figure 2.1).

The report identified above shows that at the time of writing there were over 70 start-up companies or business units in the world, with a combined annual expenditure of over $600 million. Tissue-engineering firms have increased spending at a compound annual rate of 16 per cent since 1990. It is clear that someone sees a commercial opportunity in this area, and so they seek to understand how to produce, deliver and service the products over the coming years.

Building a Vision for the Future: The 'Sine Qua Non' of an Effective Supply Chain

Each country's vision will evolve through its own political processes, and the result will tend to reflect and embody the values and culture of the society in which it is rooted. If it fails to reflect these values and culture, or is seen as too radical, it is unlikely to be implemented satisfactorily. In the fifteenth century this empirical fact was characterised by Machiavelli (1469–1527) in his book *The Prince*:

> *It must be considered that there is nothing more difficult to carry out, nor more dangerous to handle, than to initiate a new order of things. For the reformer has enemies in all those who profit by the old order, and only lukewarm defenders in those who would profit by the new.*

The vision must therefore be clearly articulated and widely understood by all those who must contribute to its delivery. I suggest that it is best framed with five key elements: control, market, access, payment and organisation.

CONTROL

Who has the power to shape the agenda and the resources to fund it? Free market, democratic economies will have a different process of reaching a consensus than command regimes or controlled economies. The USA and western Europe are examples of the former, while they are contrasted by the likes of Libya, Cuba, Iran, Kuwait and others.

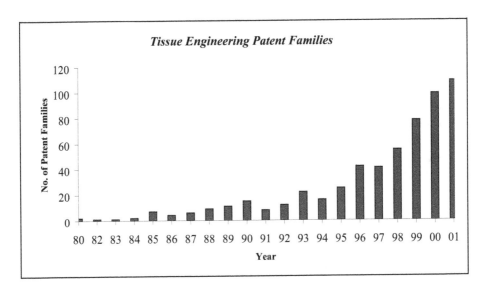

Figure 2.1   Tissue engineering patent families

Source: Adapted from 'The Emergence of Tissue Engineering as a Research Field' (14 October 2003) <http://www.nsf.gov/pubs/2004/nsf0450/start.htm>.

MARKET

The provision of healthcare services can be either from private profit-making providers, or managed and funded by government agencies. Can people spend their money as they wish, or are they obliged to obtain healthcare through government-controlled hospitals and clinics? These basic decisions will dictate the level of profitability that will be available within the market for any independent supplying organisation.

ACCESS

Will access to services be controlled on clinical grounds or on some other financial or geographic factors? Is the distribution channel restricted and regulated, and how are the clinics, pharmacies and hospitals to be controlled? This will dictate the regulatory hurdles and logistical challenges that potential providers will need to negotiate. Regulatory controls imposed by the authorities may prevent particular products or services being available within the market, or impose costs and restrictions on the suppliers.

PAYMENT

Do patients pay for their services at point of use, or do they contribute through private insurance schemes or government sick funds and via some form of co-payment? What provision is made for those who are unemployed, disabled or poor? For suppliers this is an important factor, as it will dictate the pricing mechanism that will operate. If reimbursement support can be won, the market can open up significantly.

ORGANISATION: LOCAL VERSUS CENTRALISED

In the US, individual states control the delivery of healthcare provision. In the UK, while the service is national – the National Health Service (NHS) – it is administered by a national health authority which devolves operational management down to primary care trusts (PCTs). These arguably exert increasing amounts of control over the nature of services delivered, through restricted formularies and other controlled procurement lists. Suppliers are then faced with one overall policy, delivered in a variety of operational frameworks that reflect local situations. The current interpretation of the Prescription Drugs Medication Act (PDMA) in the USA and the development of different drug pedigree requirements in different states illustrate the problems that can be faced. We will explore this later in more depth.

Social Priorities

Not only must the vision reflect a society's values and culture, it must also focus on that society's priorities. For example, when the level of infant deaths from malaria or AIDS is unacceptably high – as in areas of Africa – then that is an issue we would expect society to prioritise. Sadly we are all too aware that the political environment in these countries does not place such a high priority on these issues.

For many developed countries, cardiovascular diseases are the biggest cause of premature death, and are a prime area of focus. In the UK the NHS has developed a policy to reduce current levels of coronary heart disease (CHD, – the single most common cause of premature death in the UK, accounting for about a quarter of all deaths under the age of 65. It costs the NHS and the social services more than £3.8 billion annually and results in the loss of 35 million working days, costing industry an estimated £3 billion. The National Service Framework within the NHS concludes that:

> The Government is determined to reduce inappropriate variations in the quality of NHS care for heart disease … It aims to build an approach that allows standards and targets to change over time to ensure that the NHS can continuously improve the services that it provides. They are creating a vision for the treatment of CHD.[1]

More subtle ways in which a society can address heart disease include the promotion and encouragement of physical fitness – through popular events such as the London Marathon – and the banning of smoking in public places. History shows that this kind of prioritisation can pay rich dividends. In the 1960s and 1970s cancer was seen as the major health issue for people in the developed world: mortality rates were high, the chances of cure very low and diagnostic techniques inadequate. Governments responded by fostering research programmes such as tissue engineering, discussed above. A variety of products, techniques, diagnostics and treatment regimes have been developed

---

1   NHS   White   Paper   <http://www.archive.official-documents.co.uk/document/doh/newnhs/ wpaper8.htm>.

subsequently, such that today many cancers are diagnosed early, are curable and patients have greater confidence in their ability to survive (see Panel 1).

PANEL 1: CO-ORDINATING RESEARCH

In order to forge a truly cross-functional or multidisciplinary approach Cancer Research UK was formed to co-ordinate various researches into the disease. It merged the Imperial Cancer Research Fund with the Cancer Research Campaign and controls scientific spending of over £130 million. Seven major research centres in the university cities of London, Manchester, Birmingham and Glasgow are involved, linked to 26 major clinical laboratories and centres in 14 major cities in the UK that were in close partnership with the National Health Service. In London hospitals and medical schools, nine major clinics became associated with this radical initiative.

The outcomes have been Nobel Prizes, academic achievement awards and numerous publications – but most importantly a significant improvement in the treatment and care of patients with cancer. That was the vision, and it has been managed and delivered.

As well as working within these priorities, healthcare companies can also develop new products and services, influence policy-makers by lobbying governments, stakeholders, key opinion leaders (KOLs) and professional associations. Fostering public awareness of particular conditions can also assist. From an ethical viewpoint, many observers would consider these interventions acceptable in the case of serious issues such as smoking cessation.

We should note that, as well as pressure from pharmaceutical companies on healthcare services to target a particular area, there may also be pressures in the opposite direction: on the industry from governments. Some diseases are severe, yet affect so few patients that they are not commercially appealing propositions for pharmaceutical companies. An example is the drug Duodopa (a levodopa/carbidopa combination) that, injected directly into the stomach via a tube and pump mechanism, can be extremely effective in treating advanced Parkinson's disease. However, the total number of patients that can benefit from this drug is small, – 1.3 million in major countries – while the cost is very high and the delivery mechanism complex. From a commercial point of view, delivering a commercial return from such a drug may be very risky. Governments might therefore choose to encourage suppliers to develop so-called 'orphan drugs' in areas such as this (see Panel 2 and also Chapter 7). The range of possible incentives includes pricing, monopoly status and extended patent protection.

The extent to which this type of initiative is likely to occur depends partly on whether control of service is centralised or locally managed. Certain health problems may be practically invisible at a local level, but significant when aggregated across an entire country. This lack of visibility can also be a problem for local clinicians, who may be unable to diagnose some rare conditions correctly as they see them so infrequently; and indeed they may not recognise what they do not know.

PANEL 2: ORPHAN DRUGS

Orphan drugs are defined as 'any of the various drugs or biologicals that may be useful in treating disease but are not considered to be commercially viable'. They may be considered drugs without a parent to nurture them, hence the term orphan. The orphan drug programme was created by the US Congress and enacted during 1983 to facilitate development of drugs for the treatment of rare diseases, defined as having fewer than 200,000 patients per year. More than 20 million Americans suffer from one of over 5,000 such rare diseases and medical disorders. Often patients suffering from one of these debilitating diseases would have no other available treatments or options.

What Does a Healthcare Vision Mean for Pharmaceutical Suppliers and Medical Device Companies?

Frequently supply chain management is reduced to the tactical or operational fields within businesses; it is not considered to have a strategic contribution to make. Understanding, shaping and responding to changes in the environment lifts the discipline into the strategic and political fields. It is vital that suppliers fully understand the vision and environmental framework within which they are working in any given market. In many countries the model will be continually changing as circumstances change, and so the supplier organisations face the challenge of continually aligning their strategies with current and future states, which may look very different. Suppliers therefore need to keep their antennae out in order to get early warning of likely changes, help to shape them through lobbying and respond to them ahead of their competitors.

One example of how the model impacts on the pharmaceutical industry is the way in which prescribing decisions are made. In some models – such as the old-style NHS in the UK – doctors may have a high degree of autonomy over which medicines they prescribe, in which case influencing prescribing habits is a matter of talking to and persuading individual doctors of the benefits of your product. In other models, however – such as the one increasingly being adopted across Europe – there is a defined formulary compiled on the basis of both clinical effectiveness and commercial considerations, on the overall economic benefit rather than the price point of the prescribed treatment. In such a case the sales force must influence the handful of decision-makers who establish the formulary. A number of organisations have radically reduced their field sales forces to respond to this new influencing environment.

It is helpful to note here that pharmaceutical companies may also find they need to talk to pharmacists, who, while they cannot usually prescribe, may wield considerable influence in terms of their ability to coach patients to maintain compliance with a particular regimen (keep taking the medicine) or to suggest a referral to a doctor to consider a switch to an alternative product that may have a different adverse, side-effect profile. This point is especially pertinent to the healthcare vision in that it illustrates the complexity of the centralisation/decentralisation continuum.

While the government may be controlling healthcare policy, there are many ways in which those working at grass-roots level may retain influence. In Greece, as in many other markets of this type, patients can obtain prescription medicines directly from their pharmacist, who can then direct them to their doctor.

Again, considering the pharmacist's role, governments are attempting to reduce the burden of healthcare costs on their budgets and seek to make more medicines available for 'self-medication'. These can then be obtained directly by patients 'over the counter' (OTC) using their own funds. These OTC drugs are first made available within pharmacies where a trained and qualified pharmacist can advise the patient about best use, interactions, possible alternatives, and consider whether the recurrence of symptoms may be masking more serious underlying conditions. In these licensed pharmacy outlets the product supply is well controlled, limited in volume and managed profitably. Later, as the drugs are generally used safely by a wide range of patients and in a variety of conditions – and there is no evidence of inappropriate use or abuse – the authorities will seek wider distribution through other retail outlets. Such outlets may not have a trained pharmacist on hand; they will drive higher-volume sales through more complex channels of distribution, which will allow retail buyers to put pressure on their profitability for manufacturers and the original pharmacy outlets.

Later in the book we will see how this represents one aspect of the tensions that exist within the healthcare supply chain due to the conflict of agendas or interests of the protagonists. In this case we see that payers wish to reduce their direct support for medication and make safe medicines more easily available OTC for self-medication. This conflicts directly with the current status and business model for retail pharmacists and the control of profitability for manufacturers.

Zovirax cream is an example of this transformation. It is an antiviral treatment that is very effective against cold sores. The active ingredient is acyclovir. Having been available only as a prescription product under careful control, it was restricted to patients who visited their doctor at the early stage of their symptoms and were prescribed the product. Because advertising and promotion regulations prevented direct communication to patients, volumes were low. As the product proved to be very effective, safe and costly to the authorities it was a prime candidate for being granted OTC status. At this point volumes increased dramatically as direct advertising became possible. The price to the patient was around one-fifth of the previous reimbursement price and so the margins and distribution challenges altered substantially. No longer were the product characteristics appropriate for supply by the research-based pharmaceutical company Wellcome, so the product was transferred to a more OTC-based company, Warner-Lambert. At this time the product that had previously been the first $1 billion blockbuster drug, Zantac, was also given OTC status and transferred to the same supplier. Again the vision of making safe and efficacious products widely available to the public at as low a cost as possible was created, managed and delivered.

Using a Technology Roadmap

A technology roadmap is a very useful tool for matching strategic goals to technology capabilities and knowledge – in particular in visualising how appropriate technology developments can be realistically planned to achieve the desired outcome, specifically where the outcome depends on the development of a necessary technology capability. An example of this is the vision of connecting every doctor, pharmacist, hospital and clinic to a common information technology (IT) platform across an entire country. This vision would allow the improvement of the delivery of patient services and reduce the administrative burden. The vision will *not* be realised unless database technology, communication platforms, wireless or fixed-line broadband, software security and encryption methods and hardware production costs are all developed in harmony. The roadmap will emerge from the vision, and is a logical consequence of it. Roadmaps are used at a number of levels:

- at a national level – to provide structure to future industrial goals;

- at a business level – to develop a company's strategic direction:

  - to exploit a specific technology or
  - using technology to develop a leading business position;

- at an individual project level – to help the project manager determine how particular technologies can meet a particular business target and then generate implementation plans.

A technology roadmap is developed in response to an event or opportunity. This is characterised in a vision so that the direction and way forward are clear. From the healthcare environment such a vision would be along the lines of:

- reducing premature deaths from CHD by 50 per cent within 10 years;

- eradicating malaria in Africa by 2050;

- ensuring every doctor has online access to patient records at every consultation in the next five years;

- growing a replacement kidney from a patient's own cells so that it will not be rejected after transplantation.

The possibilities are endless. In these visions we have both triggers: what is causing us to change and targets that we will need to change and by when.

Here we have an example from another sector, the environment. The trigger is the dramatic change in the world's climate that drives us to reduce the impact of this global warming, and we are looking to develop technologies that deliver the required energy yet have very low emissions of CO_2 and other greenhouse gases (Figure 2.2).

The implications of such a roadmap developed at a strategic level for the supply chain within a country are that there will be a need for different products and services, different supply and delivery mechanisms and possibly the elimination of existing products.

If the vision and drive of the populace is to reduce cancer, then we have an opportunity to access their collective energy and political momentum. If it is to 'e-enable' all healthcare workers, then we need to understand the opportunities for this to help us provide better services. Should the developed world suddenly push funds into the developing world to eradicate malaria, AIDS and other diseases, we should work out how to support this. And, of course, if the aim is the growth of replacement organs that will eliminate rejection, we should examine our immune suppressant portfolio.

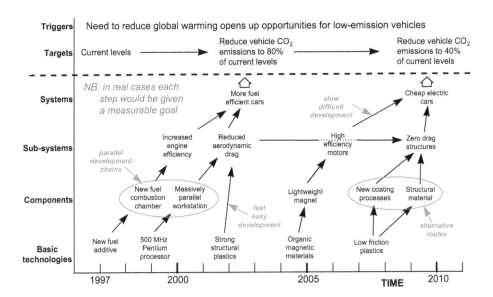

Figure 2.2   A technology roadmap to support the vision of reducing CO_2 emissions from motor vehicles

Measuring Performance Against Targets

Monitoring the impact of interventions, and measuring progress, is perhaps the most challenging area, not least because we are assuming a causal link between our intervention and the outcome. By encouraging people to stop smoking, reducing the level of unsaturated fats and salt in foods and by promoting physical activity through sport, we expect to see a reduction in the level of coronary heart disease. Many tools and techniques are emerging to support this vision. A variety of technological areas can contribute: lipid-lowering agents and blood-thinning drugs; readily accessible monitoring devices for blood pressure, cholesterol and (in the case of diabetes) blood sugar; stents to keep arteries clear; pacemakers and even artificial hearts. Which of these tools and techniques will be most useful depends on the profile of the patient population. In the UK, for example, there is an emphasis on collecting and understanding data about certain critical aspects of health, which is why patients visiting their GP are frequently invited to have their blood pressure and cholesterol levels tested. The resultant data is available not only for offering suitable advice and care to individuals, but also for understanding how blood pressure and cholesterol levels across the community relate to heart disease prevalence and prognosis.

Another example of the vision setting at national level is shown in mainland Europe, where it has had a profound effect on manufacturers supplying the market. This will be explored later in Chapters 10 and 11. Given the escalating cost of healthcare to many governments in the developed world, there is a drive to reduce the cost of drugs and to ensure greater control over what is actually spent. To this end, the authorities in Belgium, Greece and Italy share a vision of reducing or controlling better the cost of drugs. All three authorities independently imposed upon manufacturers and suppliers of reimbursed products a mass serialisation process. In this way every reimbursed pack, paid for by the government or an insurance fund, would need to be uniquely identified to ensure that the payment could be identified against a specific pack, and that no duplicate claims could be made.

Simultaneously in Belgium the authorities place restrictions on doctors and pharmacists to ensure that they prescribe and dispense the most cost-effective drugs available. The data they are collecting will eventually help them to reduce or eliminate fraudulent claims for reimbursement by pharmacists, and simultaneously monitor the prescribing practices of doctors. Suppliers are therefore facing the imposition of an administrative burden, the mass serialisation and reporting process, and are likely to have their 'branded' products substituted for low-cost generics where available. Although the governments did provide around 18–24 months' notice of the system being mandated, no suppliers developed useful ways in which this could work to their advantage. As we will see later, mass serialisation is a powerful tool that can provide many benefit opportunities. None were exploited in Belgium, Greece or Italy, until now.

To be effective such monitoring must be within the context of a suitable organisational framework and vision. What do you want to monitor, and why? The data available for monitoring is complex and extensive and will be discussed more fully in Chapter 12. Monitoring of trends is an essential tool in the policy-makers' armoury, helping them decide which technologies are likely to be most cost-effective in achieving the targets outlined in the vision; but first there must be a vision.

Working with the Roadmap

What does the roadmap mean for the industry? From a commercial perspective, pharmaceutical companies are more motivated to create treatments than they are to develop preventative methods and cures – there are few profitable companies specialising in vaccines. Vaccines have only a few courses of treatment, while treatments for chronic diseases are perpetual.

Strategic, commercial and supply chain managers need, however, to understand the roadmap as a whole in order to spot the overall implications for their products. This understanding will enable them to get their products into as wide a population as possible, for example by selling a drug that used to be prescription only in the OTC market.

Although advertising prescription drugs directly to patients is prohibited in many countries, companies can sometimes sidestep such legislation by advertising to promote awareness of particular conditions in order to stimulate demand for their products. This type of advertising has to be done with care but it can be effective, as in the case of Wellcome, manufacturer of Zovirax cream mentioned previously, which conducted an advertising campaign directing cold-sore sufferers to consult their doctors.

Companies with a sophisticated understanding of the roadmap are much better positioned to spot opportunities like these. They will also recognise that, often, it is not only their own products that they need to promote. Though putting effort into selling other people's products might seem on the face of it commercial nonsense, a company with a heart disease treatment may benefit from promoting third-party products that help people understand the use of diagnostic tools such as blood pressure monitors or products that measure, for example, cholesterol. The Oncology Therapeutic Network provides a useful example of 'selling services beyond the product'. This was set up in the US by Bristol-Myers Squibb, but then sold to One Equity Partners LLC. Via this network, Bristol-Myers Squibb promoted a full gamut of oncology-related products and services to key opinion leaders in the field, making its name a byword for oncology care.

Understanding the technology roadmap may also lead companies to rethink their attitudes to certain therapeutic areas. We have already alluded to orphan drugs, those that target very small patient groups. It might not seem worth a company investing in a treatment for Parkinson's disease that will help only a few hundred patients when the research and development (R&D) portfolio also contains, say, an obesity drug which could reach 100 million overweight patients in the US alone.

Creating a Favourable Commercial Environment

The commercial environment is critical to the success of any healthcare system in following its roadmap. The roadmap will establish the scope of the commercial opportunities that could be realised. Efficient management of these opportunities will be needed to deliver them.

The reason the commercial environment is so important is that governments cannot themselves afford to shoulder the costs and risks of the R&D implied by their vision and political ambitions. Therefore they have to find ways of persuading suppliers to the healthcare industry to take on these risks on their behalf. This implies, among other things, creating an appetite for risk; companies cannot be expected to enter risky product development areas with enthusiasm unless they see realistic opportunities of making adequate commercial returns.

In the area of medical research, the Wellcome Trust provides an illustration. At one point, the trust was putting significantly more funds into basic scientific, medical research than the UK government itself. The trust's own funds came primarily from the Wellcome pharmaceutical company, a not particularly profitable player in its industry. The UK Charities Commission pointed out that to sustain and diversify its funding activities into the future the Wellcome Foundation needed to become a profitable organisation in its own right. Recognising the extent to which the realisation of its roadmap depended on the trust, the UK government allowed the trust to be taken into public ownership. The result was the world's biggest single initial public offering (IPO) at that time.

In more general terms, there are several areas in which governments can nurture a suitable environment for healthcare R&D. They can address the treatment and protection of intellectual property (IP), for example via patents – a strategy we shall discuss in Chapter 3. They can choose from a variety of investment models within which governments can encourage and seed research, for example through the creation of 'biotech clusters' and technology parks.

Pharmaceutical companies should make sure they understand, and wherever possible take advantage of, government initiatives designed to create favourable commercial environments. Smaller companies can join a cluster, while larger ones may want to support the clusters with an eye to buying or licensing the resultant products as they become available. In this way, large companies can capitalise on smaller organisations' capacity for innovation.

Examples of Investment Models

Scottish Enterprise's Intermediate Technology Institute (ITI) is an economic development agency that aims to foster technology and technology-related employment in Scotland. This is a country with a disproportionately high number of universities for its population, so encouraging employers to invest in research facilities brings benefits for the universities, employers and the general population. To attract companies, Scottish Enterprise offers to fund research products in other parts of the world – gaining ownership of some of IP in the process – on condition that the further development of the resultant technologies is moved to Scotland.

There are a variety of technical institutes covering almost every research area, including biotechnology. Germany's Fraunhofer Institute, which performs contract research into new technologies, is an example. Some 60 per cent of its funding comes from the government and the rest is private. Another example is the Karolinska Institute in Sweden, which undertakes basic research as well as finding academic partners for large and small companies. Governments support these institutes through measures such as tax holidays and provision of suitable premises. (See also Chapter 4.)

A common thread of such initiatives is the cluster model, in which several companies, usually start-ups, are located close together to share their interests and aspirations. They can also share facilities. For example, biotech companies need not only 'wet' laboratories but also heavy-duty computing power, and setting up a science park in which companies can share these facilities is a more cost-effective way of providing them, given that each company might only need them for a short time (perhaps 18 months in the case of a wet lab).

From our previous example of tissue engineering, in a little over a decade more than $3.5 billion has been invested in worldwide research and development in this discipline. Over 90 per cent of this financial investment has been from the private sector. Currently there are over 70 start-up companies or business units in the world, with a combined annual expenditure of over $600 million dollars. Tissue-engineering firms have increased spending at a compound annual rate of 16 per cent since 1990. The commercial environment for these investors is clearly favourable, measured by the fact that investors are investing more and more with the expectation of greater rewards. The various investment models are all set up with common aims: generating and exploiting intellectual property.

Developing Skills and Capabilities to Support the Vision

This area of healthcare strategy management, like the creation of a commercial environment, is concerned with getting rid of potential constraints that could prevent the effective realisation of the vision. Having identified the type of technology required to support the vision, supplying organisations must ensure that they are best positioned to develop those technologies and deploy the resources necessary. Above all, this ability rests on having the right skills. Without proper levels of education there will be no access to advanced technologies, and therefore none of the IP necessary for a thriving economy and successful healthcare provision. Equally, to make best use of the technology there will be a need for training. In the developing world, where much of the technology could be used to the best advantage, there is insufficient skill and knowledge of capability to use it effectively.

The requirement here is not for a mass of low-skilled staff, but for relatively few exceptionally well-qualified individuals and teams. This is one reason why pure research facilities tend to be centred on universities, especially those with teaching hospitals and their own medical research facilities.

Universities are important then; but the educational requirements of healthcare also need to be addressed by schools. Governments must ensure that enough children are attracted to 'hard' subjects, in particular the sciences. One factor here is that science is often seen as boring by students. This perception might seem astonishing, but is less so given that teachers are often underqualified, and that health and safety regulations as well as financial constraints discourage schools from allowing students to perform experiments. As a teacher of chemistry for seven years after leaving university, I found students could be inspired by the appropriate use of demonstration, pyrotechnics and experimentation. Learning science requires a heuristic process, as does learning which particular technology or process is best deployed in a particular situation.

Pharmaceutical and medical device companies too have a role to play in fostering scientific education, by showing students just how interesting science and technology can be. They can achieve this by sponsoring educational events, providing input for textbooks and other educational materials and recruiting students as interns. They can pass on older equipment to school and college laboratories.

Governments also need to ensure that the relevant reward mechanisms in place for those participating in healthcare-related R&D continue to produce the desired outcomes. Consideration of an R&D facility's environment and location is a major part of this task. A proposal to adapt London's Millennium Dome as a biotech cluster was rejected because, although the project was physically achievable, local house prices in view of the character of the neighbourhood were such that it would be impossible to attract sufficient staff to work there. West London's centres of excellence such as Hammersmith Hospital and Imperial College are more appealing to staff because, although house prices are high, the environment is pleasant and the transport infrastructure more efficient.

We have already mentioned the activities of the ITI in Scotland. The living environment there is so attractive that the institute succeeds in attracting applications from all over the world. Eli Lilly's Indianapolis research facility is another example of a well-situated R&D centre (as I have been told by a number of its employees), as it is in the sort of environment where people would wish to raise their families – prosperous, pleasant and safe.

Once again, industry and government work together to identify and develop environments that can host successful R&D facilities. The amount of money companies are prepared to invest in these facilities is sometimes extraordinarily high: in Hertfordshire, GlaxoSmithKline's R&D facility was, at the time, the biggest construction project in Europe after the Channel Tunnel. To invest this kind of money (in excess of £150 million over five years) with confidence, a company must be sure that the environment it has chosen is secure, close enough to commercial centres and has access to a worldwide transport infrastructure, as well as a well-educated population.

Conclusion

While technological inventions and discoveries tend to emerge serendipitously, the application and use of technology require significant time, effort and cost, and must therefore be carefully planned.

Because technological development is both risky and involves long timescales before coming to fruition, it is arguable that governments should not commit taxpayers' money to such risky ventures, but should encourage the private sector to invest in the relevant areas. The governments' role becomes one of setting the vision, developing the regulatory framework and creating the environment where returns for private investors are in line with the risks they are taking.

As we have seen, governments need to establish a roadmap in such a way as to encourage private companies to want to take on the burden of R&D. To play its part successfully, the industry needs to have a rounded appreciation of what a government is trying to achieve and how. In the next chapter we will explore ways in which, if handled correctly on both sides, R&D can create a win-win situation for both industry and country.

3

The Economic Significance of Healthcare Investment

Healthcare institutions are employers, buyers of goods and materials, researchers, educators and more. This employment generates local wealth and opportunity; procurement generates income for local and other businesses; research represents investment in the future; education and training ensure that employees are equipped with the capability to improve services to patients. In this chapter we seek to identify the opportunities and benefits created through strategic investment in healthcare.

Three basic duties of any government are to defend the state, to keep its citizens safe and healthy and to educate those citizens. All of these requirements have implications in terms of resources and infrastructure. Some of the requirements are also interdependent. We shall argue here that a focus on healthcare positions a government particularly well to carry out its other duties.

Investment in defence, while perhaps a requirement in itself, does not, we shall argue, have the same accumulating benefits as investment in healthcare. Creating nuclear weapons, for example, has no obvious benefits for individual citizens. However, if the country is not a democracy, the decision to invest in armaments will be made without reference to citizens, whether they support it or not. Recent discussions between the United Nations, North Korea and Iran are examples of this.

A democracy is likely to prioritise effective healthcare over defence, because the former does have clear benefits for the individual enfranchised citizen. A side benefit arises from the fact that it is impossible to have effective healthcare without a really efficient educational system to develop and nurture the requisite skills and technology. A decision to invest in healthcare therefore implies a decision to invest in education.

A second beneficial effect of investing in healthcare is that it creates jobs and generates wealth for the nation. A sound educational system will also generate jobs and wealth in many other areas apart from healthcare itself.

Why not simply invest in education as an end in itself? Without the technological context provided by an emphasis on healthcare, the danger is that education will overemphasise the arts at the expense of science. For a flourishing economy, and (arguably) a rich cultural environment, both branches of education are necessary.

The position adopted in this book is that a society that focuses on developing the best possible healthcare provision will automatically produce a well-educated, highly skilled population that will enjoy interesting and rewarding employment. In fact, we could argue that, unless we reject the American Declaration of Independence's assertion that any citizen has an inalienable right to 'life, liberty and the pursuit of happiness', then in a free state healthcare has to be the highest political priority.

A Historical Perspective – How the Vision Will Be Developed

To illustrate the varying role that healthcare can play in an economy, let us trace the modern evolution of healthcare in the UK. At the turn of the twentieth century people in the developed world had to pay directly for their healthcare treatments. Those who could afford to see a doctor were treated; the rest had to depend on charity or do without treatment. Indeed my own father – brought up in the 1920s and 1930s in the industrial north-west of England among the mills and poverty – was told that he nearly died at the age of three from a raging infection of an abscess in his ear. A visit from the doctor would have cost one shilling, yet there was no shilling! A kindly lady neighbour applied a poultice to burst the abscess and clear the infection.

In the aftermath of World War I, with its millions of casualties from all classes, came a radical rethink of the status quo. There was widespread questioning of the authority of military leaders, political leaders in government and of the historic class system. Demands for reform of healthcare and education began to be heard. The movement for women's suffrage, the right to vote, also illustrated the underlying tension and dissatisfaction with the old ways. Typically for the UK much of this rebellion was subtle – the parody film *Oh! What a Lovely War* (1969) depicting the lunacy, ignorance and incompetent leadership by the 'ruling classes' during World War I is an excellent example of this irony.

While Britain did not experience a revolution in the sense that Russia did, the General Strike in 1926 and espionage activities of the Cambridge elite in the 1930s demonstrated that the government would not be able to exert the same control in the same dismissive way it had previously. The forced abdication of Edward VIII could be seen as another sign of the commoners, through the government elected by the population, asserting themselves over the traditional authority figure represented by the king. One effect of this general democratising tendency was the establishment of the National Health Service (NHS) during the 1940s under the leadership of Minister of Health Aneurin (Nye) Bevan. The fundamental principle that the service must be free at the point of use has remained unchanged ever since. However, changes to the environment in which the NHS operates have increasingly challenged and tested the scope of this principle. As a result of the post-war 'baby boom', there now is an increasing number of people approaching retirement age and, as these people have a higher life expectancy than before, it is predicted that in the 2030s there will be more than 40,000 centenarians in the UK, compared with fewer than 300 in the 1960s. As a result, there are worries that the working population will not be able pay enough tax to fund the required levels of healthcare. It is estimated that 90 per cent of an individual's consumption of healthcare resources take place after the age of 60. This theme will be explored further in Chapter 5.

The problem of funding is, of course, compounded by the increasing number and complexity (cost) of possible treatments available through the introduction of technologies and the discovery of generally expensive, new medicines. Not only do more people place demands on the healthcare resources, but there is also more for them to demand. Compounding this situation, lifestyle diseases such as obesity and its complications, depression and erectile dysfunction are now treated medically. Hitherto these conditions would have been unrecorded, unobserved; or enforced lifestyles would have altered the conditions. In general people were not affluent enough to eat excessively, and their manual work would keep their weight down. As there had been fewer support services available, depression and other psychiatric disorders were previously not effectively measured.

International Comparisons

We can shed further light on the variety of attitudes to healthcare by comparing experiences in different parts of the world. If we view healthcare as a right, then it becomes a responsibility to ensure that it is adequately funded. There are several fundamentally different approaches to this funding. If, as in the UK, the majority of funding comes directly from the government, then there must be ways to ensure that the treasury's coffers are kept sufficiently full to meet the cost of the level of healthcare that we want to provide, yet inevitably the level of care will be related to the level of funding available. Put slightly differently, if you want a good healthcare system you need to ensure that you generate the wealth to support it.

The government therefore needs to estimate healthcare spending for a given period in order to plan the amount of direct and indirect taxation it will collect in that period. In the UK National Insurance (NI) is collected through employment contributions; yet these funds do not directly fund the range of services available. General taxation contributes a major part of healthcare funding in the UK, and this is subject to the effects of changing political priorities.

In the US, by contrast, the government, while recognising a responsibility for healthcare, decided that it should be funded directly through health-specific insurance schemes into which individuals make their own payments, either directly or via their employers' contributions. Becoming unemployed, particularly with a chronic condition, can be medically and financially debilitating. Again, this topic will be explored further in Chapter 5.

Among the implications of these contrasting approaches to funding is the different level of information available to define contributions or costs of service provision. The US approach makes it relatively straightforward to understand how much government money (tax dollars) is to be spent on healthcare; whereas when a large degree of support comes from the general pool of taxes it can be quite hard to measure the amount of public expenditure going into healthcare. The US model means that the provision of the healthcare services is then 'private' and not political, subject to complaints to local operational management rather than elected politicians. In the UK the NHS, since its inception, has been a major political football as it is funded directly by the government. Hospital building and location, availability of reimbursed drugs, access to care and the standard of that care are laid directly at the feet of elected politicians. This is one reason why an established, independent management body that will oversee the management of the service, thereby insulating politicians from the operational sphere and confining them to a policy-setting steering role, has been suggested.

1990s ANECDOTES FROM WORK IN DEVELOPING COUNTRIES

The most technically advanced antibiotic in its class, Ceftazidime, was at the time the drug of last resort for people suffering from very serious infections. However, the cost of such an advanced treatment was prohibitive for many hospitals in developing countries, so they did not stock it. Instead, patients sometimes had to procure it directly from the manufacturer's distribution depots. The price equated, typically, to several months' salary for an average worker. In at least one case the patient had died by the time the remedy had been obtained and delivered to the physician.

Colfosceril palmitate, formulated with other active substances, represented another technically advanced, life-saving product for neonatal care. It is a surfactant to help premature babies clear their lungs. This product was stocked on consignment in hospitals, as its application when necessary was urgent, but it would only be provided to patients who could pay. The cost of around $500 was equivalent to a year's wages for much of the population. Paediatricians reported that parents presented with this dilemma were faced with the prospect of bankruptcy or allowing their premature baby to die. These are serious decisions with huge consequences, and I guess it is impossible for anyone to know what they would do faced with such a dilemma. Both these drugs were generally available in most western European countries at the time and were funded, and their costs reimbursed, by governments or health insurance schemes.

These political and strategic considerations impact on decisions made for the provision distribution and delivery of healthcare. While the US approach makes it easier to measure and to some extent control healthcare expenditure, at the same time it places more responsibility for the funding of that healthcare on the individual end user. The level of care that citizens receive can differ markedly according to their income. Someone who cannot afford medical insurance will become reliant on the Medicaid system, under which only a limited range of treatments is available. A colleague, recently returned from living for seven years in the USA on both the east and west coasts, suggested that an unemployed American who develops a chronic disease – say heart disease – faces bankruptcy if they have to undergo two operations; few are able to save enough to fund such an eventuality.

Healthcare Funding Reflects the Values of Society

As we can see, approaches to funding in the UK and the US not only reflect different structures, they also reflect different values. The way a government allocates funds across its portfolio reflects the relative importance it places on transport, infrastructure, energy, policing and justice, national security, international relations and so forth.

Non-democratic countries may accord a fairly low priority to public funding of healthcare, as shown by the author's experience in Central and Eastern Europe (Poland, Russia, the Czech Republic, Hungary, Bulgaria, Romania and Kazakhstan) in the 1990s, even some time after the fall of the Berlin Wall. Despite the availability of highly trained and skilled medical and nursing staff, drugs were not as generally available as in western European countries. In some former Eastern Bloc countries patients awaiting surgery were expected to buy the materials needed, even sutures. These countries often had impressive levels of technical skills and, in some cases, equipment; but they did not have money for consumables. Moreover, if a patient was hospitalised, the family was expected to bring them food; the bed was provided, but little more.

Although the unequal distribution of healthcare in some Eastern European countries might seem to be a legacy of their form of socialist, centrally planned economics, Cuba presents a contrasting picture. Healthcare there is considered highly important, with a wide range of services available to the community. According to the World Health Organization (WHO), Cuba provides a doctor for every 170 residents, ahead of the USA's ratio of 1 to 188. Cuba's local, home-grown pharmaceutical industry is also well regarded and generates export revenue for the economy. The difference between Cuba's approach and that of the former Eastern Bloc states – which have developed little by way of strategic pharmaceutical or healthcare industrial resources – seems to be the focus, priority and leadership demonstrated by the country's rulers. Ever since taking power in 1959, former Cuban President Fidel Castro wanted to create a global medical power. Whatever the cause of Cuba's political difficulties – its many dilapidated buildings, ramshackle shops and frequent power cuts bear witness to the way its crumbling, underdeveloped economy coexists with the country's advanced medical and scientific sector – healthcare has a high political priority which is reflected in the investment decisions made.

Cuba's development model is based on harnessing the nation's wealth in human resources and science to create a knowledge-based economy focused on health. These are the views of a president who was in power for nearly 50 years until his retirement in 2008. We should note that in Cuba the operative factor is not just respect for the health of citizens, but also a well-articulated recognition by leaders of the economic value of investment in the sector, and of the 'human capital' that results. In early 2006 it was announced that the growing value of Cuba's £1 billion industry would soon be exceeded by healthcare-related exports (specifically biotechnology, vaccines and healthcare for foreign nationals).

The Role of Citizens' Expectations

These different models help us see that, while democracies tend to prioritise universal healthcare more than totalitarian regimes, there are exceptions. In non-democratic countries total wealth and the views of those in power are likely to determine the prioritisation of healthcare. The expectations of citizens about healthcare also vary between nations, reflecting (among other factors) the extent to which citizens feel responsible for their own health. These expectations can, to some extent at least, be managed by the state.

As part of a consultancy assignment, I had the privilege of interviewing senior politicians and managers within the healthcare industry in the US and Japan, and noted a marked contrast in national attitudes towards responsibility for healthcare. In Japan the attitude came across that every individual has a level of responsibility to maintain their own health and prevent illness as far as possible, for example through eating healthily and exercising regularly. The government supports this by licensing healthy foods and drinks and helping to promote them. This promotion also occurs in the USA, as evidenced, for example, by the Food and Drug Administration's (FDA) promotion of healthy foods.

A related contrast between the two cultures would appear to be the attitude of the individual towards 'authorities', as distinct from 'authority'. In Japanese culture there is innate respect for hierarchy and professionals such as doctors. Consequently Japanese citizens are more likely to follow their advice or instruction. In western cultures, epitomised by the USA, individuals seem commonly to deride the 'nanny state' and ignore such things as nutritional advice, while relying on medication to combat problems created by lifestyle diseases such as obesity.

Another facet of this attitudinal difference is the US citizens' propensity to sue suppliers for injuries associated with their products. For example a successful suit against McDonald's after a scalding with hot coffee was followed by an out-of-court settlement relating to a hot pickle. There are signs that consumers also want to blame food vendors for obesity – so much so that in late 2005 the House of Representatives passed the so-called 'Cheeseburger Bill' – or more officially H.R. 554: Personal Responsibility in Food Consumption Act of 2005 – aiming to discourage the public from suing food companies over any obesity that they suffer. The official header to the bill identifies the purpose as:

> To prevent legislative and regulatory functions from being usurped by civil liability actions brought or continued against food manufacturers, marketers, distributors, advertisers, sellers, and trade associations for claims of injury relating to a person's weight gain, obesity, or any health condition associated with weight gain or obesity.

The introductory finding that led to the bill being enacted includes the following statement:

> (4) because fostering a culture of acceptance of personal responsibility is one of the most important ways to promote a healthier society, lawsuits seeking to blame individual food and beverage providers for a person's weight gain, obesity, or a health condition associated with a person's weight gain or obesity are not only legally frivolous and economically damaging, but also harmful to a healthy America.

Europe is probably somewhere between these two extremes in terms of public attitudes to healthcare. Like some parts of Japan, southern Europe has a traditional diet that appears to be conducive to good cardiovascular health. What elements of the diet are most healthy is difficult to establish, yet there are several candidates. Lycopene, for example, is found in tomatoes. It is fat-soluble, and so a diet featuring tomatoes cooked in olive oil, as favoured in southern Europe around the Mediterranean, could help reduce heart disease (as well as some other illnesses such as prostate cancer).

We see, therefore, that public attitudes as well as prevailing politics may affect the priority given to healthcare, particularly in democracies. These attitudes are by no means fixed within a single population. Technology may influence attitudes: as more devices for monitoring one's own health become available – bathroom scales, blood pressure gauges, cholesterol tests, blood sugar meters and so on – individuals may become more inclined to take control of their health. In addition, changing demographics may cause attitudinal changes: an ageing electorate might place more value on affordable healthcare, and thereby influence strongly their political leaders.

On the other hand, a country with an increasingly ageing population will also, other things being equal, have less money to spend on it. This consideration reminds us of the complex relationship between the ability to provide healthcare and the capacity to deliver it. Not only skills and technology are needed, but also cash.

Healthcare Investment Decisions

To summarise the argument of this chapter so far, our contention is that, compared with prioritising investment in defence or education, it is more beneficial to prioritise healthcare because this necessitates an improvement in education: adequate healthcare cannot be provided without good education. In the long term, maintaining a focus on healthcare creates a virtuous circle, with education and healthcare feeding one another. The views of Fidel Castro illustrate this well. What is the secret? It lies in the solid fact that human capital is worth far more than financial capital. Human capital involves not only knowledge, but also – and this is essential – conscience, ethics, solidarity, truly humane feelings, spirit of sacrifice, heroism and the ability to make a little go a long way.

An investment that will stimulate scientific education, in particular, has much to commend it. In the UK at present the level of science teaching in schools is poor. Even at more senior levels it tends to be so general – many practical, experiment-based activities are restricted either through health and safety regulations, cost or difficulties with classroom management – that the teaching is by demonstration or becomes simply theoretical studies from textbooks. This is seen as extremely boring for students. This is achievement of a kind, given the intrinsic fun and wonder available through personal exploration and experimentation in scientific subjects. I write here from some authority, having spent my first seven years out of university as a teacher of chemistry to teenagers (as mentioned earlier). It was truly rewarding to see the students marvel at the wide range of effects: from the squeaky pop of hydrogen burning in a test tube, through their delight at the 'firework' effect of the Thermite reaction; to the wonder of how brilliant yellow crystals of lead iodide can form slowly like golden snowflakes out of a completely colourless, hot solution. To illustrate the sophistication of the human body a comparison of the catalytic action of various inorganic chemical agents such as manganese dioxide on the decomposition of hydrogen peroxide can be compared with that of a small piece of liver containing organic catalysts or enzymes. Even the most indifferent student meets the resulting eruption with gasps of amazement. Ensuring that scientific education is more closely driven by the needs of the healthcare industry in its widest sense could result in a more practical focus, a more interesting style of teaching and thus in a richer supply of educated, motivated and trained healthcare professionals.

In part because of a lack of focus on healthcare, scientific education is underfunded; therefore science courses tend to have a disproportionate number of overseas students who bring money into the economy. Evidence suggests that these students, unfortunately, are more likely than others to drop out of their studies.

Given that there is a strong case for investing in healthcare, what exactly should we be investing in? There are several parameters in this decision, of course; yet the major consideration is to create the right portfolio of provision in terms of infrastructure in order to meet the needs of the population. A balance of specialists and generalists in each area will be needed, otherwise those with heart or eye problems may find themselves having to travel 200 miles to see the right specialist. As well as specialists, the appropriate range and number of technological assets are required. Different specialities will require different technologies: radiography, CAT scanners, monitoring instruments for intensive care and so on. To make these assets work to best advantage there will need to be a corresponding number of professionals trained to operate them.

Not only do these technologies have to be funded, they also have to be developed in the first place. Although it is possible to rely on others to develop medical technologies, developing them locally has clear strategic and financial benefits.

What Is the Correct Investment Model for Healthcare Technology?

It is not feasible for governments to fund healthcare technology development directly. Recent research from Tufts University (a private research establishment near Boston, USA) and others shows that it costs around $200 million and takes ten years to develop and approve a new drug. The chance of any newly discovered molecule reaching the market is only 1 in 8,000. This is not the type of investment that a government is likely to make; nor should it using public funds. Instead, it is better to encourage private enterprise to undertake the R&D and create, through regulation and price control, a favourable environment for these enterprises to carry it out, and then to sell their products for a reasonable commercial reward. In return for its contribution the regulator (government) will get three returns: the advanced products it needs to provide a high level of healthcare to its citizens; export revenues; highly skilled jobs and the economic benefits that follow.

The validity of this model can be seen in the technology clusters that have been instituted since the 1970s and 1980s. We shall be exploring these in more detail in Chapter 4. Whether it be a science park, a technology centre or a 'Silicon Valley', we see small start-ups being funded either by 'angels' – people who like the ideas and are prepared to make early investments for potentially very high returns – or, at a more advanced stage, by venture capital companies. These start-ups often come from within universities or similar research establishments. Within these incubator environments the small, embryonic organisations can share resources. Support functions – such as office or laboratory accommodation, through to legal, logistical and administrative resources – can then be provided centrally by the site management company. This makes all of the contributors more effective and reduces costs. Experienced management expertise too, such as marketing, finance and operations, can be provided at a group level. Such facilities are a often essential to support the more creative skills that invent the original ideas, yet may have less understanding of how to nurture, harness and commercialise them.

Individuals within organisations working in these environments can then efficiently generate valuable intellectual property: patents, trademarks and copyrights. If the state allows them to sell their resulting products and services at reasonable, perhaps protected, prices, they can grow and will in due course generate potentially enormous amounts of export revenue. The UK's two biggest revenue earners are the defence and pharmaceuticals sectors. In 2005 pharmaceuticals accounted for a net £3.7 billion of export revenues, while in 2001 the defence industry earned £4.1 billion.

A Note of Caution

The model we are advocating has worked successfully in many instances – the UK, the US, Switzerland and Germany are among countries demonstrating that developing drugs generates export revenues as well as improving local healthcare standards. However, it should be pointed out that there is no clear or predictable relationship between the level of expenditure on healthcare and the success of these outcomes. While the European Union (EU) and the US have similar populations of around 200 million, R&D expenditure in the EU averages around 10 per cent of gross domestic product (GDP), whereas in the US it is nearer to 15 per cent; yet Europe has lower infant mortality and higher life expectancy.

The relationship between input and output is clearly different in the US and the EU, but we would need much more information about the dynamics of this complex system before we could offer a responsible explanation. If we were to hypothesise about the reasons for the differences in life expectancy between Europe and the US we would need to test our assumptions very carefully, using a vast amount of data and possible underlying causes. For example, we might find that there is a difference in deaths due to heart attacks. This is the *reason* for the death, not the *cause* of the illness. To get at a possible solution we need to examine the causes of heart disease itself: genetic predisposition, lifestyle, social situation, diet and so on.

The Dangers of Heavy-handed Control

The choices that a government makes will inevitably be constrained by other calls on public funds at the time, and also by the need to keep total public expenditure, and the ensuing taxation burden, within a politically acceptable limit. While most western countries have increased their expenditure on healthcare since the 1990s, there has also been mounting pressure on healthcare organisations to control their costs. Regulatory bodies have been put in place to assess the costs and benefits of healthcare elements and make purchasing recommendations or decisions accordingly. In the UK, for example, the National Institute for Clinical Excellence (NICE) has judged that certain popular

Alzheimer's drugs do not confer sufficient benefit at the early stage of the disease to justify the cost of prescribing them on the NHS – to the consternation of patients and relatives' lobby groups.

Even when executed with the best of intentions, heavy-handed regulation of the drugs market can result in a commercial environment that is less attractive for healthcare companies. The multinational pharmaceutical company Novartis's decision to move its research and development laboratories from Europe to Boston, USA, and GlaxoSmithKline's threats to move its research from the UK to the US following an unfavourable ruling on its drug Relenza can be seen as symptomatic of this danger. The US has a free market with higher prices and currently looks like a more attractive environment for R&D than do many, budget-constrained European countries.

In an extreme case, parallel trade may undermine the drug company's business case for marketing a particular item at all. This is true, for instance, of diagnostic kits to help diabetic patients monitor their blood glucose levels. A common business model in this industry is to lease or lend the basic equipment to patients. The capital cost of this equipment would preclude them from acquiring them at all. The revenue and profit are then recouped over a longer period as they sell the consumables at affordable costs to patients.

Given the wide variation in government-imposed prices across the European Union, where parallel (cross-border) trade is encouraged, profit margins on consumables can be eroded to the point where it is simply not worth the company's while to invest in the kit. The alternative to withdrawing altogether from the market would be to decline to supply the product below a certain price, which in practice would mean withdrawing from the lowest-priced countries. This cannot be good for patients or for governments as they will have to fund more expensive acute care as patients lose control of their conditions; and it is certainly bad for manufacturers, employees and wider community stakeholders.

In particular, Europe's encouragement of parallel trade, which will be discussed in full in later chapters, inevitably reduces the profits available for drugs companies. While this practice at first sight would appear to provide benefits in terms of cost reduction (around 5 per cent on average), these benefits are arguably tiny compared to the disadvantage, and possibly unintended consequence, of losing a large proportion of highly paid and rewarding jobs in R&D to other countries, as we shall argue in the next chapter.

4

The Importance of Intellectual Property: Its Development and Protection

The cost associated with the research and development (R&D) required to create a new drug is unrealistic for any organisation in a capitalist economy without some guarantee of suitable returns. This guarantee is achieved by protecting intellectual property (IP): copyright, trademarks and patents. Governments that wish to foster a 'knowledge-based' economy will recognise IP as an engine of economic growth and can foster it in a variety of ways. Research grants, tax holidays, price protection for favourable new products and so on are common formulations of this protection mechanism. Governments or societies that fail to provide this protection – or that even encourage patent infringement – pose a significant threat in the long run to the development of their own economies, the industry and its consumers.

The protection of intellectual property in the pharmaceutical sector creates a very attractive market (~$500 billion per year globally) and provides opportunities for the 'vultures'. The complex nature of the pharmaceutical supply chain – with outsourcing, toll manufacturing, contract manufacturing, third-party logistics, co-marketing and parallel trading – provides ample opportunities for fraud against an unwary IP owner. A variety of structural and tactical measures can be taken to protect this IP and its realisable value. These will be discussed later (principally in Chapters 10 and 12).

Anecdotal disasters due to IP infringement pepper the last decade. Cough syrup prepared with a chemical found in antifreeze killed nearly 100 children in the Haiti region; a fake meningitis vaccine led to 2,500 deaths in the Niger region; and in 2001 the Chinese government estimated that 192,000 people died from taking counterfeit drugs.

Drug development is difficult, risky and expensive. This chapter suggests that strategic investments in healthcare technologies will be made only in environments that are favourable to the generation of returns through the use of measures that will value and protect that intellectual capital. The chapter discusses what is involved in creating and exploiting a favourable investment environment, both from the point of view of the government, as guardian of the welfare of its citizens and their taxation revenues, and from that of a wealth-generating pharmaceutical industry.

The Parameters of Investment Decisions

Investment in healthcare technologies is risky and expensive, and the returns, if any, will only be gathered over the long term. As previously mentioned, only 1 in 8,000 drug items discovered eventually makes it to market, and only 30 per cent of those that are launched achieve significant return on investment (ROI).

> The Tufts Center for the Study of Drug Development today announced that the average cost to develop a new prescription drug is $802 million. Other sources have similar estimates; 'on average it takes 12 years and costs £550m to bring a new drug to market'.1

Yet what they all have in common is that costs, and therefore risks, are increasing – from $231 million in 1981 to $802 million in 2002; while at the same time there are significant pressures on pricing from state sick funds, private insurance companies and government healthcare institutions.

Out of necessity, therefore, the healthcare environment is subject to a high, and increasing, degree of state control. Healthcare technologies are subject to considerable regulatory scrutiny to ensure that they are safe, effective and provide clinical value. The level of control varies between countries. For the manufacturer, regulation adds costs, in the form of constraints. Extensive clinical trials, safety submissions, testing of materials and ingredients, validation of manufacturing processes, maintenance of detailed personnel and training records, control over the marketing, sales and promotional messages and other

---

1   Association of the British Pharmaceutical Industry (30 November 2001) <http://www.abpi.org. uk/statistics/intro.asp>.

literature that can be conveyed to prescribing doctors, dispensing chemists or patients – all these cost ever-increasing amounts of money at a time when pricing pressures are curtailing the opportunities for 'double digit' growth.

A contributor to the success of new product development which is at the heart of the research-based pharmaceutical industry is the level of educational provision and attainment available or encouraged in a given country. Research, development, manufacture and use of healthcare technologies require a sophisticated, knowledgeable and skilled workforce. Before investing in suitable facilities, companies need to be sure that they will be able to staff them. The development of biotech clusters around universities and other technology institutes testifies to this fact.

Here we identify a few simple model healthcare institutes that have clear ambitions. These ambitions require loose collaboration with established and high-performing academic institutions. Other examples of organisations and institutions that have been established in order to generate intellectual property, and hopefully long-term benefits, include the following.

NATIONAL INSTITUTE FOR HEALTH (USA)

The NIH is regarded as one of the world's foremost medical research centres and comprises 27 separate components, mainly institutes and centres. It has over 18,000 employees, over 4,000 of whom hold professional or research doctorates. Although difficult to compare because of the sheer scale of investment, funding and number of projects, the NIH does provide some useful precedents in terms of its governance, management structure, method of peer review and also of selecting projects. Of particular interest are the role of the director and the method of choosing the research programmes.

THE JOHNS HOPKINS UNIVERSITY (USA)

The JHU comprises of eight academic divisions – the most famous of which is the school of medicine that is the largest recipient of NIH research grants to medical schools. The JHU offers an interesting model for commercialisation: the role of the business development group is clearly identified. It is there to serve the interests of the university; it does not operate as a business in its own right. On this basis, it is not a proactive group; nor is it purely commercially focused. Instead it serves to ensure that the university gets the best out of whatever it does.

THE FRAUNHOFER INSTITUTE (GERMANY/USA)

The Fraunhofer-Gesellschaft is a leading organisation for applied research in Europe, undertaking contract research on behalf of both public and private sectors. The institute maintains 56 research establishments and employs 11,000 individuals – mainly scientists and engineers.

While it does not have a specific mandate to spin out companies, the Fraunhofer offers a key service to a wide range of medium/large companies in terms of assisting them to overcome technical/commercial challenges. It has a very active customer-base in Germany and has been successful in generating revenues through offering a wide range of services for which there is a demand. A further benefit of this is that its researchers are actively involved not only in basic research but also in interacting with the marketplace, thus ensuring that much of the activity within the institute is commercially focused.

The Fraunhofer's sister institute in the US also works on a similar model. The institute serves the need of its local region, usually an industrial area comprising many chemical and environmental plants. Hence the research focus of the US organisation is 'chemicals and environmental studies' (bioremediation for example) for which there is a ready, local demand.

TEKES (FINLAND)

Tekes is the principal promoter of R&D within Finland. It does this by funding the research projects of a range of stakeholders, including universities, research institutes and commercial organisations. Tekes provides a very interesting example of an institute focused on increasing the level of technology applications within Finnish industry. It does not undertake any research itself but will select and support projects, and offers a tailored technology mentoring service to companies. Existing knowledge, combined with coaching, can then be used to stimulate the development of new technology companies. To date the approach has worked, with the development of over 30 technology-based companies.

KAROLINSKA INSTITUTET INNOVATIONS AB (SWEDEN)

Karolinska Institutet Innovations (KIAB) manages the intellectual property and related commercial activities of the Karolinska Institute. The success of KIAB is reflected in the formation of over ten new biotechnology companies in 2001–03. Commercial exploitation is achieved through the creation of biotech start-ups and licensing to pharma/biotech both within and outside Sweden. Key factors that have contributed to the success of KIAB have included the recruitment of commercially minded dedicated inventors, early legal protection for any IP that it develops, the effective management of portfolios of patents and the recruitment of experienced industry managers.

BUCK INSTITUTE (USA)

The Buck Institute is an independent non-profit research centre focused specifically on the science of ageing. The institute is young, and its success is measured in its general contribution to the body of knowledge into ageing research; it shows the advantage of bringing together top scientists in different disciplines to work on similar problems. It undertakes research onsite.

STANFORD RESEARCH INSTITUTE INTERNATIONAL (USA)

SRI was founded in conjunction with Stanford University. However, it has since split from the university and operates as a non-profit scientific research institute. The group has started more than 20 spin-off companies leveraging core technologies in new commercial applications.

SRI is another example of a Silicon Valley organisation that has scientists and labs onsite to achieve its goals. SRI International's model has achieved exactly what other similar institutes want to achieve, namely intellectual property generated, companies spun out and technologies licensed to generate revenue and wealth. This success would seem to support the 'incubator' model, or a model whereby the institute directly addresses the development of key enabling technologies and knowledge in its own facility.

BIRD FOUNDATION (USA)

The mission of BIRD – Israel-US Binational Industrial Research and Development – is to stimulate, promote and support industrial R&D that mutually benefits the United States and Israel. It achieves this by providing matchmaking services between US and Israeli companies.

BIRD's individual investments range from $500,000 to $1 million over 2–3 years for full-scale projects. The total project cost to the companies is at least twice the BIRD grant. It also provides funds of $100,000 for up to a year for mini-projects (where total costs are at least $200,000). Neither investment buys the institute equity or intellectual property rights. What it does get is a simple commitment to receive repayments from successful projects, up to a modest maximum. Repayments in the year 2000 totalled $6 million. Since the establishment of the foundation in 1977 accumulated repayments have totalled $64 million.

The 'matched investment' model is an interesting idea and certainly does ensure that all projects undertaken have a clear commercial justification. However, the focus of the institute is very much based on developing stronger ties and ensuring the research projects reach their economic potential.

To demonstrate the importance of a vision when establishing any form of organisation to develop healthcare services, the following examples are offered (see Table 4.1). Each was established with clear aims and ambitions, utilising some specific resources and capabilities available while setting clear criteria for success.

Figure 4.1 lists some of the attributes that are important for the establishment of high-growth biotech regions that will ultimately support the healthcare sector. While it would be ideal for any one geographic region to have all of these attributes, this is usually unrealistic. However a region should possess at least a few of the attributes identified if it is to develop into a high-growth sector stimulating the emergence of many high-growth technology companies.

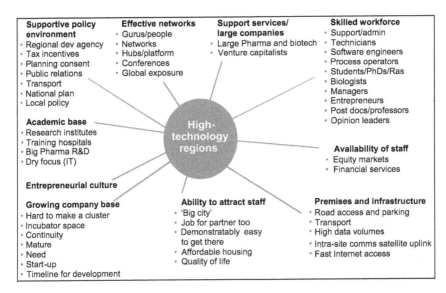

Figure 4.1   Key considerations about the location of major R&D facilities

Table 4.1   Factors demonstrating the importance of a vision when establishing healthcare organisations

Institute	Ambition	Drawing upon	Success factors
Wellcome Trust Clinical Research Facility, Edinburgh	One of five new clinical research facilities founded by the Wellcome Trust in a £16m initiative. With research becoming increasingly difficult to carry out in the NHS, the new centres will provide major sites for patient-oriented research, helping to ensure that advances in biomedical research feed through into improvements in healthcare	Multidisciplinary clinical research with ~22 specific research projects, including atherosclerosis and cholesterol and homocysteine reduction	Has successfully attracted charitable, academic and public-sector funding
Wellcome Trust Cardiovascular Research Initiative (CVRI), John Radcliffe Hospital, Oxford	Main goals are to promote recruitment and career progression of talented young clinical and basic science researchers in cardiovascular medicine, and to provide a platform for collaboration on existing and future cardiovascular research	Draws from: Oxford University departments of Anatomy & Genetics, Biochemistry, Cardiovascular Medicine, Pharmacology, Physiology; Nuffield Dept of Clinical Medicine; Sir William Dunn School of Pathology; Wellcome Trust Centre for Human Genetics. The Oxford CVRI draws on some 20 independent, but interactive, research groups from seven university departments, the Institute for Molecular Medicine and the Wellcome Trust Centre for Human Genetics	Leverages existing academic/clinical networks through focused funding support
The Interuniversity Cardiology Institute of the Netherlands (ICIN)	The ICIN is one of seven life science institutes overseen by the Royal Netherlands Academy of Arts and Sciences (KNAW), an alliance of all eight university cardiology departments in the Netherlands, that together co-ordinate and execute cardiovascular disease research. The ICIN seeks the optimum platform for its research, including co-operation with non-academic hospitals, institutions of basic science or fellow institutes of the Royal Academy	ICIN research projects are carried out in the participating cardiology centres or the laboratories of other partners in research. The ICIN does not have research facilities of its own, but uses the infrastructure best fitted for the research projects in hand. For clinical studies patients are recruited in the participating hospitals. More basic studies are performed in the research laboratories of universities or research institutes	ICIN organisation avoids duplication and waste of talent and money

Pharmaceutical companies typically spend anywhere between 15 and 25 per cent of their revenues on R&D, as shown by the extract from their annual reports for 2006 (Table 4.2). Investment decisions of this order of magnitude, between $3 billion and $8 billion, are not taken lightly.

A common criticism of the pharmaceutical industry is that it spends nearly twice the level of R&D funds on sales and marketing. In answer to that we can suggest there is little point spending all that money to discover, develop and commercialise a drug if no doctors get to hear about it and prescribe it.

What Makes the Commercial Climate Conducive to Long-term Investment in Healthcare?

Here we focus on the major parameter – the commercial climate in which to develop intellectual property that will return only in the long term. We shall consider both purchasing and pricing strategies together with the legal and enforcement frameworks that protect investors from unscrupulous competitors. This climate will be among the most important determinants of the decision to invest in a given country.

DRUG COMPANIES' DECLINING WINDOW OF OPPORTUNITY

The climate in which drug companies operate is getting tougher in several respects, one of which is the increase in competition when it comes to discovery of new treatments. Since the 1990s we have seen a striking reduction of the

Table 4.2   R&D spending by pharmaceutical companies

Company	Global sales ($m)	R&D spending ($m)	%
Pfizer	48,371	7,599	15.7
sanofi-aventis (Euro)	28,373	4,400	15.5
GlaxoSmithKline	23,225	3,457	14.9
AstraZeneca	26,475	3,902	14.7
Novartis	37.020	5,364	14.5
Johnson & Johnson	53,324	7,125	13.3
Amgen	14,268	3,366	23.6
Wyeth	20,350	3,109	15.2
Roche	42,041	6,589	15.7

window of opportunity in which drug companies can exploit a new discovery without any competition. As Table 4.3 shows, post-launch product exclusivity has declined, and the time taken for competitors to arrive on the market after the launch of a new drug has fallen drastically. For example, the arthritis drug Celebrex was only on the market for four months before the arrival of Vioxx. This means that, while development costs of new products are rapidly increasing, the products themselves have a shorter period in which to recover these costs and provide the expected return to their shareholders. This makes it doubly important to find, or influence, the optimum operating environment, and to make the most of it.

INCREASING COMPETITION AND CONTROL

Decreasing exclusivity is evidenced by the fact that Vioxx was launched only four months after the launch of Celebrex, and more than 53 of the top 100 pharmaceutical products in 2001 will have come off patent by the time of writing. Where appropriate, governments seek to exercise increasing control over their healthcare budgets and so exercise strong price control.

At the same time regulations regarding testing, validation and approval of new drugs are increasing costs and reducing the likelihood of approval, as well as limiting the patent-protected time in which the massive investment costs can be recovered.

Table 4.3   Post-launch product exclusivity

Leader drug (year of launch)	Follower drug	Years of exclusivity
Inderal (1968)	Lopressor (1978)	10
Tagamet (1977)	Zantac (1983)	6
Capoten (1980)	Vasotec (1985)	5
Seldane (1985)	Hismanal (1989)	4
AZT (1987)	Videx (1991)	4
Mecacor (1987)	Pravachol (1991)	4
Prozac (1988)	Zoloft (1992)	4
Diflucan (1990)	Sporanox (1992)	2
Recombinate (1992)	Kogenate (1992)	0
Invirase (1995)	Norvir (1996)	1
Celebrex (1999)	Vioxx (1999)	0

Source: PricewaterhouseCoopers (1999), '*Marketing to the Individual*'.

SHAREHOLDERS' EXPECTATIONS

Shareholders expect a minimum level of return. This, for public companies, can be represented by their weighted average cost of capital (WACC). Companies will invest in regions where they can be confident of making at least that level of return; otherwise the shareholders may exercise their right to question the strategy of the Board of Directors. They could do better investing their money in more secure funds.

ASTRAZENECA – WHY NEW PATENT PROTECTED PRODUCTS ARE IMPORTANT

In 2006 there were questions about the strategy of AstraZeneca. The company was suffering from a depleted drugs pipeline, prompting financial analysts to speculate that the company must use some of its $4 billion (£2.1 billion) cash pile to buy another drugs company.

The Chief Financial Officer appeared to acknowledge the need to seize a pipeline from another group when he said: 'We have substantial resources and a balance sheet with few constraints.' In some cases, where no shareholder-value generating investment opportunity exists, management may choose to return benefits to the shareholders through buying back shares.

Then in July 2007 job cuts were announced in a major restructuring exercise following the acquisition of Med-Immune for $15.2 billion (£7.4 billion).

The company then planned to cut 7,600 jobs in a major cost-reduction programme as it announced a fall in its in second-quarter profits for 2007. The programme was as a result of restructuring and acquisition expenses.

In 2007 financial analysts agreed with the underlying strength of AstraZeneca's existing business, as its top five products increased sales by 15 per cent in the first half of 2007, a remarkable achievement indeed; yet they were more concerned about the future. For the business to sustain itself at this level these key products – Nexium, Seroquel, Crestor, Arimidex and Symbicort – must be replaced by newer products as their patent-protected lives expire. Although AstraZeneca, like other major drug companies, had been buying products at all stages of development to fill its pipeline, analysts needed to see evidence of delivery, and so the shares were traded at the time at a 15 per cent discount to its competitors.

Governments that place a high priority on healthcare and on fostering a healthy pharmaceutical industry will adopt or promote reasonable purchasing strategies, allowing manufacturers to charge realistic prices for their products, and permitting or encouraging healthcare providers to buy a reasonable range of products. Insurers, trusts or national sick funds will approve a particular formulary: products they agree to support with reimbursement to patients or pharmacists.

In the UK the establishment of the National Institute for Clinical Excellence (NICE) represents another hurdle which manufacturers must negotiate in order to ensure their products are listed on approved formularies, even within the overall markets in which they have gained marketing and regulatory approval from the regulator based on the safety and efficacy of their products as shown by results of extensive and expensive clinical trials.

In other European countries the formal approval to license products for sale due to their safety and efficacy is separated from the negotiating processes necessary to agree reimbursement prices (that is those the government or sick fund will pay). This may represent the entire cost of the product or a partial cost, giving patients the responsibility to make co-payment contributions. Without such an agreement products have only a private market, where volumes will be small and the products unlikely to be viable. This 'pricing' process effectively acts to manage and control the amount of money the government will pay for the drugs.

In France new product pricing is approved based on an expectation of the volume of sales or prescriptions. Where this expectation, and therefore the cost of the therapy, is exceeded the government will demand a rebate.

How Governments Can Reduce Confidence in Investment by R&D Companies

In 2006 Pfizer launched a product for the treatment of diabetes, using a novel formulation and delivery by inhalation. Previously all patients were expected to self-inject using needle devices. Despite diabetes being a life-threatening disease, compliance with therapy has been lower than required, and therefore the eventual costs for the health service provider has been high. In Germany the inhaled product was initially deemed to have no increased therapeutic value, yet in France the product was supported with reimbursement. This possibly reflects the consideration given to patients' experience of administering the product rather than to the expected outcomes. It is likely that this ruling will be challenged by the manufacturer, Pfizer, on the grounds that increased patient acceptance and compliance with the regimen will inevitably lead to the reduction of overall healthcare costs to the provider, the government.

Possibly the first ruling of NICE that began to increase the nervousness of the research-based manufacturers about their future in the UK was the decision not to approve the novel GlaxoSmithKline flu treatment product Relenza for general use and reimbursement.

Working in Glaxo Wellcome, as it was at the time, I understood that this product had the capability to cure flu by disabling the virus if treated quickly, not just alleviating the symptoms. The product therefore provided the opportunity to mitigate the effects of the pandemics that have afflicted the world in the twentieth century as such occurrences still threaten the world today. Relenza's mode of operation against the virus was novel and ingenious. Its method of application was complex and required a certain level of education, understanding and sophistication on the part of the patient. Patients, however, regularly misunderstand the disease influenza. Patients with common colds and other minor infections consider they have 'flu' when in fact they are suffering from 'flu-like' symptoms. These patients therefore often fail to visit their doctors in the narrow window of opportunity available to administer effective treatment.

The rapid spread of flu across the globe is evidenced by the global outbreaks, or pandemics, in 1918 immediately following the World War I, and in the 1960s with 'Hong Kong' flu, when millions of people of all ages and backgrounds died. The mutation of the so-called 'bird flu' (avian influenza) virus in 2006 is considered to represent a similar, if not greater, threat to young people across the globe.

Developing a treatment, or better still a cure, for such a disease would represent a significant and valuable breakthrough. Glaxo Wellcome felt it had developed just such a product. The complexity and logistical risks around the manufacture and supply of this product were enormous, however:

- Estimates of demand were related to the 'explosions' of infections during pandemics.

- The provision of inventory and manufacturing capacity to replenish supplies in the short time available would require huge investment by both government agencies and manufacturing companies at a number of strategically sited locations around the world.

- The possibility of failing to supply during what could become a major public and political issue also needed to be taken into consideration.

The decision to proceed to develop a product that could potentially save lives was a brave one, and typical of the decisions, some successful some not, of the research-based industry. Clearly the vision and the perspective of the pricing and regulatory authorities were different, and they failed to recommend the product for widespread use and reimbursement. This is perhaps a function of the view of private equity money versus public funds and public funding. Private equity is based on risk and improving potential return with greater risk, whereas public investment is managed by civil servants who have the duty to ensure public money is *not* at risk and who therefore guard all spending fiercely.

Protecting the Investment

For those seeking to foster a favourable environment for the healthcare industry, the problem is the more liberal the purchasing strategy, reflected in the ability to charge higher prices, the greater the risk of attracting less desirable entrants and competitors. This is evidenced by the sudden and numerous interceptions by the US Food and Drug Administration (FDA) and customs authorities of counterfeit 'Tamiflu' in 2005. Tamiflu was the product considered most likely to protect against the expected bird flu epidemic. Any market that has a high commercial potential will attract competitors, both legitimate and less so. From the purchasing point of view, whether within a healthcare authority or a supply chain intermediary, the pricing policies necessary to generate an adequate return on investment will encourage buyers to seek a variety of competitors and alternatives.

It is therefore necessary to put in place protective frameworks – both physical and legal – to allow manufacturers to both protect and exploit their IP to a reasonable level. Protective frameworks not only depend on the laws and regulations operating within the country concerned; they also should control and manage the way in which intellectual property is discussed inside and outside the owning organisation. A few examples will illustrate these points. All employees should:

- understand what intellectual property they own and what they do not;

- recognise that all intellectual property should be safeguarded and handled in a secure manner;

- manage and control documents and the physical environment in which these will be handled and stored;

- ensure that appropriate due diligence is shown, that legally binding confidentiality agreements and contracts are necessary before any IP is discussed with third parties;

- secure their laptop screen against the overlooking competitor in the seat behind you on a 7-hour trip across the Atlantic;

- use a client rather than company name, and first names only if necessary to identify an individual;

- adhere rigorously to the terms of any non-disclosure or confidentiality agreements in place;

- not refer to site, location, company, or names in public places, especially in poor reception areas for mobile phones that cause one to speak louder; in other words, guard their mobile phone discussions in public places.

Working as a consultant on behalf of major pharmaceutical company clients, the concept and adherence to 'consulting guard' is paramount. Sadly, this is not always the behaviour of those directly employed by a company. For example, while sitting on a train from Newcastle to London opposite four senior managers from a food company, I overheard enough confidential information that would embarrass their employer, and no doubt influence the company's share price if the information had been made public.

The Importance of Protective Frameworks in Promoting a 'Knowledge Economy'

An objective for government in designing frameworks for the protection of IP should be to strike the right balance, encouraging long-term entrepreneurial investors while discouraging short-term, value-destroying opportunists or arbitrageurs.

Without adequate protection of IP, the risk is that a market will degenerate into one that competes only on labour costs. This is pretty much the case today in, say, car assembly. Western industrial markets developed and manufactured the vast majority of the world's cars in the early twentieth century. At the beginning of the twenty-first century the major producers of these items are in the lower-cost economies of Asia. In January 2006 that giant of the industry, General Motors, with its heartland in the USA, announced the closure of a number of plants in its home market, with the loss of thousands of jobs.

An economy that is based on low labour costs, and competing on that basis, is one where the standard of living is consequentially low too. Governments will not have sufficient funds to finance education and healthcare; nor will individuals be in a position to take advantage of any such services that are provided.

For the pharmaceutical and medical devices industry the risk is that if prices are driven down too far the market will become one of commodity manufacturer, as innovation becomes choked as it is unaffordable. The threat by manufacturers to move their R&D and manufacturing plants overseas is not an idle one. As we saw in the previous chapter, Novartis moved some of its activities from Switzerland to Boston, no doubt attracted by the proximity of Harvard and MIT and the implied availability of a skilled and educated resource, as well as by the favourable market pricing conditions of the USA.

For an economy in the developed world to thrive into the future, it must build up a base of knowledge and intellectual property rather than abundant supplies of cheap labour. This will only happen if governments take a long-term strategic view and take steps to protect and nurture their knowledge base. The dilemma for this industry, where returns are delivered over a 20–30 year horizon, is that it requires the support of politicians whose term in any one government is four or five years, while the development cycle of these complex products exceeds that by four times.

How the Pharmaceutical Industry Can Shape Its Own Environment

As well as choosing judiciously the countries in which they operate, pharmaceutical companies can sometimes influence an environment to meet their needs better. Lobbying is an obvious way of exerting such influence.

It is also possible to offer governments a quid pro quo; for example building a factory in an area of unemployment might encourage the government of a particular country to agree to a higher price on a given project. It might even undertake to use a subsidised national airline as its preferred carrier. However transparent some of these agreements, or understandings, may be, they are a fact of life. These practices could be considered covered by a definition of politics – 'the art of getting things done' – yet to my knowledge and experience the research-based pharmaceutical industry has upheld the highest code of ethics in such matters. Perhaps that is why it has limited operations in areas of the world that are known to be overtly corrupt, while still maintaining a presence to support the desperately poor and sick in spite of the basic provision of food, water, sanitation that is so important to raise the bar on healthcare management (as already discussed in previous chapters).

Ethical or not, these deals can be risky in that the agreements or frameworks may not be accepted after a change of government. This is among the reasons why pharmaceutical companies will not generally make infrastructure investments in locations where the political environment is seen to be unstable; Africa, the Middle East, Latin America and significant parts of Asia are to be included here. Pharmaceutical companies then need to seek out (and shape) areas that will favour achievement of the required ROI by providing suitable environments. Within their chosen environments, however, companies themselves also need to take steps to maximise their profitability.

This is an industry beset by uncertainty. Inputs are notoriously hard to estimate: a development may easily cost ten times the original projection. Competition too is difficult to predict, and (as discussed earlier) there are cases where a competing drug has appeared within months of the initial launch and expectation of a period of exclusivity, free from substitution.

Other imponderables relate to the environment: a drug that appears to have massive commercial potential may founder when government agencies or healthcare providers, seeking to manage burgeoning drugs bills, refuse to pay the expected price. Buyers or regulators may also decide to restrict a drug's use to a narrower field than that envisaged by the vendor. At other times they may demand that prescribers try cheaper alternatives first; for example, insurance companies or other payers in a number of markets are insisting that doctors try cheaper, generic statins first before prescribing Lipitor, even though clinical opinion might favour the immediate use of Lipitor. Such payer practices inevitably result in slower market growth than anticipated.

Investment decisions will have to be made in the face of uncertainty as to both inputs and outcomes in areas where the buyer-related decision-making processes are relatively stable and the environment is favourable. This has always been true of the pharmaceutical industry, but is becoming more problematic as the pressure to get more investment decisions right increases.

How can pharmaceutical companies manage this uncertainty? As well as doing their best to get accurate estimates of costs, they can also acquire a better understanding of how their market works, so obtaining better projections of outcomes. By striving to learn how factors such as promotional expenditure, sales force investment and marketing influence profitability, they will position themselves better to compare alternative investments.

Getting an accurate picture requires a very detailed model, showing, for example, to what extent visits by salespeople to doctors increase sales and where they might be counterproductive as doctors become impatient through excessive interruptions. A system dynamics model can aid this understanding (see Figure 4.2).

System dynamics models can capture four fundamental characteristics of real-world environments:

1. cause–effect relationships (for example, between marketing expenditure and market share);

2. time delays (how long such expenditure takes to influence market share);

3. non-linear responses (marketing expenditure may exhibit diminishing marginal returns as the market becomes saturated);

4.   feedback (for instance, increased market share allows more marketing expenditure, or a lower price encourages greater uptake and leads to a high overall cost to government).

After the model is built, it can be tested against a range of real-life scenarios in order to check whether the relationships depicted are accurate and to refine the parameters defining the relative strength of each relationship. Although these system dynamics models can look intimidating, they are invaluable for rigorously testing options and evaluating trade-offs. More details of how these models can be applied will be covered in Chapter 13.

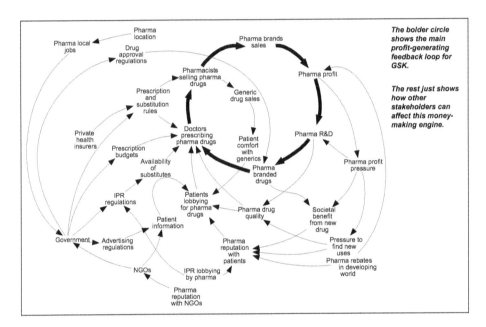

Figure 4.2   Mapping relationships and influences in the healthcare industry

Case Study: Applying System Dynamics to the Management of Cardiovascular Disease

Spiralling costs led a US state Board of Health to seek a new strategy for reducing the impact of cardiovascular disease. To formulate its strategy the board needed to understand what types of programmes were most effective in reducing the morbidity, mortality and costs associated with this disease, and what combination of these programmes worked best.

PA Consulting helped the board to develop a model (Figure 4.3) simulating utilisation rates for a range of health services, including physician care, diagnostic procedures and surgery. The model was also able to test the impact of extending or introducing services such as hypertension screening and lifestyle programmes. This analysis indicated that it would be cost-effective for the state to implement preventative and lifestyle programmes alongside existing emergency and acute care programmes.

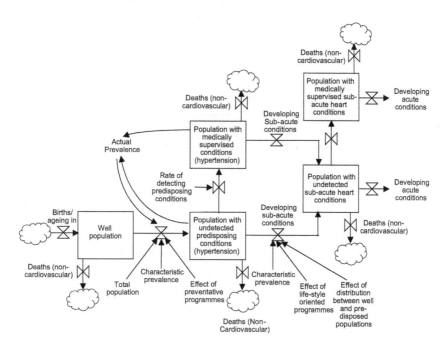

Figure 4.3   Partial view of model-predisposing and sub-acute heart conditions

For pharmaceutical manufacturers, system dynamics modelling can greatly clarify their understanding of the relationship between inputs that they can (to some extent) control and the eventual outcomes of their projects. Figure 4.4 shows the types of relationships that are likely to prevail in this industry: by assessing the strength of each, companies can reduce the level of uncertainty they have to live with.

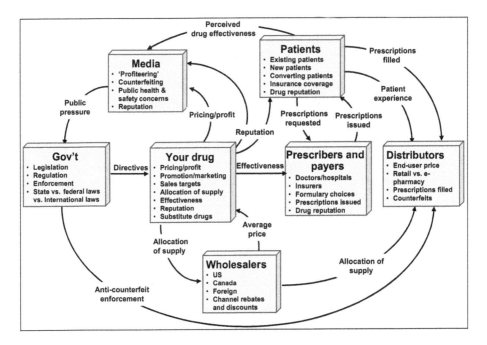

Figure 4.4   Some key dynamics in the pharmaceutical, commercial and supply chain environment

Modelling a problem with system dynamics would make it possible to compare the effects of proposed expenditure on activities such as lobbying, patient awareness and so forth, thus exploring different strategies for allocating budgets more effectively. As well as helping to optimise a given project, systems dynamics models can be used to compare investment propositions, markets or, indeed, countries as potential operating environments.

Models like these, as well as enabling better decisions, are helpful in explaining those decisions to investors in a way that inspires confidence in the company's ability to manage. It is vital to be able to explain why you have decided to move your production facility from Switzerland to Singapore, or to redesign your R&D processes; system dynamics provides a way of doing so.

Each Company Must Balance Its Portfolio of Intellectual Property

Although it is important to maximise the return on individual projects, the most powerful way to satisfy investors is by managing the entire investment portfolio to minimise risk and maximise total return, both long- and short-term. The list below shows some of the risks that can derail a product, either during development or after launch. Some types, such as poor productivity, can be managed, while others, such as the political environment, are usually outside a single company's control. Portfolio management makes it possible to hedge against most risks. Projects within the portfolio need to be continually evaluated since they compete for constrained resources: skills, capacity and cash. An effective portfolio management process will assess all projects in terms of their costs, possible returns, timescales and probability of success, and prioritise them accordingly. Factors that can adversely affect a project include:

- patent expiry;

- poor R&D productivity;

- increasing technical challenges and regulatory demands;

- increased costs of development;

- project attrition;

- hostile political environment;

- pricing constraints;

- patient (non)compliance;

- supply chain arbitrage;

- brand/reputation damage.

There must be clear criteria for success, together with a structured process for making portfolio decisions. Ailing projects need to be killed off without compunction. Such apparently draconian measures need not cause undue loss of morale within the company as long as it is clear why the decision has been made, and that the decision is in line with the company's stated aim and strategic direction.

This advice applies not just to drug development but to all projects, particularly in an industry where all initiatives are long-term ones. A well-known drug company holds the distinction of having run the world's most expensive systems, applications and products (SAP) implementation. It is hard to believe that its project would have been allowed to reach the point where it was three years behind on a three-year schedule if success criteria had been defined up front.

Applying Good Governance to Decision-making

In addition to making comparisons between initiatives within the portfolio, it is important to have a governance process for deciding, at a high level, how money should be allocated. Typically, companies put 35 per cent of their sales revenue into sales and marketing, up to 20 per cent into R&D, 5 per cent into manufacturing and so on. However, these practices are not set in stone. It might be appropriate, if one product has a complex, unique ingredient, to spend money on setting up a project either to buy the supplier or create a competitor to it. Conversely, when a product is coming off patent, the company might decide to invest in buying up spare capacity that another company might use to compete.

With the right governance procedures in places, a company can ensure that it evaluates all its options, instead of just repeating the past. A model for governance is shown in Figure 4.5. This is a way of managing short-term improvement projects against long-term transformational ones while keeping within resource constraints. Such a model allowed a consulting client to maintain and prioritise hundreds of improvement projects; previously it had been inclined to drop all projects except the one that needed immediate attention.

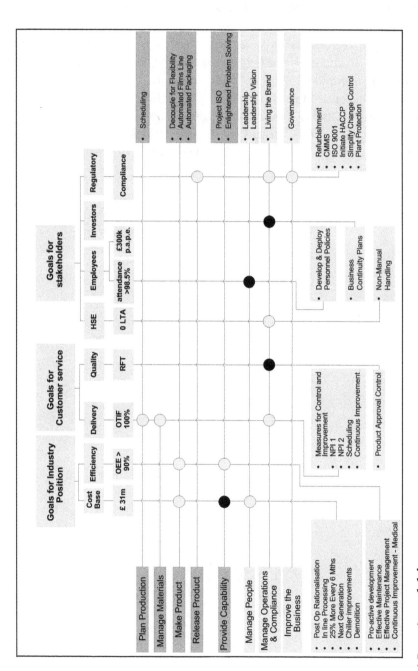

Figure 4.5　A model for governance

Conclusion: A Better Business Environment Based on the Development of Intellectual Property

Pharmaceutical companies have several ways to improve their chances of success. They can choose – and help to shape – the best environment for their activities. They can model their activities so that they understand them better and predict their outcomes with maximum reliability. They can manage their portfolio of intellectual assets so that resources are suitably allocated. In all cases it is a given that they ensure that their decisions are aligned with their overall strategy – development of improved healthcare provision.

5

The Operational Provision of Healthcare

Societies that share a vision for the healthcare and welfare of their citizens must inevitably structure the market by providing the regulatory framework within which providers must operate. The ability of any service providers to operate with freedom conflicts with the need for the society to control costs and establish minimum standards of service expected within that market. This chapter examines a number of healthcare frameworks and discusses how a supplier can optimise its position within any one market. Few people would question that the security, education and welfare of its citizens are fundamental responsibilities of any government. The degree of emphasis placed on each aspect, and the chosen characterisation of each, provides us with a whole array of societies that are markedly different in character.

Firstly, maintaining the security of the citizens can be interpreted as mainly home affairs such as immigration, policing, prisons and so on. This would mean protecting society from individuals within that society, and from those seeking access to that society, who might cause harm. This indeed is a government obligation. The police will uphold and enforce the law as defined by that government through its judicial processes. Maintaining state security through a defence department is also understandable, and here we see the development of military forces and intelligence services.

Secondly, education is critical to the development of citizens who understand and respect the norms and the laws that operate within the society. Also nurturing a generation that can sustain the society through learning, teaching, constructive debate and application of new techniques and technologies that are discovered enables sustainable, peaceful development of the society.

Thirdly we also recognise the responsibility of the governing authorities to provide healthcare services for their citizens. Each government must then find the funds to pay for these duties or responsibilities, and allocate those funds proportionately. Governments levy taxes on their citizens in a variety of forms to pay for services to satisfy these responsibilities. In democratic societies, where governments are routinely called to account for their policies and actions, the raising of taxes and the allocation of funds will reflect the needs, priorities, fears and wishes of the electorate at any stage. These subjective criteria will inevitably change through time as events occur. The responses by the authorities to the changes will also be a reflection of the culture, values and norms of the society.

We can see that military regimes such as those in North Korea or the former Soviet Union tend to prioritise spending on what is euphemistically called 'defence'. It has been suggested that the arms race – continual increases in spending on defence equipment in the attempt to stay ahead of the USA in the Cold War – led directly to the bankruptcy of the USSR. Education and provision of healthcare follow on with a strong degree of central control. These forms of government cannot be defined as democracies; in the medium term their demise is inevitable, as power ultimately resides in the people, and no dictators are immortal.

Where we do have democratically elected authorities we do not see such obvious bias in spending provision. A more balanced approach is adopted. It is in the creation of the systems that will provide and deliver these services where we see the variation in cultures, values and norms. This chapter outlines a generic model of healthcare provision and then provides some specific examples that show interesting variations. This is done to help understand how an organisation can best position itself within any one market and gain an optimum and sustainable position.

A Model of Healthcare Provision

The model in Figure 5.1 has been created to illustrate the arguments developed later in the chapter, but is not meant as an exhaustive study of the field. I suggest that there are four basic roles in the provision of healthcare products and services:

- the consumer, who has the initial need;

- the provider of the products or care services;

- the regulator, who has the responsibility of setting standards of provision, monitoring and inspecting their delivery;

- the payer, whose role is to find ways of raising funds to cover the costs.

It is in the different ways in which these funds are raised and allocated that the market and supply chain challenges are created for the provider. What do they have to do to get a large share of these funds? How do they establish their operations to provide best service at lowest operational cost, perhaps across a range of different systems in different countries?

The diagram maps the key relationships and parameters within the framework and attempts to illustrate the complexity that exists in any one country's healthcare system. The levels of prosperity and employment, the demographic profiles of age, location and disease will mean that even within one country there needs to be a range of techniques and systems to deliver

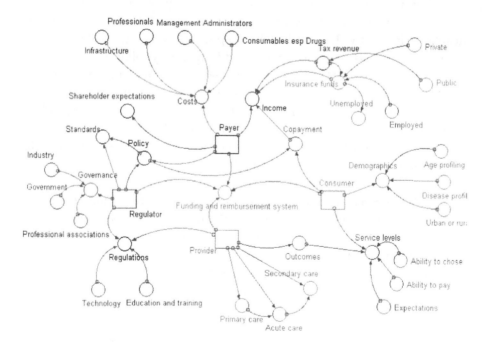

Figure 5.1   A generic model of healthcare provision

effective products and care for all. Rhetoric was used to rally voters behind an ideal or a specific policy, such as in the UK when establishing the National Health System (NHS) shortly after World War II. 'Free at the point of use' rapidly becomes meaningless as soon as we begin to question what will be free. If the provider does not have the resources, if funds are not available, or not seen as a priority over other services, and if the regulator suggests the particular product needed does not provide sufficient benefit, then what may be needed may not be provided without some form of charge or co-payment. This complexity has recently been the subject of controversy within the UK over the provision of Herceptin, an innovative breast cancer treatment. Here we see the complexity of the choices and difficulties with decision-making.

Examples of the Application of Policy

THE USA

At a policy-making level within government, the degree of public funding direct from tax revenues is a key initial question to be answered. All modern societies provide emergency care for those who need it, regardless of status; yet any additional care is expected to be funded through insurance, either private or publicly managed. In the USA citizens are expected to purchase their own healthcare insurance. These privately run profit-making organisations take on the risk of the costs that may be incurred if the policyholder becomes ill and requires long-term care. The costs are covered by a regular, monthly premium. Unfortunately, the costs of healthcare products and treatments tend to rise faster than the general range of products that make up the cost of living indices. Combine this factor with the fact that life expectancy has increased, and that the population age profile is changing, and then we can begin to see an inevitable 'crunch' looming on the not-too-distant horizon.

The 1950 US census showed the aged population (proportion of over-65s) had grown from 3 million in 1900 to 12 million in 1950. Two-thirds of these older citizens had incomes of less than $1,000 per year, and only 12 per cent had any form of private health insurance. Between 1950 and 1963 the aged population grew to 17.5 million, or 9.4 per cent of the population. One in ten citizens was of retirement age. At the time of writing, this figure was 12.7 per cent.

Pressure from this powerful voting and lobby group increased and was heard by their representatives, who then demanded government action. The issue at stake was to provide some federal support or contribution that would afford older Americans access to an acceptable level of healthcare at affordable costs. A bill enabling the Medicare programme was enacted in 1962.

Medicare is the set of insurance schemes established by the federal government to provide long-term care for elderly uninsured citizens; while Medicaid provides hospital care for people on low incomes and other groups eligible through disability or disease type. Thus, the US government effectively began to provide funds through these programmes to ensure all its citizens received a minimum standard of healthcare. Since 1962 the aged population has continued to rise, particularly in Florida, the sunshine state, where large numbers of Americans relocate on retirement. The costs of products and services continue to rise substantially above the background rate of inflation, and so demands for government money to support them grow ever louder.

A report published in 2004 by the National Center for Policy Analysis (NCPA) identified rather starkly how the costs of funding the Medicare programme would escalate in the coming years. The study reported that:

- 2004 was the first year that the federal government used general revenue to pay for social security and Medicare benefits – around $45 billion, or 3.6 per cent of federal income tax.

- The general share of revenue needed to fund these programmes would be about 7 per cent five years from this date (2009) and roughly 14 per cent in a further five years.

The report suggested that after 15 years 1 in every 4 tax dollars would be needed.[1] Figure 5.2 illustrates these points. 'The choices are going to be difficult,' said Andrew Rettenmaier, executive associate director of the Private Enterprise Research Center at Texas A&M University and the study's co-author. 'Beginning in the next few years we are going to have to start raising taxes, cutting benefits or squeezing other federal programs.'[2]

---

1   Bartlett, B. 'Buyer's Remorse for Drug Bill', *National Center for Policy Analysis* (8 March 2004) <http://www.ncpa.org/sub/dpd/index.php?Article_ID=3822>.
2   Rettenmaier, A.J. and Saving, T.R. 'With an Eye to the Future' (May 2004) <http://www.tamu.edu/perc/perc/Publication/may04.pdf>.

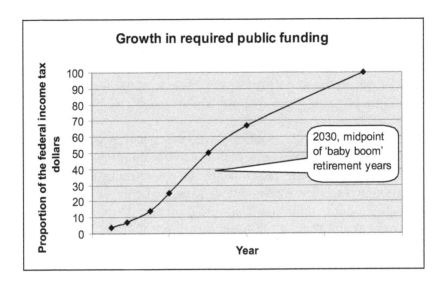

Figure 5.2   Growth in required public funding for healthcare[3]

This is, of course, a serious problem for the US government. It is mirrored in other modern economies in a similar way. What is not identified in these numbers is the ever-increasing pressure there will be on suppliers of healthcare services to reduce costs. In the USA there is a free market and suppliers are able to set their own prices. In most of Europe, the prices paid for products are controlled by a variety of reimbursement mechanisms that are effective price, or spending, controls. For many global pharmaceutical or medical device companies the USA represents 30–60 per cent of their revenues. As the largest single market in the world for healthcare products, the USA will always remain vital to any global provider of healthcare services; yet it seems clear that it will not be as easy in future to make the same level of profit.

The emerging political furore is seen in newspaper headlines which discuss 'cuts in Medicare or Medicaid'. These cuts are reductions in the projected expenditure. As we can see from Figure 5.2, costs will rise for the foreseeable future. The actual sum spent will rise inexorably.

THE EUROPEAN UNION

At the time of writing the European Union (EU) consists of 27 independent states. The initial reasoning behind the treaty was to create a mechanism that

---

3   Adapted from Rettenmaier and Saving (2004).

would prevent another world war within Europe, and provide a platform for democracy, peace and prosperity into the future. The fact that there has been no further world war must confirm the success of the venture in this regard. Other significant conflicts have taken place in continental Europe between the Soviet Union and its former Warsaw Pact states, the current Russian republic and its neighbours in central Asia; and between the Balkan states as the former Yugoslavia broke up.

Comparing and contrasting the European Union (27 countries) and the USA (50 states) we see that the EU has a population of around 491 million and the USA 301 million. The EU land area is 4.3 million sq km, while that of the USA is 9.8 million sq km. In the US the dollar is the currency across all 50 states, while in Europe not all eligible countries agreed to adopt the Euro, and there are a number of smaller, weak economies that are not yet eligible to join the currency mechanism. Federal law is supreme in the USA, and European Union law overrides individual countries' laws (with certain opt-outs). The most important law from our point of view is that regarding competition in trade. This law postulates that there should be free movement of goods, services and capital between member states as the ideal, yet it has four areas of exception:

- Article 28 prohibits quantitative restrictions or equivalent measures;

- Article 30 – exceptions of public health and industrial property;

- Article 81 controls agreements which may affect EU trade;

- Article 82 prohibits abuse of a dominant position.

Supply chains within the healthcare sector are therefore managed under Article 30. We will discuss the impact of some of these other Articles later in Chapters 8 and 13. Article 30 effectively means that each member state is free to define and manage its own healthcare system, impose its own regulations for the supply of products and, most importantly, set its own pricing mechanism. In reality the regulatory agency for Europe, the European Medicines Agency (EMEA), and a process for licensing products known as Mutual Recognition Process (MRP), makes sure that there is no bar to the technical availability of one product throughout all member states. Regulatory approval enables the product to be available for sale in each market, yet pricing needs to be subject to local control. Otherwise the imposition on a small economy to pay for drugs at a centrally agreed price would be prohibitive. This means there can be no 'single pricing' across Europe for the foreseeable future.

Here is the major difference for pharmaceutical and medical devices companies serving both US and European markets: you can set your own price in the USA because you are effectively supplying to independent, profit-making healthcare providers paid by private insurance funds. In Europe each member state effectively pays for the majority of healthcare through its own independently administered sick funds and insurance schemes. There is a small market, funded privately, consisting of the rich or those who can afford to buy private health insurance, and it is often associated with high-status employment. Agreeing a reimbursement price with the authorities is, however, the key to gaining access to the majority of the population within any European market. The pricing mechanism is a way of ensuring that products are made available at an acceptable cost to the state, and is increasingly seen as one of the major levers with which to manage the escalating cost of healthcare. The challenge for the suppliers of products is that they have to understand 27 different systems and manage them separately from both commercial and supply chain perspectives. Table 5.1 shows some of the regulations and their impact on supply chains.

As discussed earlier in this chapter, the proportion of healthcare spending funded directly by taxation is a major political factor in the debate, and one that will dictate the attractiveness of a market to a supplier. This will reflect the values and culture of the local market population. We know that one of the enriching characteristics of Europe is the variety of languages, cultures and customs that can be experienced within a relatively short geographic distance. Driving south from Scotland through England, while remaining within the UK, you will find a variety of attitudes and two separate governments responsible for setting healthcare policy: the devolved assembly for Scotland and the UK parliament for England and Wales. Crossing the Channel into France and going north to Belgium we find ourselves in a federal state with three main communities with their own official languages. Continuing on to the Netherlands and across to Germany, Denmark and, crossing the magnificent Øresund Bridge near Copenhagen, we can move freely into Sweden and Norway. Through this journey we see a range of cultures. Their healthcare systems reflect this.

Table 5.1 **Some regulations and their impact on supply chains in the European market**

Factor	Practical interpretation	Impact
Individual pricing by state	Variation in margins across the region	Profitability is difficult to assess and forecast ahead of launch
Reference pricing between states	Price cuts can be imposed in one market because of the launch in a lower-priced market	Profit forecasts and budget allocations are difficult to predict Launch sequencing across markets is imperative (see Chapter 12)
Free movement of goods	Channel partners divert products between member states where price differentials occur	Forecasting of demand will be highly variable and subject to availability of parallel traded products. A customer (pan-European wholesaler) in one market becomes a competitor in another
Product and packaging regulations are set by each member state	Possibly 27 different packs required to serve the entire market	Inventory control is complex Packs are produced in small lots and so manufacturing costs are relatively high Central distribution and customisation is more difficult than for other consumer packaged goods where these regulations are not applicable Quality standards may differ, increasing the cost of analysis
Variety of languages used	Printed packaging materials are more complex to manage Supply of commercial and promotional literature and other documentation is complex	More complex and costly packaging process Material and inventory handling costs are high Shared services centres require different resources and skills

Figure 5.3 compares the level of total healthcare expenditure for each country shown as a percentage of its gross domestic product (GDP). We can see that there is a general consensus that between 6 and 10 per cent is an acceptable range. This will obviously depend on the state of each economy and the level of services that are provided from this spending. As people can travel within Europe easily they, as voters, can assess for themselves the standard of healthcare provision in neighbouring countries compared with their own. Indeed there are currently considerations that if patients can get more effective healthcare or medical procedures in France than in UK, then the UK authorities should provide funds to ensure patients receive the best treatment available. This debate will no doubt continue for some time before finally being resolved

by the European Court. Whatever the outcome it will provide challenges to payers, providers, regulators and consumers alike.

If we analyse the proportion of this expenditure that comes from private sources such as insurance schemes, patient contributions or co-payment, then compare this with the expenditure from tax revenues in each country, we do get a rather more colourful picture.

Greece stands out as providing the lowest proportion of its healthcare expenditure direct from public funds, and is well known as the lowest-priced market for products in Europe. The expectation here is that patients will provide a significant level of co-payment. This market is indeed characterised by the coexistence of a national health service and an extensive voluntary private health insurance system.

At the other end of the spectrum, healthcare expenditure in Sweden is worthy of note. The entire resident population is covered by a compulsory, tax-based system. This limits the need for any voluntary coverage and payment, and represents the highest and most generous level of publicly funded healthcare

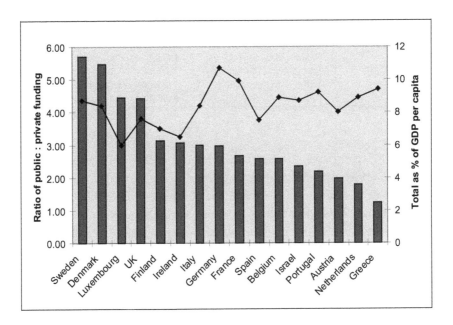

Figure 5.3   Expenditure on healthcare in the EU

in Europe. We can track here in Sweden the changes that have been forced by the pressures that such levels of public funding generate. Responsibilities have been decentralised gradually, with more responsibility for provision being transferred to local governments and healthcare providers. Similarly internal market reforms have been developed in response to the rising pressure of cost increases. As with many things that I have personally experienced with Sweden and Swedish organisations, they have been remarkably successful in their efforts, and the Swedish healthcare system is considered to be among the best performing in the world.

Pressures and Trends into the Future

Healthcare provision costs are expected to rise at a significantly greater rate than general price increases. This is due to a number of complicating factors, but demographic changes leading to a gradually ageing population and the implementation of costly new technologies and techniques are significant drivers. Irrespective of the proportion of healthcare covered from public funds, this means there will inevitably be increased demand on public tax revenues. This is accentuated by the rise in the average age of the population, with its consequent rise in demand for healthcare services. Figure 5.4 clearly shows that the growth rate of healthcare expenditure across Organisation for Economic Co-operation and Development (OECD) countries is slowing, while historically the growth rate of healthcare expenditure has been higher than that of GDP. This means that the proportion of government money spent on healthcare provision up to 2005 has been increasing steadily.

Government providers are responding in a number of ways:

- creating guidelines for prescribing doctors to favour generic products;

- reducing the amount of central control over provision, pushing down accountability to more locally funded providers (to meet local services most appropriately);

- making demands, through reimbursement policies, on dispensing organisations to encourage them to use cheaper, parallel traded products;

- development of payment of 'diagnosis related groups' for treatment in hospitals rather than reimbursement of costs as incurred, thus providing an incentive to lower-cost hospitals;

- increased approval of over-the-counter (OTC) product licences to place the cost of treatment onto the individual rather than the state;

- comparing and collaborating across EU markets in developing pricing and reimbursement strategies.

These changes are seen within the relatively recent EU entrants – Poland, Hungary and the Czech Republic (joined 2004). Previously their governments were the major providers and payers of all healthcare costs. The share of healthcare funding provided by these governments has fallen since 1990. By contrast, where public healthcare costs were relatively low – for example in the USA, South Korea, Mexico and Switzerland – we find that the proportion is increasing due to inflation and demographic changes. Figure 5.5 shows that the proportion of direct public expenditure in drugs is quite revealing; this is further illustrated in Table 5.2, ranked in order of the ratio of public : private expenditure.

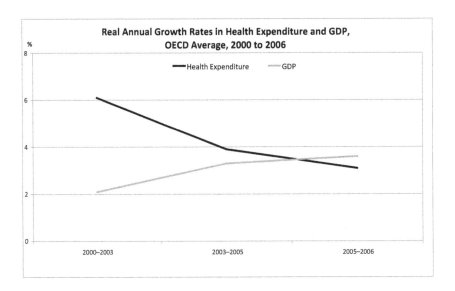

Figure 5.4   Real annual growth rates in health expenditure and GDP

Source: *OECD Health Data 2008* (June 2008) <http://www.oecd.org/datao-ecd/46/4/38980557.pdf>.

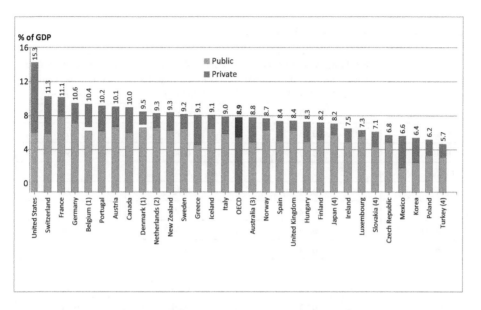

Figure 5.5   Health expenditure as a share of GDP, 2006

Note: (1) Public and private components are current expenditure, that is, investments are not separated; (2) current expenditure; (3) data refer to 2005/06; (4) data refer to 2005.

Source: *OECD Health Data 2008.*

Here we can see clearly that the ratio of public: private expenditure on drugs reflects the overall political view regarding the responsibilities for healthcare funding in general. The USA has 70 per cent of all drug expenditure paid for by private insurance companies or individuals; most systems have around 30 per cent to 50 per cent of total drug expenditure paid for privately, and the large majority borne by the state.

Understanding these systems is vital to ensuring that the supplier gains access to as large a market as possible at appropriate pricing and profitability levels. Where the proportion of public expenditure is high we see strong control over pricing (Greece) and encouragement of prescribers to focus on equivalent generic or parallel-traded products (Germany, New Zealand).

Table 5.2   Pharmaceutical and other medical expenditure, 2006[4]

	Total pharmaceutical and other related expenditure/ capita (US$ PPP)	Public pharm. and other exp./capita (US$ PPP)	Private pharm. and other exp./capita (US$ PPP)
United States	1.00	0.30	0.70
Canada	0.76	0.39	0.61
Belgium	0.69	0.50	0.50
France	0.67	0.70	0.31
Spain	0.63	0.72	0.28
Italy	0.62	0.50	0.50
Germany	0.59	0.74	0.26
Japan	0.58	0.71	0.29
Hungary	0.55	0.67	0.33
Portugal	0.53	0.56	0.44
Austria	0.53	0.69	0.31
OECD	0.52	0.60	0.40
Iceland	0.52	0.60	0.40
Greece	0.52	0.93	0.07
Switzerland	0.51	0.68	0.32
Australia	0.51	0.55	0.45
Sweden	0.51	0.59	0.41
Finland	0.46	0.56	0.44
Norway	0.46	0.57	0.43
Korea	0.45	0.53	0.47
Slovakia	0.43	0.74	0.26
Czech Republic	0.41	0.71	0.29
Luxembourg	0.41	0.83	0.17
New Zealand	0.36	0.67	0.33
Denmark	0.34	0.56	0.44
Poland	0.29	0.39	0.61
Mexico	0.22	0.15	0.85
Ireland	–	–	–
Netherlands	–	–	–
Turkey	–	–	–
United Kingdom	–	–	–

---

4   Adapted from *OECD Health Data 2008*; PPP = purchasing power parity.

Free market pricing, where an equilibrium position or market price is reached between supplier and consumer, will not be possible within a centrally managed healthcare environment. The payer will not be the consumer; a regulator will control access to and the nature of the service provided; and the entire topic will be overlaid with political priorities and pressures. The role of marketing, to negotiate pricing and generate demand, will be completely different from that within a market where the patient can be influenced directly through advertising and more traditional consumer marketing campaigns.

Given that disease and the need for care are not confined to political boundaries, the key questions for any supplying company when considering any single, geographic healthcare market are:

- What level of return is potentially available from this market?

- How do we create a profitable and sustainable position in this market?

- What are the risks, and how can they be mitigated?

- Or, more simply, how much, how to make it happen and what if ...?

It is possible to answer these questions in a dispassionate, logical and objective manner only. For example, by identifying the number of patients who will need the treatment on offer and the price likely to be negotiated for that market we can judge the commercial potential of that market. This is a good start, yet rather too easy. The complexity, subjectivity and politics associated in reality show that a different approach is often required.

It is, of course, necessary at first to demonstrate that the treatment on offer exists and can treat the condition claimed. This will be represented by the submission of marketing approval for the product to the regulator in that country. It may be that the submission is specific to the country, or that the country recognises the mutual recognition process (MRP) to enable many country submissions to be obtained by reference to one submission. This gives authorisation to offer the product for sale in that market. This satisfies the authorities that they are allowing products within their market that are efficacious and safe, and protecting their citizens against charlatans selling snake oil.

The supplier will need to establish and agree a price for the product within the market. Since the overwhelming majority of sales will be purchased by national healthcare systems, to have any long-term success it will be necessary to agree a price at which the government will reimburse the dispensing pharmacist, setting any co-payment necessary from the patient or consumer. As the government or healthcare provider will be spending government or taxpayers' funds we can expect that negotiations will be protracted and involve rather complex discussions, such as:

- Is this treatment necessary, and why do we need to buy it?

- How should we prioritise this spending alongside other important spending considerations: other treatments, defence, police, education, road and other infrastructure projects?

- Why should our country effectively give your organisation money, taking it away from our citizens to pay your shareholders? (This really means, what can you do for us?)

From our perspective of supply chain management, it is the third of these questions that still poses the major issues. In order to answer the questions in a positive, supportive light that will demonstrate to the payer that your organisation is one of substance, has longevity and fully accepts its obligations of corporate and social responsibility, it is appropriate to respond in ways which result in generating local employment and funding for research grants at prestigious institutions. These and other varied mechanisms illustrate a willingness to 'give something back' and to become a long-term partner working with the authorities to improve healthcare in their market.

As a result the map of pharmaceutical facilities across Europe is littered with beautifully equipped secondary manufacturing plants, packaging facilities and distribution warehouses. Many of these facilities have been installed to create local employment that will ease the reimbursement price negotiations for new products. This is massively inefficient from a viewpoint of a supply chain professional, yet supports completely the business case for a product with a gross margin of over 90 per cent where the objective is to create sales.

Many of these facilities have been underutilised and were therefore inefficient and created a problem that emerged only when the facilities were rationalised as part of strategic review cycles that inevitably take place following mergers. Indeed a merger of two companies always leads to a manufacturing strategy review as the new company now has two underutilised, inefficient facilities in each market. Rationalisation is then a major opportunity to reduce costs to justify the investment.

Indeed when Glaxo Wellcome and SmithKline Beecham came together to form GlaxoSmithKline in 2000, it had been felt that other recent mergers had threatened to leave Glaxo Wellcome and SmithKline Beecham behind in the race to gain market share. This, together with the opportunity to seriously rationalise the cost base, is thought to have catalysed this merger. Pharmacia had joined with Upjohn, and then acquired Monsanto; Pfizer were in discussions with Warner-Lambert; Zeneca and Astra merged; and German company Hoechst joined with the French Rhône-Poulenc to form Aventis. Since that time we have seen further consolidation as Pfizer digested Warner-Lambert and then acquired Pharmacia; and similarly Aventis was acquired by Sanofi to form sanofi-aventis. The year 2006 also saw a wave of activity among medium-sized companies, with Bayer and Schering, Merck and Serono, Solvay and Fournier, and Nycomed and Altana coming together. As we can see from Figure 5.6, many mergers since 1985 have failed to deliver expected value.

Many of the mergers of the past 20 years have failed to deliver expected value

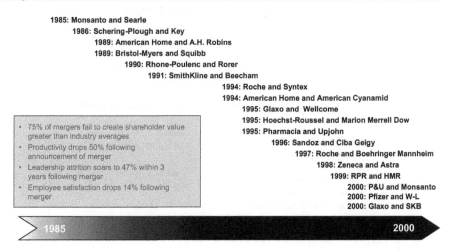

Source: PA Consulting Group

Figure 5.6   Global healthcare sector mergers, 1985–2000
Reprinted with kind permission of PA Consulting Group.

The main driver behind these marriages is undoubtedly the need for companies to extend their portfolio of new drugs in development while providing the resources, through cost reductions, to promote and deliver them. The result will be a major review of their physical assets and resources so that efficiencies can be gained and the cash redirected towards development and marketing activities, often known as profit generating. All very sensible, yet the actual rationalisation and the transfer of product manufacture from one site in one country to another facility in a new country are fraught with regulatory changes resulting in delays and further inefficiency in terms of inventory build. Any subsequent withdrawal of a product from any market can never be good for patients.

The drive for any research-based company is to maximise sales of its products while they have patent protection and can command high prices. Regardless of the nature of any particular market, they will seek some sort of presence in every market. The matrix in Figure 5.7 illustrates the types of investment in infrastructure that might be appropriate as the commercial attractiveness of the market varies.

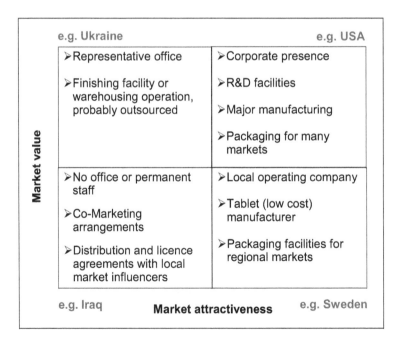

Figure 5.7   Typical infrastructure investments within markets

Conclusion

We see that suppliers respond to market conditions by adapting their infrastructure investments to the perceived level of opportunity available, balanced against their perception of risk involved.

Although we agree that there is no free market within healthcare provision, as the influence of the payer is overwhelming, suppliers are free to determine the level of commitment and risk that they are prepared to make. This can be a win-win situation as there are potential benefits to the local economy, as discussed in Chapter 3, and the payers and regulators have the opportunity to make the market as attractive or unattractive as they wish. The actual operation of healthcare provision within a market will be related to the level of investment and resources that suppliers are prepared to make, given the attitude of the regulator manifest in the regulatory and pricing framework that they establish.

6

Conflicting Goals within the Supply Chain

In the previous chapters we identified that when the healthcare provider and the supplier of healthcare products have objectives that are aligned, they both win from the establishment of a robust and vibrant healthcare market. This chapter deals with the other parties in the supply chain and their different roles, between the original manufacturer of a product and its final delivery to patients. Since my involvement in pharmaceutical manufacturer and distribution around the world from 1983, I have seen this area characterised by continual tension and even conflict between parties. This is what makes pharmaceutical supply chain management fascinating and a completely different challenge from that experienced in other industry sectors.

The situation described in the previous chapter related to the fact that both the paying authority and the regulator share the same goal as that of the supplying companies: namely the availability of the product on the market for their patients. Clearly there is tension around the cost of the products, yet a balance is generally found and the products are made available, providing a win for both parties.

In the supply chain situation that we are going to explore in this chapter win-win cannot be possible for the parties involved: any win for one is a loss for the other. There is only one pot of money, and the balance is about who is able to get the biggest share. That pot is, of course, the difference between the selling price to the first party and the eventual price to the final payer or patient. That is the amount available for the supply chain and distribution partners to share.

Supply Chain Configuration

One small factory producing only one product to one customer nearby will have a very simple supply chain: they will deliver directly. As the number of customers increases the task becomes more complicated, as delivery times and schedules for customers may vary and not be controllable. Here the supplier may employ a specialised delivery company to take the goods from the factory and deliver them according to customers' needs, while leveraging that specialist organisation's existing infrastructure to gain cost efficiencies. Here we have the first trade-off: the manufacturer is relinquishing direct control over the product and service to its customers to an expert distribution company that aims to deliver at lower overall costs for a given service level. If the service and costs are acceptable to both the customer and the manufacturer, then we can have the start of a beautiful, if tense, relationship.

Customers may also require more than one product and ask the supplier (manufacturer or distributor) to either manufacture or procure the additional product on their behalf, or procure the additional product themselves from other sources. This represents good business and customer service, building and enhancing revenue opportunities for the manufacturer or distributor at relatively low additional cost. If the product is procured from outside the existing local facilities again we see another trade-off. The manufacturer is handing off direct control of product quality and the service available via the third party. This may in fact be another division or factory location of the wider organisation, particularly if the product is 'off-patent' and the generics division of that organisation is able to supply it. These decisions are made in order to increase the profit available (revenues minus costs) from the customer, and increase the share of that customer's available budget.

As the manufacturer begins to increase the number of customers an additional challenge arises. Some customer orders may be large enough for the manufacturer to supply directly, efficiently. Other customer orders may be small and therefore very expensive to service via dedicated facilities. Here again a third party with existing infrastructure and reach that can break down a large load, repackage, collate and deliver a set of small orders to distant customers alongside other items from other manufacturers for that same customer may be a better option.

This is, of course, a simplistic way of describing the 'Logistics Twist' – the way in which customers have supplies from many manufacturers, while manufacturers have many customers. The challenge is to set up and configure the supply chain organisation to provide the best service–cost–control balance. This will inevitably mean that some part of the distribution is outsourced, and the manufacturer must therefore spend some of the available margin with the third party in return for an agreed service. Assuming that this service can be acquired at lower overall cost than could be achieved by the manufacturer, this outsourcing will be a positive and sustainable model. There will always be tension in this model, as the manufacturer will seek an improved service from the suppliers at ever-reducing cost, possibly using a number of different contractors, defining and managing the contract within continually improving service level agreements (SLAs).

This model is a pretty traditional distribution arrangement that operates in a whole variety of business sectors – a straightforward payment for service and expertise. The manufacturer can focus on its core business of manufacturing; the distributor can leverage its warehousing and distribution infrastructure to provide benefit to customers through economies of scale by attracting new business and therefore improve its own profitability.

This simple model becomes complicated as the ambition of each party changes and where the title to the goods, or ownership, is transferred. To illustrate this I will reduce the argument to the absurd. The postman does not own your mail; he simply conveys it from the originator to you, for which he is paid a fee via the cost of the postage. This is the essential difference between a distribution arrangement and a wholesale or reseller arrangement. A wholesaler will purchase goods in bulk and will assist the manufacturer by attempting to extend its reach to a wider group of customers, possibly those to whom a manufacturer would not choose to sell due to the misguided concept of economic order size; misguided in as much as a major manufacturer of a patent-protected product requires every item possible to be sold during that protected period in order to recover its massive research and development (R&D) costs. Typically distribution costs in the pharmaceutical industry represent around 1–2 per cent of sales revenue. Margins on the patented molecules can be over 90 per cent, and so to refuse the opportunity of a sale, even at a high distribution cost, is commercially unacceptable. Unfortunately I have had direct experience of situations in which local supply chain managers have failed to meet customer needs due to parochial budget and cost constraints – a question of the tail wagging the dog.

By purchasing the product, the wholesaler now has the opportunity to make profit in a variety of ways: by trading and also by optimising its expertise in receiving, handling and distributing the goods. The wholesaler can negotiate better deals with suppliers based on increased volumes, while selling the product(s) at higher prices due to extra services and reach that the infrastructure provides. These services will often include some link from the end user to the wholesaler to manage demand and place orders; for example, an installed computer system linked directly to the wholesaler. This of course ties the small end customer into a main wholesaler, thus protecting future business for both parties. The smaller customers accept the higher prices in return for guarantees of good service and delivery. The larger customers may well maintain a certain proportion of business through a second source to protect the supply and to maintain leverage over prices.

As a manufacturer in a growing market, this is perfectly fine. My goods are sold as widely as possible and I choose to use a variety of channels to reach an ever-growing number of customers. I also choose to sell to a wholesaler, in large volume, to ensure that even the smallest customer is able to receive my product in order quantities and with delivery schedules that, for me, would be impossible or uneconomic.

The Service Imperative in Healthcare

As I visit my local supermarket in the UK at various times of day I am always amazed by the range of fresh produce that is available. With some experience and understanding of the complexity of the food distribution industry I am impressed by the skill, organisation and techniques used to replenish the shelves a number of times a day to ensure that fresh products are available for customers that the retailer has managed to attract into the store through their marketing and brand awareness. This is one aspect of understanding the complexity of the supply chain.

Another aspect is the relationship of a customer to a particular store. If I, the customer, arrive at the store as it opens in the morning I am likely to be greeted with full shelves, beautifully arranged in a manner that will entice me to browse, examine the goods closely and hopefully purchase them. Arriving at midday, I may well see the display in a used state, the neat arrangement disrupted by other customers picking the items; yet I would still expect to see plenty of produce available from which to choose. Stock availability in retail is the overriding imperative; if the goods are not available when customers have taken the effort to travel to the store the retailer cannot take their money, and the customers may well go to a competitor to procure the missing item – reducing that store's market share of the available budget.

Now, arriving at the store towards the end of the day, when most people are returning from their shopping sprees, it is likely that the fresh produce shelves are dishevelled or possibly in the process of having damaged goods removed and shelves cleaned to prepare for the delivery of new items overnight. As a customer I may go away without being able to acquire the fresh vegetables and other perishable items that I need. At this stage the retailer may well apologise for not having products available, yet it will not be worth replenishing stocks at this time of the day as the cost to do so would not be covered by the level of sales from the demand that would be seen at that time of day: the marginal cost outweighs the marginal revenue. As consumers we come to accept this state of affairs and plan our shopping carefully so as to arrive when a wide choice of goods are likely to be available. To ensure that every available penny is extracted from customers, some supermarkets in heavily populated areas remain open for business 24 hours per day, six days of the week.

Customer service in healthcare is rather different. The service is being demanded and procured at the highest level by the government on behalf of the public. It is being delivered through a set of partners and organisations that are offering their skills, products and expertise to operate within the established framework set up and monitored by the regulator. The actual delivery of this service cannot then be left to the vagaries or the perceived profitability of one outlet. A patient cannot conceivably be turned away from a hospital or surgery because it is not worth it staying open at that time. The consequences of failure to supply the service at this point would be rather more severe than being unable to provide an exotic vegetable for a dinner party. Delivery of the service at the point of use is critical; cancelled operations could be life-threatening.

The severest consequence of failure to deliver an approved, regulated item of healthcare such as a medical device used in surgery, blood for transfusion or use in operations, transplant organs or a treatment for an acute condition whose treatment requires immediate attention, such as anaphylactic shock, is death. The sentiments are appropriately summed up in the rhyme:

> *For want of a nail the shoe was lost.*
> *For want of a shoe the horse was lost.*

For want of a horse the rider was lost.
For want of a rider the battle was lost.
For want of a battle the kingdom was lost.
And all for the want of a horseshoe nail.

By way of more detailed explanation, goods and services distribution within the developed world use the same techniques and operational management processes as those within healthcare distribution. The consequences of an ambulance driver being delayed while transporting a patient to hospital are potentially terminal. The consequences of a vehicle delivering consumer goods late to the retail store will be costly and inconvenient. The attitudes, beliefs, management processes and rewards for those operating in the healthcare environment must reflect the importance of the potential consequences.

The Complexity of the Wholesale Operation

In Europe there are two categories of wholesaler: the full-line wholesaler and the short-line wholesaler (see Figures 6.1 and 6.2). The difference is that full-line wholesalers accept a responsibility to stock, service and deliver every item approved for sale in their market. Short-line wholesalers deal in those items in which they can see a regular demand that will allow them to trade and turn over their stock regularly and profitably.

To illustrate this, in France over 3 billion packages of pharmaceuticals are distributed from wholesalers to pharmacies every year, yet 75 per cent of these products are distributed to less than one pharmacy per month. Wholesalers deal with many items and their expertise lies in managing the complexity of holding many items and delivering them efficiently to many customers at very short notice, frequently only hours.

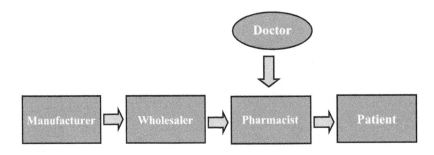

Figure 6.1   The traditional model of the medicine supply chain

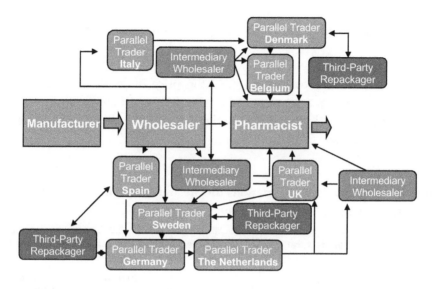

Figure 6.2   A contemporary model of the medicine supply chain

GIRP is the European Association of Pharmaceutical Full-line Wholesalers (Groupement International de la Repartition Pharmaceutique). The members of GIRP employ around 140,000 people. They hold stock from over 3,500 suppliers and manage over 100,000 different medicinal stock-keeping units. In total they distribute across Europe to over 133,000 pharmacies. Their role is to deliver medicines in a timely, safe and efficient way, and thereby guarantee access to all medicines for the 450,000 patients treated daily throughout the continent. In 2004 there were 673 licensed full-line wholesalers in Europe operating from 1,458 warehouses. The three largest wholesalers – Celesio, Alliance Unichem and Phoenix – are pan-European and had a market share of 46 per cent in 2004, rising to over 60 per cent in 2006.

By contrast in the USA, a market of comparable geographic size, over 90 per cent of all items are delivered by only three major wholesalers: AmerisourceBergen, Cardinal and McKesson. At the time of writing there were only 27 independent wholesalers supplying the rest of the market, and this is number is shrinking gradually.

Pressures on this sector in both markets are resulting in consolidation to optimise size and gain efficiencies of scale. These pressures are coming from both ends of the supply chain; the manufacturer wishes to regain margin while the payers for the products are seeking to limit and reduce their acquisition price. Wholesale market growth in Europe has consequently declined steadily since 2000.

As discussed in previous chapters, the price of products is set by the regulatory authorities across Europe in a variety of different, locally specific models. The wholesale margin is similarly fixed and allows little room for manoeuvre (see Table 6.1).

Table 6.1   How different markets dictate and divide margins available within local distribution channels

Market	Manufacturer price as % of final	Wholesale margin	Retail pharmacist margin	VAT payable
UK	75–77	~12.5%	10–15%	0% for Rx, 17.5% for OTC
Czech Republic	69	5–7%	25–27%	
Greece	49.2	7.78%	35%	8%
Sweden		4.2% average	20% average	
Italy		6.65%	26.7%	10%

Examples of pricing arrangements in France, Germany and Italy are shown below, and all provide some level of commercial protection for both pharmacist and wholesaler. These were collected in discussions with distribution managers within local operating companies of a major pharmaceutical manufacturer. They were accurate at the time (2003) and are subject to regular review and amendment. They serve here as an example of the complexity, not as a definitive source of information.

The specific regulations in each market are very complex and the impact of imposed and frequent price changes can be significant. To illustrate this complexity I identified a couple of the calculations for three of the biggest markets in Europe, collected from similar sources.

FRANCE

- Of the retail price of a medicine, the industry receives 68.1 per cent, wholesalers 6.3 per cent, pharmacists 23.5 per cent and the state 2.1 per cent in the form of taxes.

- A new distribution margin system was introduced on 1 September 1999 with the aim of encouraging pharmacists to substitute generics and to increase the eroding pharmacy margin.

- Under the pharmacy margin regulation, pharmacists started to submit reimbursement claim forms electronically from January 1999 for a fee of €0.05 per form.

- Margins are not controlled for non-reimbursed products.

To promote generic substitution, the value of the wholesaler and pharmacist margin on generics is equal to the value of the wholesaler and pharmacist margin on original products.

Reimbursed products

The overall wholesaler margin is calculated using a different mark-up for two slices of the manufacturer's price:

- 10.74 per cent for the part of the ex. man. price ≤ €22.9;

- 6.00 per cent for the part of the ex. man. price > €22.9.

The margins are not controlled for non-reimbursed products, illustrating the importance of government, payer control.

GERMANY

Until 2003, pharmacists were only allowed to own one pharmacy. Since 2004, they may run a maximum of four, and the three branch pharmacies must be in the same or a neighbouring county as the main pharmacy. The margin system is in the form of a capped upper price band:

- eight price bands;

- average margin 4.3 per cent;

- average mark-up 7.8 per cent;

- lowest-priced drugs (<€0.84) gain mark-up of 21 per cent;

- highest-priced drugs (> €684.77) gain mark-up of 3 per cent, plus fixed sum of €61.63.

ITALY

- Both wholesaler and pharmacy margins are fixed for reimbursed medicines.

- Pharmacies exploit competition between the large number of wholesalers and use discounts to supplement their margins.

- No discounts are allowed for generics.

- Margins for reimbursed products apply, regardless of the marketing authorisation route (the previous rule which laid down five calculation bands for centralised procedure was abolished by the 2003 Finance Act).

- There is a fixed wholesale margin of 6.65 per cent of the price to public (excl. VAT) for reimbursed products.

- There is a fixed pharmacy margin of 26.7 per cent of the price to the public (excl. VAT).

- Pharmacies have to grant the national health system compulsory discounts on the prices of medicinal specialties (claw-back), proportional to prices, five price bands.

- Discounts are strongly reduced for 'low sales' pharmacies.

- Compulsory discount only applies to branded medicinal specialties (including off-patent branded products), with the exception of those specialities with prices equal to the reference prices.

- Generics are excluded from the compulsory discount.

This serves to illustrate that although the customer service requirements are given for wholesalers distributing to pharmacies, and therefore their cost-to-serve is largely fixed, the calculation of their profits and even revenues available across their whole portfolio is difficult to estimate. Every time one government amends the reimbursement terms, or a manufacturer alters their pricing strategy, the wholesaler must recalculate the impact on their business, and their response.

As with any other commercial organisation, the wholesalers will seek to purchase at the minimum price possible, sell for the highest price possible (largely fixed in our case) and closely manage their cost of operations. The fact that European law allows wholesalers to trade pharmaceuticals, within specific regulations, means that pan-European wholesalers have the opportunity to transfer products purchased in low-priced markets within their operations to sell them in high-priced markets. This parallel trade is the main cause of tension between manufacturers and wholesalers in Europe and will be discussed in later chapters.

'When negotiating with my wholesalers I do not know if I am talking to a partner in healthcare distribution, a customer, or a competitor.' This is a quote from a European logistics director of a top-three pharmaceutical company. In the USA similar tensions were previously caused by wholesalers speculating and stockpiling in advance of an expected price increase by the manufacturer. This would cause massive swings in demand which resulted in significant overstocking of the distribution channel, arbitrage between channels to reduce the working capital exposure and a distortion of the real, sustainable profitability of key products and their owners. This was most clearly evidenced by the Consolidated Class Action against Bristol-Myers Squibb in 2003, as shown in the panel.

BRISTOL-MYERS SQUIBB SECURITIES LITIGATION US DISTRICT COURT, SOUTHERN, DISTRICT OF NEW YORK

The claimants held that Bristol-Myers Squibb (BMS) had engaged in a fraud of massive proportions – involving over $2 billion of improperly recorded sales.

They claimed that the scheme misled the expectations of Wall Street and the investors into believing that they were meeting their targets. In reality they 'made their numbers' by recognising revenues in violation of generally accepted accounting practice (GAAP).

Bristol-Myers Squibb did admit to improperly booking billions of dollars of revenue from inventory that it 'stuffed' into the distribution channels. The company also admitted that senior management were engaged in a concerted effort to artificially inflate the company's earnings at the end of financial quarters. This involved the improper use of incentives to wholesalers to increase purchases of BMS products to sufficient amounts to meet the quarterly sales targets.

The company admitted that there was no legitimate reason for 'channel stuffing' other than to mislead investors.

The overstatement of the company revenues is quite staggering:

1999 $ 376 million

2000 $ 521 million

2001 $1,284 million

It was estimated that $3 of every $10 earnings was due to this fraudulent activity, and it rates as one of the biggest frauds in history to that time.

This course of events was hastened by the pressure on the company's blockbuster drugs – Pravachol, Glucophage, Taxol and BuSpar – which faced competition from both generic and other brand-name products. Simultaneously the productivity of the R&D operations was falling so there were insufficient new products in plan, meaning that the company would inevitably see a future reduction of revenue.

In the process of adding new products to the portfolio, BMS management entered into an agreement with ImClone to develop and market the potential blockbuster cancer drug Erbitux. It came to light that the company knew that the product was unlikely to pass FDA scrutiny, and made misleading statements, overstating the potential revenue earning and their timing for this product.

When the FDA officially announced its rejection of the drug in 2001, the scandal came to light. In submissions in 2002 the company admitted that the wholesalers were holding three months of excess inventory. Full disclosure was made in 2003 and the company admitted its attempts to manipulate earnings and deceive shareholders. During the overstatement of its revenues the share price had been $77.94; by the end of the period it had fallen to $22.51.

Conclusion: Where distribution and manufacture are effectively decoupled from the generation of demand and consumption, the trading between supply chain parties will seek to optimise their own parochial agendas, which will effectively sub-optimise the efficiency of the overall supply chain.

Consolidation of the industry across Europe is therefore inevitable as wholesalers seek to leverage scale and purchasing power. As mentioned above, the three major wholesalers in Europe have increased their market share from 46 to 60 per cent in two years.

Despite being involved in complex operations, the existence of wholesalers does, in fact, reduce the total number of transactions that would need to occur directly between manufactures and all end pharmacies across all products, given the existing service expectations. GIRP has estimated that their 2004 level of 28 billion transactions annually would rise to over 528 billion if direct distribution was the norm.

Integration to Gain Control

In the basic three-tier model that we have identified – manufacturer, wholesaler and pharmacist/patient – there are many more wholesalers than manufacturers and many more pharmacies than wholesalers. Pharmacies have the ability to buy their products from a number of wholesalers, who must compete for their business, and manufacturers can find that, if there are competitive products available, the wholesalers can influence demand.

With this freedom of choice for the pharmacist comes the consequence of variation in demand, revenues and profits of the manufacturers. It will be the role of the management of the manufacturers and wholesalers to stabilise this variation by finding ways to 'tie in' their pharmacist customers.

Manufacturers of patented products, with full-line wholesalers, have the luxury of knowing that when their products are prescribed they must be supplied and therefore purchased from the manufacturer. When the patent expires there will be greater freedom for wholesalers and pharmacists to decide on which product is dispensed, driven by the generic competition that will flood into the lucrative market. One example that illustrates this occurred in 2008 when the patent on Fosamax (Alendronate sodium) expired. In Belgium this product was the third largest pharmaceutical brand, selling around 7 million units with a retail price of >€90 for a standard pack. On the day the patent expired, generic providers offered their own versions of the product, selling at <€40 per pack. Within two months six generic companies were offering their own versions: ratiopharm, Sandoz, Teva, Eurogenerics, Mithra and Mylan. In response to a prescription for Alendronate the pharmacist and wholesaler can now offer one of seven different items. No doubt the one they choose will reflect their own specific objectives and local profitability.

Wholesalers providing a wide portfolio can attempt to win over their pharmacy customers with 'bundle' discount deals and other arrangements. One common form of tie-in is to provide the pharmacist with sophisticated software that will manage their dispensing process, inventory replenishment and reimbursement submissions.

There is also the possibility of manufacturers acquiring wholesalers, and wholesalers buying retail pharmacies. Indeed the freer markets allow the loose consolidation of pharmacies into buying groups or cooperatives, and consolidation of pharmacies into chains such as Walgreens, Boots and Multipharma. Some of these chains become integrated with wholesalers groups – Celesio/Lloyds, Alliance/Boots – although there are restrictions in some markets to limit such consolidation. The logic of these restrictions lies in the reluctance of the payers (governments) to assist any one commercial organisation in exercising power over the provision of a service it has defined and regulates. Again, healthcare supply chain management has a significant political overlay with which to contend.

In the USA we see organisations such as Rochester Drug Co-operative (RDC). This organisation is an arrangement of independent pharmacies across New York State and Pennsylvania that wish to remain independent, and have aggregated their demands to provide themselves with purchasing power and guarantees of service. The resulting wholesale operation boasts over 1,000 independent pharmacy retail outlets as customers in only three states. RDC is one of 27 independent wholesalers supplying less than 10 per cent of the market demand in USA. Only three others; McKesson, AmerisourceBergen and Cardinal, cover the remaining 90 per cent.

There was a wave of integration between manufacturers and wholesalers during the 1980s as manufacturers attempted to exercise greater control over demand. The most notable of these was Merck-Medco. Merck is a major research-based company whose portfolio was in decline, and Medco is a prescription management organisation that provides medicines to patients via employee insurance schemes. This relationship eventually broke up as their business models and strategies were too diverse.

This example illustrates that the requirement to integrate along the supply chain brings a level of operational and management complexity that must not be underestimated. Such changes cause the management to pose the question 'What sort of business are we?' The skills and competences required to run a research-based manufacturing company or a wholesale distribution and customer order management organisation are very different; we need both.

Conclusion

Markets that have established a national healthcare framework and governance impose a level of service to which all regulated pharmacists, wholesalers and manufacturers must conform. This imposes restrictions not only of service, but also of price.

Within this framework manufacturers must compete with each other for their share of the overall healthcare budget by negotiating an acceptable reimbursement price. Full-line wholesalers accept their obligation to manage a huge range of slow-moving items and compete with each other, and manufacturers, to secure their portion of the available margin. Short-line wholesalers could be considered unfair competitors in this market as they enjoy the opportunity to supply fast-moving, profitable items without the obligation to supply slower-moving items. They do, however, provide the opportunity for governments to pay less for the goods through the mechanisms of parallel trade and the resultant government 'claw-back' of reimbursement price.

Hence we see conflict between payers and providers of the services: government or insurance funds, manufacturers, wholesalers and pharmacists. This can only represent a positive opportunity to create competition while maintaining service levels.

7

Diversion and Parallel Trade

In Chapter 6 we discussed the complexity of typical healthcare supply chains, the large number of partners and therefore the diversity of possible channels to market for any product. Diversion is defined here as the unauthorised and unwarranted movement of products between these channels initiated by supply chain participants. The result of this diversion is the potential lost opportunity to realise higher revenues and profits that would be achieved if all products were sold only at their highest realisable price. In this chapter we will discuss the causes of diversion and its impacts, both real and perceived. In the next chapter we will identify ways in which organisations can respond to minimise this lost opportunity.

Introduction: Three Dilemmas That Make for an Ineffective Supply Chain

Three dilemmas beset the healthcare industry and prevent it from being fully effective. These relate firstly to the question of how to tackle risk; secondly, to the choice of product areas; and thirdly, to pricing and promotional policies.

ATTITUDES TO RISK

The pharmaceutical and medical devices industries operate under conditions of high commercial risk. To bring any new product to market requires sizeable investments of time and money: Tufts University data from 2003 suggests that it costs $800 million and takes between 10 and 15 years to bring a new product successfully to market. It can easily be seen that in this period a great deal can go wrong, so that in the worst case there may be no return at all on a huge investment.

Companies attempt to optimise the risk/return by careful analysis, selection and management of the projects they prioritise through the development pathway. Central to the strategic business planning process is therefore management of the portfolio of these development projects. This may mean 'licensing-in' products from other companies and 'licensing-out' products that, through the development activities, are seen not to fit appropriately into the desired portfolio due to their profile of risk, cost or resource required to achieve their commercial potential and fit with the existing strategy. A 'blockbuster' drug such as Zantac, Prozac, Lipitor or Viagra will bring enormous rewards, yet these are the exception. Many pharmaceutical companies were originally founded on the success of just one product. The success of biopharmaceutical specialist Amgen is such an example. Originally founded in 1980 as Applied Molecular Genetics, Amgen pioneered the development of novel and innovative products based on advances in recombinant DNA and molecular biology. More than a decade ago, Amgen introduced two of the first biologically derived human therapeutics, Epogen (Epoetin alfa) and Neupogen (Filgrastim), which became the biotechnology industry's first blockbusters.

Historically, we can trace similar block company histories, developing and commercialising rapidly through the launch of one or two blockbuster products: Wellcome with Trimethoprim (a chemically produced antibiotic); SmithKline with Tagamet; Glaxo with Zantac; Astra with Losec (all anti-ulcer drugs); Lilly with Prozac (the antidepressant). There are many examples, and this is why large, now cash-rich organisations continue to invest significant proportions (10–25 per cent) of their sales revenues back into research and development (R&D).

At the same time regulators, who safeguard public safety, have increased their control and require more rigorous study to produce increasing levels of clinical trial data that demonstrate the safety and efficacy needed to gain marketing approval for a product. This increases the cost burden, the risk, at a time when pricing pressures are reducing the commercial potential of the products. The marketing investment also required to exploit the potential of the product launch are immense and beyond the resources of smaller organisations. Licensing deals are therefore common. These allow small, innovative university and research organisations to maintain their ability nimbly to incubate early research projects and allow the 'Big Pharma' investors to absorb these into their overall portfolios. Only these Big Pharma corporations have the resources available to invest the necessary level of funding to give products the best chance of getting to market and realising their potential.

CHOICE OF PRODUCT AREAS

The subject of portfolio management in the area of research and development is entire in itself. Here we will merely touch on the topic by considering the impact of decisions on management of the supply chain.

The directors of a publicly listed company have a number of fiduciary duties, among which is the duty to promote the interests of the company. It can be argued that to 'maximise the current value of the future cash flows, or revenue streams' is a summary of this duty. The company's share price is based on future cash flow, and maximising any revenue stream will support this.

This business imperative, more sales at highest possible prices, drives all decision-making. In order to create products that will be profitable for their investors, companies put most of their R&D funding into the development of products within therapy areas that have the greatest commercial potential. The products might not be in the therapy areas that relieve the greatest suffering to the greatest number, but rather those that realise the greatest commercial opportunity.

The consequences of these decisions have unappealing consequences for healthcare consumers. There is a tendency to develop drugs to *treat* rather than *cure* diseases. It is easy to see that treatments will generate an ongoing revenue stream, while cures will not. Indeed for that reason, vaccines which have brought untold benefits to millions since their development are the seen by marketers as the poor relations of their more celebrated (western) lifestyle-enhancing pharmaceutical products.

There are also areas of acute need for which drugs are either not developed at all, or are not available because they are too expensive. As we have seen in Chapter 2, governments do sometimes try to offset the commercial influence on drug companies by allowing exceptional prices to be paid for 'orphan drugs' so that companies can recover their costs in a therapeutic area that would otherwise not be commercially viable.

Orphan drugs

In the United States orphan drugs are defined as those that treat diseases that affect fewer than 200,000 people, or 5 per 10,000 in the community. Some examples include Huntington's disease, myoclonus, amyotrophic lateral sclerosis (ALS, or Lou Gehrig's disease), Tourette syndrome and muscular dystrophy.

Legislation in the United States, Japan and Europe provides financial incentives to biopharmaceutical companies producing orphan drugs. The Orphan Drug Act in the United States provides seven years of marketing exclusivity for orphan drugs approved by the US Food and Drug Administration (FDA) for the treatment of certain rare diseases. Tax credits for clinical research are also available to ensure that the necessary level of data is available through clinical trials for marketing approval.

Similarly, Japan and the European Union (EU) have their own orphan drug plans that allow for market exclusivity and commercial protection following approval of successful products. Examples of such drugs are:

- Fabrazyme from Genzyme, a treatment for a rare condition where patients suffer from a low level of, or are missing, an essential enzyme;

- Zavesca from Actelion, a treatment for Gaucher disease;

- Trisenox from Cell Therapeutics, a treatment for acute promylocytic leukemia;

- Pfizer's Somavert – a treatment for acromelagy, a rare hormone disease;

- Carbaglu, marketed by Orphan Europe, is a treatment for a disease where patients suffer from high levels of ammonia in the blood.

All of these products have very small patient populations and as a consequence are unlikely to generate annual sales in excess of $100 million globally.

Glivec from Novartis, as a treatment for chronic myelogenous leukemia (CML), does generate global sales of more than $1 billion as it also has great potential for the treatment of non-orphan indications. Similarly Tracleer from Actelion, a treatment for pulmonary arterial hypertension (PAH), has significant commercial potential for its opportunities in other disease areas.

These examples are by way of illustrating that the pharmaceutical industry does exist to develop products that will improve the human condition, which benefits us all. In doing so it takes on significant risk and it is in our long-term interests to ensure its commercial interests are protected so that it can build sustainable businesses.

PRICING AND PROMOTIONAL POLICIES

The same dilemma between balancing obligations to investors and to the community at large relates especially to decisions in sales and marketing. From a moral point of view most of us would say that medical treatment should be affordable; yet management's obligations to their investors mean that they are duty-bound to charge as much for each product as they can achieve. The next section will look in more detail at how companies approach this pricing challenge.

Morally, once again, it seems desirable to distribute a medicine to all who need it, yet publicly traded commercial companies will promote their products to the widest possible audience of people or organisations that can afford to pay for it. It is noteworthy in this context that most companies spend around 30–35 per cent of their revenue on sales and marketing – significantly more than the 10–25 per cent that usually goes on R&D.

Table 7.1 compares and contrast the pharmaceutical supply chain structure and drivers with other businesses with which we, as consumers, have more direct experience; we all buy food from retailers for example.

Regardless of the industry sector, companies will seek to manage their product portfolios and their supply chains in a way that satisfactorily addresses risk. Their goal is to develop products for which there is a profitable market, and to manage the cost of marketing, sales and distribution of those products to maximise the resultant profits. Where diversion or parallel trade is an issue it will be important to analyse the effect of increasing the complexity of the product portfolio and availability to markets in an attempt to prevent or reduce the opportunities for channel partners to exploit the variation in price. This occurs in all business sectors, so we see right- and left-hand drive models of car, front- and top-loading washing machines allegedly designed for consumer preferences in different markets, as well as different specifications for electrical goods. On the one hand these subtle product variations drive costs within the manufacturing environment, and on the other they can be exploited by marketers to ensure they work to optimise pricing and profit where such market idiosyncrasies exist. Where the Cost of Goods Sold (COGS) is a small proportion of the sales revenue the focus will be to increase the number and range of market-specific products. The pharmaceutical industry is an excellent example of this, with huge final, market-specific pack ranges, low COGS and a wide variety of government-imposed prices. For white goods and automotive products the balance of effort is to minimise the complexity of the product offering, which, together with the resultant impact of parallel trade, will lead to narrow price bands between markets.

Of those illustrated in Table 7.1, it is only in the pharmaceutical industry that we see the additional pressure of morally equivocal implications of business decision-making. In this book we contend that in a mixed economy the profit motive produces the most beneficial overall outcome for patients through the development of sustainable enterprises.

The Impact of Diversion and Parallel Trade on the Supply Chain

The three areas of risk, portfolio management and pricing strategy provide challenges to efficient supply chain management. We are considering scenarios

	Pharmaceuticals	Food/FMCG	White goods	Automotive
Demand generated by	Doctor	Retailer	Consumer	Dealer/consumer
Change of ownership	Manufacturer to wholesaler	Manufacturer to retailer	Manufacturer to retailer	Manufacturer to dealer
Lead time/availability				
- Expectations	Instant (minutes)	Instant (picked)	Days delivered	Weeks to dealer
- Reality	Return visit	Alternate brand	Days delivered	Weeks to dealer
Value of a sale to				
- Consumer	Prescription charge	~ £10s	~ £100s	~ £Ks
- Manufacturer	~ £10s	~ £10s	~ £100s	~ £Ks
COGS (% sales)	<20%	~ 60%	~ 60%	~ 75%
Dist. cost (% sales)	>12%	~ 4%	8%< costs >4%	Contribution by customer
Key supply chain driver	Manufacturer	Retailer	Manufacturer (Brands)	Manufacturer
Order transmission	Prescription (paper)	Visit or Internet	Visit or Internet	Visit or Internet
Decoupling point	Wholesaler	Manufacturer (factory)	Manufacturer (RDC)	Manufacturer (storage)
Manufacturers' driver	Terms of licence	Availability	NPI	Cost reduction

Table 7.1   Comparing key supply chain parameters across different industry sectors

from the perspective of a supply chain manager and I offer some examples to contrast the nature and management of risks within the functional areas of the business.

In the research and development processes there is little control over the ability of the molecule itself to be efficacious, safe and of adequate commercial potential. Project and portfolio management methodologies help to ensure that work is directed towards the most profitable areas. The skill associated with the management of these decisions will minimise the risk of investing in unprofitable projects. It is the decision-making process that is critical. We do not expect to get it right all of the time.

In the production and supply chain environment, however, we do expect to manufacturer reliably and consistently to ensure that we get it right all of the time. Machine failure, missing items on a delivery, 'off-spec' batches are all unacceptable within the supply chain environment, particularly in the healthcare industry where patient or consumer safety is critical. The number of individual factors to be managed and controlled throughout the development, manufacturing and distribution processes is enormous. This makes the creation of robust processes critical in reducing the risk of failure and ensuring that we get it right first time and every time. We strive to understand the capability of the entire supply process, eliminating unnecessary steps and refining the remaining processes by applying business management strategies and methods such as Lean, Statistical Process Control, Six Sigma, Just in Time (JIT) and so on, all of which seek to minimise the risk of poor performance and unacceptable outcomes.

In the commercial areas of sales and marketing things are a little less tangible and often unquantifiable. The risk of inappropriately investing the 35 per cent of sales revenue is clearly enormous, so the successful managers are those who get the big decisions right. Building 'the brand', creating 'the messages', developing tools to create and influence the market that will generate demand are all areas which prove difficult for rational, logical production folk to grasp. Yet without the creation of demand we will have nothing to produce.

I offer one example from my past that illustrates the complexity of activities required to address the issue. Decision-making was reactive and tactical rather than considered and strategic. This took the focus away from the cause and addressed only the symptoms of the underlying problem. The price differential between France and the UK for a particular product meant that a very high degree of parallel importation occurred. At one point about 80 per cent of the UK demand was covered by imported products. To counteract this, two new improved products – a dispersible tablet and a non-dispersible tablet – were developed and the existing products discontinued. Only the dispersible tablet would be registered for marketing approval in France, thereby eliminating the diversion of product back into the UK. Given margins in excess of 98 per cent the additional complexity and development costs were small in relation to the opportunity. Success would be inevitable.

Generation of excitement and frustration were natural human responses associated with anticipation as the approval decision that brought the product launch grew ever closer. Now, despite hours and hours of meetings to plan and schedule the manufacturing and packaging of the final formulation, we found that the initial three validation batches of the dispersible product had not been successful. A rapidly developed formulation process proved less than robust and involved high wastage together with an inability to manufacture in humid weather – in England. Irregular assays and quality problems were also generated as the analytical processes had not been sufficiently refined. To compound the problem the tooling for the tablet compression machine had been damaged in storage and long delays for new parts were anticipated.

The short-term result was the failure to bring the dispersible tablet to the market on time, and in the long term the inability to produce the dispersible product consistently led to its withdrawal. This example illustrates the importance of reviewing the entire product strategy fully before launch. Parallel trade was already a feature of the market. The original formulations had been developed using tried and tested methodology, and the resultant process was efficient and capable of producing excellent product consistency. The problem had been caused by the acceptance of a price in the French market that would immediately destroy the UK market. In this case we see that the lack of regional control of the prices, together with a set of management incentives which allowed local sales and marketing organisations to act independently, destroyed millions of dollars of shareholder value. The situation would have been far better if:

- The marketing strategy had taken full account of the fact of parallel trade and made an assessment of the possible impact on the region at the low price achieved in France. This would have given enough time, pre-launch in France, to formulate different options.

- The local decision to launch in France at the low price could have been reviewed by regional management in the light of possible impacts of parallel trade.

- Local management incentives could have a major component of their remuneration being calculated according to regional profit and not just local sales.

Pricing Strategies Examined

Accepting that to be sustainable in developing new products companies have to make a commercial return, how do companies price products in order to deliver the necessary return? As one major company's chief executive officer (CEO) stated at an annual general meeting (AGM) when discussing his remuneration package, 'I'm not Mother Theresa' – meaning, I think, that he is in business to make money.

An important aspect of the environment in which pricing strategies have to operate is that different countries differ in their ability, and their willingness, to pay for a given product. In addition the picture may be different for different products. This means that any given product has different prices in different markets.

The highest-priced market in the world for pharmaceuticals is the US. In Europe, prices in Italy and Spain can be 50 per cent of those charged in more affluent countries such as Germany and the UK. This is one context where the European single market has not brought about any noticeable unity. Europe considers healthcare provision to be a local issue; therefore, in accordance with the principle of subsidiarity, as discussed in Chapter 5, the pricing of pharmaceutical products is set by local governments.

While trade barriers restrict opportunities for importation from outside the EU, within the EU there is free movement of goods and services. That freedom, combined with the pricing differential mentioned above, creates the paradox of a market that is free (in terms of movement) and yet not free (in terms of pricing).

The freedom to charge different prices in different markets presents drug manufacturers with an opportunity to maximise profit by charging what the market will bear in each country it targets. It also means that the launch sequence is important. In negotiating a price for a new product, governments rely on 'reference pricing', which means that they consider the prices of the product in neighbouring or otherwise related economies, applying a predetermined formula to arrive at the price they themselves will pay. For a pharmaceutical company to maximise the commercial potential of a product, it therefore needs to make sure it launches the product in the right markets, at the right price and in the right volume. It must have a regional pricing process and management incentives that encourage the generation of regional profit and not local sales revenue.

Profitable Pricing and Arbitrage – Two Sides of the Same Coin

Differential pricing, coupled with the free movement of goods, creates a major opportunity for arbitrage. Buying in a low-price market and reselling in a high-price market can generate huge profits, especially if the trader also takes advantage of exchange rate fluctuations. (In the US, by contrast, there are no legal arbitrage opportunities since importation of drugs is prohibited.)

From the healthcare industry's point of view, arbitrage threatens a company's ability to maximise the profits from its products by tending to drive prices in all markets down towards the lowest price in any market. The next section will discuss how companies try to combat or limit arbitrage.

While a number of schemes designed to prevent arbitrage have been developed, none is really satisfactory. The reason is inherent in the market structure. If a company can charge a high price in one market, its obligations to shareholders oblige it to do so. By the laws of economics that means there will automatically be an arbitrage opportunity. Therefore it could be said that the existence of arbitrage is a sign that a company is getting its pricing policy right. The following tactics are among those adopted by manufacturers to try to prevent arbitrage.

DUAL PRICING SCHEMES

This is where products sold for local use are priced lower than those sold for export. This tactic, tried by Glaxo and others in Spain, was ruled illegal by the European court as it was judged to have been imposed to reduce the movement of goods from Spain.

QUOTA SYSTEMS

These aim to restrict the supply of products to low-price markets. Bayer had adopted this tactic with respect to its anti-hypertension drug Adalat. The practice was ruled legally acceptable because Bayer did not have a monopolistic position in this market and because there was no contractual arrangement between supply chain partners.

ALLOCATION OF PRODUCT TO THE MARKET CHANNEL PARTNERS

This is the most commonly used system across Europe and is employed by many pharmaceutical companies. It relies on the ability to predict forward demand within a market and sell to partners who, it is hoped, will meet local demand ahead of more profitable export opportunities. It is flawed on both premises: real demand data is of generally poor quality and inherently inaccurate; and the channel partners have their own business profitability to nurture.

How *Not* to Promote the Product

In Germany it has been common practice for drug companies to give medicines – principally those relating to chronic conditions – to patients free at their first use in hospital, the idea being to build brand awareness and attachment to the product. The resultant loyalty, the companies hope, continues after the patients leave hospital, leading them to want to be prescribed the same item on a continuing basis.

The strategy can be successful, as can be seen from the example of Wellcome's azathioprine, branded as Imuran, an anti-rejection product which was given free to kidney transplant patients for the first few weeks following their operation. When the drug came off-patent, the volume of branded Imuran sold did not drop substantially, which is not characteristic of the patterns of other molecules at patent expiry (see Fosamax in Chapter 6). In view of the fact that the end of a patent is typically associated with an immediate and substantial drop in sales, that result is a marked success. We might explain it by surmising that transplant patients familiar with a given brand would be nervous about switching to a generic alternative and would influence their prescribers accordingly.

The problem with this policy, however, is that the free-of-charge product often turns up being resold in a secondary marketplace. Since the product is being sold by its rightful owners this practice is legal, even though it goes against the spirit of the manufacturer's offer. The manufacturer cannot impose a restriction of use or further sale by the purchasers, as its intellectual property rights are deemed to be exhausted by the sale. This is not so if the product remains the property of the manufacturer until sold to the end patient; that is, it is consigned to the pharmacy until dispensed against a prescription.

Similarly, wherever discounts or samples are provided, the opportunity to make money by reboxing and reselling exists, even within a single market. For example, large pharmacy chains that have secured discounts from manufacturers may resell to smaller pharmacies at a lesser discount. One manufacturer of a contraceptive product discovered that while the UK's 5,000 dispensing doctors accounted for 16 per cent of the total UK demand for the product, they were writing only 6 per cent of the prescriptions. That implied that the products were being traded in a secondary channel to local pharmacies as well as prescribed and dispensed to these doctors' patients. When the practice was discovered, the manufacturer withdrew the discount. From direct experience across Europe no doubt there is a good deal of this type of activity still going on, and that it is generally understood as common practice. Certain local sales managers are able to use these secondary channels to manipulate short-term sales activity.

Trade Via the Internet

The Internet, like conventional mail order, allows people to buy at prices lower than those offered in the main marketplace. Even in the US this practice is legal, provided drugs are supplied only to patients with legitimate prescriptions. In the UK – where Pharmacy2U is a leading player – this market is likely to be stimulated by the advent of e-prescriptions.

In the US, reimportation is a growing threat for the healthcare industry and is taken very seriously indeed: because of the country's status as highest-priced market, it can represent up to 50 per cent of global sales for some organisations. For example, a whole new industry has developed in Canada where doctors consult, as it were, across Niagara Falls, converting US prescriptions into Canadian ones so that patients can buy their drugs from Canadian pharmacies. In Mexico, there are entire streets in border towns given over to pharmacy shops. While it is illegal to ship drugs from Mexico, it is legal to buy the drugs in Mexico for personal use and bring them back over the border.

In Greece, where products are sold by the pharmacist without prescription, there is a practice whereby traders will buy, say, ten packs of a certain product from each of ten or more pharmacies, and export them to achieve a significant trading cash benefit. Greece prides itself on having the lowest reimbursed prices in Europe and, as a result, is a major source of parallel-traded product to other high-priced European markets. Such sales have the effect of distorting the data that is used to calculate the 'local demand' for input to company quota or allocation schemes described above. This distortion enables excess stock to be present, which leads directly to parallel trade – a vicious circle.

The governments in low-priced countries also wish to ensure that supplies to their own local patients are secured. To this end manufacturers are given preferential pricing arrangements for items that can be proved to have been dispensed to local patients. However, in practice, the supply chain configuration between manufacturer and pharmacy, with its variety of partners and intermediaries, makes it difficult to realise any of these opportunities. Later we will see how mass serialisation of packs and authentication at the point of dispensing could enable this to be managed to the advantage of all but the arbitrageur.

Conclusion

Parallel trade does have benefits. Some are debatable, but there is no doubt that it can reduce costs to governments and patients, at least in the short to medium term. Some governments, such as of the Philippines and New Zealand, actively encourage drug imports as a way of reducing healthcare costs. It is also arguable that those governments are more interested in short-term cost saving than long-term development of a profitable and politically desirable, research-based industry.

As we have seen, parallel trade is in many ways the price of the freedoms that manufacturers themselves enjoy. However, as well as reducing profitability for the manufacturers, parallel markets create problems for consumers. In particular, they open up opportunities for fraudulent supplies to enter the supply chain. These problems will be described more fully in Chapter 10. In the next chapter, however, we shall look at some of the tactics adopted by manufacturers as they attempt to combat parallel trade, and propose an approach that could be more effective.

8

Tactical Responses to Diversion

In Chapter 7 we identified the causes and impacts of diversion. Here we will discuss the ways in which diversion and its impact can be reduced. These actions cover a range of concepts, functions and organisational boundaries. Some are discrete, straightforward projects. Others are complex and require considerable coordination and stewardship to ensure success. The nature of the problem is complex, as described above, and so we can expect the solution options available to be equally sophisticated. Whatever options are adopted we can be sure that the responses from the diverters or counterfeiters will be equally nimble and imaginative. The strategy is clear: minimise lost opportunity through diversion or counterfeit. The tactics must be ever changing to stay one step ahead.

As we have already identified, reimportation into the USA is not allowed; yet it exists and is growing in line with increases in Internet use. In Europe parallel trading is legal, is growing and is encouraged through the legal framework and competition laws. This chapter will focus largely but not exclusively on the problems for research-based manufacturing companies caused by this legal diversion – generally termed parallel trade or unwarranted trade in Europe – and describes how companies attempt to minimise the impact of this activity on revenues and profits. Many of the solutions will be equally applicable to prevent diversion anywhere in the world the problem exists. As we shall see, pricing differentials drive trade, and pricing affects revenue in many ways (Figure 8.1).

Diversion Is a Fact of Life

As we saw in the previous chapter, arbitrage and other forms of diversion are a fact of life in many industry sectors, and especially in the price-regulated healthcare industry. While these activities are arguably a valid form of

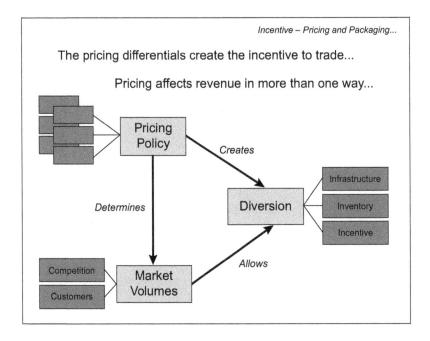

Figure 8.1   Pricing differentials create the incentive to trade

competition, and even a useful aspect of a (mostly) free market mechanism, for the primary manufacturers of patent-protected products they represent a severe loss of potential profit.

As described above we see that all the major branded, patent-protected products that are distributed through the accepted channels are impacted. Every research-based manufacturer suffers this problem. Generic products are not usually affected because they do not command enough of a premium in any market. If they are affected the impact is less due to the existing high level of competition in this area and the lower prices pertaining. The Association of the British Pharmaceutical Industry (ABPI) identifies the top-selling drugs in the UK as shown in Table 8.1.

It is certain that every one of these products is at risk from diversion, either within a particular market or across borders. In many instances the difference between the lowest price and the highest price in any one legitimate trading zone can be as much as 50 per cent. As part of my MBA dissertation in 1994 I showed that prices for antibiotics across Europe ranged from £0.12 in Austria to £0.27 in Germany. These countries are both in the European Union (EU) and share a

Table 8.1   Top UK pharmaceutical products, 2006

	Product	Manufacturer	Launch date	Primary sales £m[*]	Hospital sales £m	Total sales £m
1	Lipitor	Pfizer	Jan 97	495.68	9.88	505.56
2	Seretide	GSK	Mar 99	325.56	11.95	337.51
3	Plavix	sanofi-aventis	Jul 98	178.77	14.63	193.40
4	Enbrel	Wyeth	May 00	100.24	57.87	158.11
5	Zyprexa	Lilly	Oct 96	134.19	20.35	154.54
6	Omeprazole	Generic	Apr 02	147.43	5.27	152.70
7	Cozaar	MSD	Feb 95	109.53	1.56	111.09
8	Simvastatin	Generic	May 03	102.93	1.18	104.11
9	Efexor	Wyeth	Jan 95	100.37	3.67	104.04
10	Coversyl	Servier	Jan 90	96.48	2.73	99.21
11	Symbicort	AstraZeneca	May 01	94.57	2.63	97.20
12	Spiriva	Boehringer Ingelheim	Aug 02	89.35	4.85	94.20
13	Serevent	GSK	Dec 90	77.89	1.68	79.57
14	Lansoprazole	Generic	Dec 05	76.07	1.60	77.67
15	Seroquel	AstraZeneca	Sep 97	62.60	11.81	74.42
16	Herceptin	Roche	Sep 00	9.35	62.24	71.59
17	Amlodipine	Generic	Mar 04	69.81	0.66	70.47
18	Lantus	sanofi-aventis	Aug 02	64.27	2.14	66.41
19	Clexane	sanofi-aventis	Nov 90	8.88	56.31	65.18
20	Zoladex	AstraZeneca	Mar 87	56.55	7.76	64.31
21	Alendronic	Generic	Mar 05	62.03	1.26	63.29
22	Avandia	GSK	Jul 00	62.48	0.79	63.27
23	Nexium	AstraZeneca	Aug 00	58.92	1.68	60.60
24	Glivec	Novartis	Nov 01	55.10	4.26	59.36
25	Remicade	Shering Plough	Sep 99	0.04	59.20	59.24
26	Aricept	Eisai	Apr 97	49.58	9.64	59.22
27	Viagra	Pfizer	Sep 98	57.05	1.60	58.65
28	Xalatan	Pfizer	Jan 97	54.49	2.35	56.84
29	Crestor	AstraZeneca	Mar 03	56.09	0.60	56.69
30	Diovan	Novartis	Oct 96	56.01	0.65	56.66
31	Risperdal	Johnson & Johnson	Jun 93	49.20	6.07	55.28
32	Lyrica	Pfizer	Jul 04	51.57	3.16	54.73
33	Novorapid	Novo Nordisk	Sep 99	52.95	1.42	54.38
34	Mabthera	Roche	Jun 98	0.28	54.05	54.33
35	Gabapentin	Generic	Dec 03	49.82	2.52	52.34
36	Actonel	Procter & Gamble	Apr 00	49.33	2.49	51.82
37	Arimidex	AstraZeneca	Sep 95	49.34	2.07	51.41
38	Aprovel	sanofi-aventis	Sept 97	48.97	0.73	49.71
39	Ezetrol	MSD	Apr 03	47.49	0.64	48.12
40	Casodex	AstraZeneca	May 95	42.91	4.65	47.56

[*] Primary sector sales are prescription and OTC medicines not dispensed in hospitals.

Source: IMS link via ABPI <http://www.abpi.org.uk/statistics/section.asp?sect=2#29>.

common free-trade border, and indeed the same language. I also identified a basket of products where the relative prices ex-manufacturer to wholesaler in each market was seen as Austria 42 – Germany 100. Who can hope to prevent diversion in these situations? The general level of pricing across Europe has changed little since this date, and these opportunities for arbitrage have been exploited, as we shall see in the next section.

The cost to the UK pharmaceutical industry of parallel trade has been estimated by a number of sources to be over £1.4 billion in lost potential revenue in 2006. The level is believed to be growing at 25 per cent per annum. The growth in the number of licences granted to import parallel-traded products (legally diverted) into the UK is shown in Table 8.2 and has been referred to in previous chapters.

Table 8.2   UK licences granted to import parallel-traded products

Year	Licences
1993	239
1994	266
1995	426
1996	447
1997	541
1998	757
1999	1354
2000	1363
2001	1546
2002	2014
2003	2916

Given these figures, parallel trade is high on the agenda for any national manager of a research-based pharmaceutical or medical devices organisation marketing patent-protected products.

Although I am focusing largely on the pharmaceutical industry due to its specific nature and high intellectual property content, the same issues are faced by manufacturers of medical devices and diagnostic products. Again the prices, if the products are subject to National Health Service (NHS) reimbursement, are largely controlled and can differ substantially between these national markets. As Figure 8.2 shows, parallel trade is a contentious subject and arises due to the differences in price in neighbouring markets. Figure 8.3, meanwhile, outlines some potential problems associated with parallel trade.

Medical Devices

The following predicament was relayed to me by the European logistics director of a global company that manufactures hospital equipment in the form of saline drips and other bags, together with the associated tubing and connectors. Following his presentation at a conference in London in 2001, entitled 'European Distribution in the Pharmaceutical Industry', he explained some of the frequent and recurring issues that his organisation faced.

Bags, tubes and connectors are manufactured in different locations. Some factories supply all items to a number of different markets; in other cases bags from one factory are supplied separately from the tubes, which come from another location. This is a result of manufacturing strategy and the need to balance capacity across the different facilities. That seems fine apart from the fact that different product specifications are registered in different markets – an

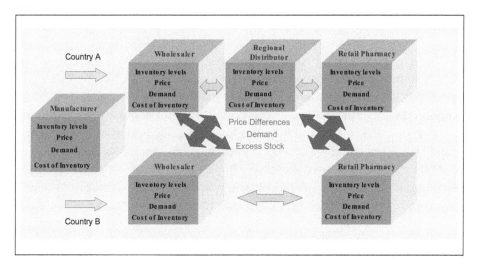

Figure 8.2   **Parallel trade arises through price differences in neighbouring markets**

Source: PA Consulting Group.

Is parallel trade a problem, to whom?

- Immediate sales revenue loss for the manufacturer
- Potential long term damage to the research based pharmaceutical industry as investments are reduced
- Possible impact on quality and safety of medicines through re-packaging and non-essential handling
- ~15% of prescriptions in UK are dispensed using a parallel traded product
- The re-packaging operations presents opportunities for the introduction of counterfeit or substandard product to enter the supply chain

- Savings accrue to the national health budgets (2.4%)
- Profits accrue to the parallel traders (49%)
- Profits accrue to pharmacies (~£67k p.a. in average UK pharmacy) Source: PA
- Pharmacists spend time 'hunting down' the cheapest prices from various wholesalers at the expense of providing 'patient time'
- Patients in low priced markets may not get access to products as they are exported into higher priced countries
- Legal costs associated with defending cases and prosecuting actions absorb valuable time and resources

Figure 8.3   Is parallel trade a problem, to whom?

excellent tactic to prevent movement of goods across borders, as discussed in the previous chapter. Unfortunately, to an untrained eye the items appear very similar and are packaged with the company branding, albeit in multilingual packs. This company also suffers from counterfeiting of their products and they clearly have no control over the specifications or quality of these counterfeit items.

The major problem this situation presents to the company is that customers, large hospitals, buy the items from traders as they are available at much lower prices. As the nurses attempt to assemble the items they find that they either do not fit together or are loose. This results in a poor company image among the users of the products, and therefore has a negative impact on the company brand. I am uncertain whether the company has analysed the benefits in revenues and profits from maintaining the different specifications and supply matrix against lost future sales associated with poor image in the minds of end users, but suspect that such an analysis has not been undertaken.

Diagnostics

Figure 8.4 illustrates the business model operated by many of the large companies manufacturing and marketing equipment for patient use. Here we have the typical situation for the routine testing necessary in patients with diabetes. The patient pricks their finger to release a small drop of blood. This sample is then added to a small prepared strip impregnated with a specific reagent, and then placed into a sophisticated analytical device which calculates the blood sugar level and informs the patient of the level of treatment appropriate at that time.

The analytical device is sophisticated, calibrated and validated. It is consequently rather expensive – probably too expensive for a patient to buy and maintain – although its use is critical to the treatment regimen. The consumables on the other hand, although high quality, are less sophisticated, manufactured in very large volumes and consequently lower in cost. In this case the manufacturers may subsidise the cost to the patient of the analytical device as its use will generate sales revenues into the future through use of the drugs and consumables. The pricing of the device, the drugs and consumables can then be calculated according to some assumptions of use, such as number of patients, their compliance with the treatment and so on. These devices have had a dramatic impact on the patients that use them, helping to transform their lives significantly as they gain better control over the effects of their disease.

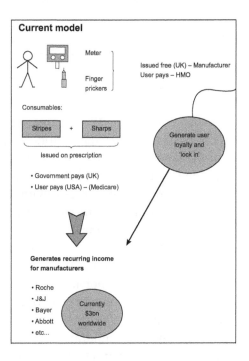

Figure 8.4   A typical business model for the supply of diagnostic materials

We can see that either parallel trade, diversion within a market or the ingress of counterfeit consumables will disrupt this business model and can make the subsidy of the devices a very expensive, though necessary, activity. In discussion with the UK CEO of a European devices company in 2002 it emerged that his UK affiliate was practically unable to supply any significant volume of consumables at UK prices into the home market, such was the flood of low-priced, parallel-traded items from other European countries. In 2005 most diagnostic companies in the world suffered major impact from diversions from Canada and grey market trading within the USA, while some have identified and acknowledged significant counterfeit product being available in the USA, Greece, India and Dubai. This is clearly then a problem across the range of healthcare products, and it is likely that the actions required to address it are similar. We shall group the tactics into four major categories:

1.   regulatory;

2.   supply chain management;

3.   product design, technology and branding;

4.   commercial.

Regulatory

Organisations can seek to prevent reimportation by creating a regulatory barrier to the high-priced market. One mechanism had historically been by licensing a different formulation of the same product for specific countries. For example, Wellcome – as it was in the late 1980s – developed a variety of formulations of their top-selling drug Acyclovir (brand name Zovirax). A specific 800-mg dispersible tablet was developed and produced, at extraordinary cost and complexity, to differentiate it from the standard tablet product. The standard product had been eroding profits and revenues in the UK and German markets through parallel trade. The dispersible formulation was to be licensed and sold in the low-priced French market and was not at the time registered elsewhere in Europe. This was a good plan at the time, and no doubt prevented significant loss of revenue from the higher-priced UK and German markets for a period. We saw in the previous chapter that the withdrawal of marketing authorisation on grounds other than patient safety would be ruled anti-competitive. In this instance the emerging regulations in Europe were moving towards mutual recognition: if approved in one EU market a product would be considered approved in them all. Despite the supply chain issues identified in the previous chapter, the tactic stalled and reduced, but did not eliminate, cross-border trade.

ANTI DIVERSION REGULATIONS

A more extreme version of this tactic can be seen in the market for HIV anti-retroviral drugs: drugs destined for Africa may be made in a completely different formulation from those sold in northern Europe. GlaxoSmithKline (GSK), the largest manufacturer of these products, took steps to minimise the threat of preferentially priced products destined for the impoverished markets in Africa returning to Europe. Such diversion takes away necessary medicines from the HIV/AIDS patients in Africa and only benefits the diverting traders. This is not a situation which a developed democratic market could tolerate, in spite of its commitment to free trade.

New 'special access packs' and tablets dyed red were registered in over 25 African markets under the European Union's Anti-Diversion Regulation, and were sold at prices no greater than 25 per cent of the prices available in Europe. Here we have a case of the regulator working with the manufacturer to protect patients even if, in this case, those patients are in another market (see Panel).

COUNCIL REGULATION (EC) NO 953/2003 OF 26 MAY 2003

To avoid trade diversion into the European Union of certain key medicines is intended to enable producers to significantly increase supplies of medicines at lower prices, to countries or destination as specified in the Regulation, while keeping higher prices for the same items in the EU. Exporters are invited to put their products on a list run by the European Commission which constitutes the basis for subsequent enforcement by customs authorities. Both patented and generic products can be registered. In order to be added to the list, medicines have to be made available either with a price cut of 75 per cent off the average 'ex factory' price in OECD countries, or at the cost of production plus 15 per cent.

There are 76 countries concerned, including the least developed countries, the countries with the lowest per-capita income, and those countries where HIV/AIDS is particularly prevalent. Most of these countries have no local production facilities of their own.

In April 2004 the EU commission announced the placement of seven GSK products on the list of products given protection.

EU Trade Commissioner Pascal Lamy said: 'The anti-diversion mechanism the EU put in place last year is essential to ensure that manufacturers of HIV anti-retrovirals, such as GSK, actively engage in providing cheap medicines to poor countries severely affected by the AIDS pandemic. I have little doubt that other producers will soon follow this example.'[*]

The products on the list bear a logo allowing customs to identify them easily. Being on this list and bearing the logo means that imports of these products into the EU for free circulation, re-exportation, warehousing or trans-shipment is prohibited.

[*] <http://ec.europa.eu/trade/issues/global/medecine/pr210404_en.htm>

SPECIAL PRODUCT CHARACTERISTICS THAT ATTRACT DIVERSION

The extent of diversion and other illicit trade in HIV products or similar lifestyle drugs, especially via the Internet, is extraordinary. Viagra, Cialis and Levitra are products used to treat male erectile dysfunction. This is a common ailment in some patient groups, yet normally is not a topic for open discussion with strangers or work colleagues. These items are available through a variety of sources on the Internet or through 'grey' market activity. They have a high price and the purchasers/patients would prefer the trade to be discreet. Similarly the powerful painkilling drug OxyContin suffers from a high level of grey market and counterfeit trade. It is abused by criminals who wish to take part in violence and have their pain threshold increased. Methadone, a treatment for heroin addicts, and HIV treatments are also regularly being 'sold back' by patients to pharmacies. These items have a significant 'street value' which proves very attractive to patients. The manufacturers of these products provide a major benefit to those people who have genuine need for the drugs, and bear a major responsibility to protect those innocent patients and traders who may, unknowingly, receive illegally diverted, substandard or counterfeit product through these activities.

EXPLOITATION OF DIFFERENT STANDARDS

The classification in some countries of dangerous drugs which do not have the same restrictions on use and supply in neighbouring markets can create problems of illegal supply and abuse. Subutex in Europe is one example of this. In many European countries the supply of this drug is very closely restricted due to its potential for recreational use and social problems that can result. In France, a major market for the product, Subutex is classified as a *'stupéfiant'* (psychotropic drug). Additional unique numbered forms and procedures are required to accompany all prescriptions, but Subutex is not required to be kept under lock and key. There are many attempts to obtain Subutex on forged prescriptions, but these are usually easily detected because of attempts to make gross modifications. When a pharmacist dispenses this product they must at least talk to the patient and verify that there are no overlapping prescriptions that could indicate overconsumption. The pharmacist must also keep the original prescription and make a record of each supply in the record book for Subutex. Nonetheless, product is often seized in a range of countries across Europe by police investigating narcotic abuse and trafficking. This is a major embarrassment for the manufacturer, who is expected to provide some control over the supply and use of the product, yet is prevented via the need to ensure free movement of goods and services in Europe.

The complex nature of the distribution channel for the product in France, in conjunction with the legal framework in Europe that facilitates free trade, arbitrage and cross-border activity, restricts the purely commercial control solutions that might otherwise be available to manufacturers. Examples of these commercial solutions are US-style Inventory Management Agreements (IMAs), or the restriction of supply to those customers who agree to buy exclusively from the manufacturer. European competition law prevents these arrangements between supply chain partners.

The addition of sophisticated or even simple coding technologies to the product packaging, both carton and blister, is in itself a complex task. This solution would, however, be rather meaningless and the investment largely wasted unless the pharmacies, sales representatives, investigators or law enforcement officers could quickly and effectively identify and authenticate the items.

The wide variety of legal dispensing outlets and wholesaler distribution locations across France alone means that the costs of implementation of any fixed infrastructure solution to monitor and control this specific product would be both enormous and unrealistic.

Some countries have, or have had in the past, different levels of standardisation for labelling strengths; companies have sometimes been able to exploit this difference, and regulatory authorities have used them as a barrier to entry. This can take a variety of forms.

Certification approval of the manufacturing sites and processes

The US Food and Drug Administration (FDA) strongly regulates and inspects all manufacturing sites around the world that produce products for the United States market. Importation of products specifically intended for the US market is governed by the FDA and is legal. Importation of a product that has been initially intended for sale in a market other than the USA is illegal. This market is by far the largest in the world, so if manufacturers want their products to have access to that market they must bear the cost of the regulations.

Special formulations or product specifications

In spite of the efforts of many international groups to develop global standards and requirements, some countries and regions adopt different standards for the same product. This prevents manufacturers from accessing the economies of scale that can be enjoyed by producing in bulk to a common standard. In a commodity market this might cause problems and prevent profitable sale of those items in a market with such specific regulations. Counter-intuitively for the products under discussion, high-value patented items whose prices are largely controlled, this barrier is an advantage. It prevents diversion either to or from the 'special requirements' market.

In 1994 the EU adopted the Convention on the Elaboration of a European Pharmacopoeia, drawn up by the Council of Europe. This harmonised the specifications for the manufacturing and quality control of pharmaceuticals to enable them to circulate freely within the European Union.

Detailed quality and analytical inspections prior to release from customs

In many developing markets, imported, patented healthcare products represent significant costs and loss of revenue for manufacturers and the local industry. Border controls can necessarily cause delays, fines and rejection of a product following quality inspection of both the product and its documentation. From my own experience, these barriers were a regular feature and everyday challenge to distribution.

Japanese quality standards are known to be very demanding. If blister packs of tablets are found to have print imperfect or misaligned, or tablets chipped or pitted, the whole product batch can be rejected and lost. Rigorous inspection takes place during production and prior to shipment, and agreed quality levels must be achieved. Upon inspection at customs in Japan, there are regular rejections as inspectors identify additional problems. In one instance a special formulation of Zovirax 200-mg tablets, made only for the Japanese market, was rejected before leaving the factory. The note placed against that particular batch by the quality assurance team read: 'Zovirax 200 mg (Japan) – Restricted not for Japan', thus illustrating that regulatory frameworks and restrictions create a major obstacle to efficient stock management and supply.

In Moscow in 1995, as Russia was transforming itself from the USSR, I had the fantastic opportunity to assist in the establishment of the supply chain into Russia for Glaxo Wellcome. Truckloads of Calpol, Septrin and Actifed Syrup would be despatched from the UK, and other products sourced from Italy, France, Germany and South Africa, while their invoices would be sent from either the UK or Switzerland, depending on the financial trade routes applicable. Time after time goods would arrive without the original documents, with the wrong documents, or the documents would not correctly match the product description on the Bill of Lading. Fines would then be levied, generating welcome foreign currency revenue. The products would also need a Russian certificate of analysis, at a cost of $50 per batch. This was a direct translation of the original, prepared within minutes on an old typewriter. Effective supply chain management requires the coordination of goods, documents, cash and data. If these are not all aligned, delays and additional costs will result.

These two examples are cited to illustrate that, while these barriers would be of significant advantage in markets that were net importers of diverted products, they tend to exist in markets that are net exporters due to their lower prices. Indeed, the trend in the more developed markets is to remove barriers and harmonise standards, which only increase the opportunities for diversion.

Local packaging requirements

In Belgium, Italy and Greece products that attract reimbursement by the authorities must have a specific identifying label attached to the packaging. The dispensing pharmacist must attach this label or unique number to the claim for reimbursement. They will not purchase packs that do not have these labels as they will not be able to receive reimbursement from the relevant authorities.

Again, these markets are lower-priced European markets and are net exporters. The importing markets such as the UK, the Netherlands and Germany have few, if any, specific packaging requirements and they present no real penalty to the traders.

Lobbying governments

Companies within the industry – through national or regional trade organisations such as the ABPI in the UK, SFEE in Greece, Farmidustria in Italy, the European Federation of Pharmaceutical Industries and Associations (EFPIA) or the Pharmaceutical Research and Manufacturers of America (PhRMA) – seek to influence their respective governments to maintain or impose regulations that will restrict the flow of products. This process can be clearly seen in the US, where healthcare companies vigorously lobby to prevent legalisation of drug reimportation from Canada. The move to develop track and trace 'pedigrees' to accompany every consignment of drugs is one such initiative. This has effectively stalled the implementation of the Prescription Drugs Medication Act (PDMA) in the USA, which could have opened the door to the US market for regulated and approved (yet much lower-priced) medicines from Canada and Europe. Such a policy would completely reshape the whole industry due to the impact it would have on profits available from the largest market in the world.

Major manufacturers such as Pfizer – which suffers diversion and counterfeiting of two of its largest-selling drugs, Lipitor and Viagra – have campaigned publicly about the issues and dangers of substandard medicines reaching patients. This could be seen as an issue of protecting patients or, more cynically, an attempt to persuade governments to introduce regulations that render reimportation impractical, thus protecting their future profits.

Supply Chain Management

STOCK ALLOCATIONS

Licensed full-line wholesalers accept an obligation to supply their local market in preference to the more lucrative export market. Manufacturers may seek to use quota restrictions to limit exportation. For example, a manufacturer wanting to prevent the export of a drug from the lowest-priced market in the EU, Greece, could decide to supply wholesalers with only enough to meet the needs of patients in Greece itself. Given the vast amount of data available regarding doctors' prescribing habits, switching, historical sales and patient numbers it should be relatively straightforward to assess the total market size for any given treatment, perhaps adding 10 per cent to cover short-term or regional variation.

However, such quotas are regularly challenged in courts by parallel traders and their associations, which see them as a restriction to trade or abuse of a dominant market position by the major pharmaceutical companies. Courts have tended to support the parallel traders' case, although two exceptions are worthy of note.

Bayer and Adalat

Bayer's Adalat drug is a treatment for coronary heart disease and hypertension. There are many such drugs, and Adalat had only a small market share of this major market, as defined by the courts. Prices in France and Spain were approximately 40 per cent lower than in the UK. French and Spanish wholesalers saw the opportunity to divert their stocks and placed increasingly large orders with the French and Spanish affiliates of Bayer, as a consequence of which sales of UK-specific products fell dramatically. Bayer unilaterally reduced supplies to the exporting wholesalers, who cried 'foul' and took their complaints to the European Commission. In 1996, eight years before the final ruling in 2004, the Commission ruled against Bayer and imposed a fine of €3 million.

Bayer appealed to the European Court of First Instance, the Advocate General, stating that there was no 'agreement' between supply chain partners to restrict the supply (Article 81 EC Treaty), the action being unilateral on the part of Bayer. Equally the small share of the overall market as defined meant that such actions could not be construed as abuse of a dominant market position (Article 82 EC Treaty). The Advocate General reviews each case and makes a statement that is likely to become policy. The original decision, the penalty of €3 million, was suspended in October 2006 and it was later ruled that the initial decision was to be annulled, based on an incorrect assessment of the facts and the absence of an agreement. The court also recognised that:

> *Provided the manufacturer does so without abusing a dominant position, and there is no concurrence of wills between him and his wholesalers, he may adopt the supply policy which he considers necessary, even if, by the vary nature of its aim, for example to hinder parallel imports, the implementation of that policy may entail restrictions on competition and affect trade between Member States.*[1]

Syfait vs. GlaxoSmithKline (GSK)

In Greece, GSK implemented a strategy that limited supplies to its wholesalers, meaning that their orders – especially large orders from wholesalers known to be engaged in export activities – were not supplied in full. This would prevent wholesalers from buying products at low Greek prices and reselling them in markets with higher price levels, such as the UK and Germany. Some wholesalers complained to the Greek Competition Commission, which suspended proceedings in order to obtain clarification from the European Court of Justice (ECJ). They asked the ECJ whether and in what circumstances a dominant pharmaceutical company may limit supplies to its wholesalers in order to limit parallel trade in its products.

In his opinion in this case, issued on 28 October 2004, Advocate General Jacobs concluded that the general rule on restrictions of supply by dominant companies should not apply to restrictions of supply put in place by pharmaceutical companies as a means of coping with parallel trade for the following reasons:

- The European pharmaceutical sector is subject to close regulation, including price controls, which themselves give rise to significant price differences between member states. Attempts by pharmaceutical companies to restrict parallel trade are not aimed at reinforcing these price differences; they are an obvious and legitimate reaction to them.

---

1   Hancher, L. (2004), The European Community dimension: coordinating divergence <http://www.euro.who.int/document/e83015_4.pdf>.

- Unless pharmaceutical companies are able to take steps to limit parallel trade, the adverse effect on their revenues could undermine their incentives to invest in research and development.

- In the case of pharmaceutical products, it is the parallel trader, not the patient or purchaser of the product, that benefits from parallel trade, because lower prices are not passed on by the parallel trader, but rather taken as profit.

Justice Jacobs effectively ruled that it was not his position to rule on the matter in Greece as member states gain no significant benefits from parallel trade, and patients in Europe do not benefit either. Limiting parallel trade therefore has a negative impact only on the traders.

When the Greek Competition Commission rules on the case the losing party will undoubtedly appeal. This is not yet over, and even so many companies have confirmed or introduced allocations to wholesalers in low-priced markets, particularly with products that do not provide them with a dominant position in the defined market.

DIRECT DISTRIBUTION

A perhaps less controversial tactic for managing the supply chain against parallel trade is that of cutting out the wholesaler and distributing goods directly to the customer (which could be a hospital, pharmacy or patient). Companies whose biopharmaceutical products are almost exclusively for hospital use tend to establish a direct delivery service using specialist distribution companies. The product characteristics, storage and handling conditions required (for example a cold chain) also militate against distribution through numerous supply chain partners. This would make it complicated and expensive to manage, administer and audit.

Direct distribution will appeal particularly to companies launching a new, high-priced product for the first time. While it will be practically impossible to change an existing supply chain arrangement, the point of launch is the ideal opportunity for the manufacturer to choose to supply that product direct rather than through the typical wholesaler route. Considerations of diversion apart, manufacturers will welcome the opportunity to save the wholesaler's substantial margin on a high-value item. We referred in Chapter 6 to the level of wholesaler margin: in the UK 12.5 per cent of the sales price. One manufacturer of consumer medicines who has chosen to deliver direct to about 50 per cent of pharmacies in Belgium was able to reduce the channel costs from 16 to 2 per cent within a year.

The legitimacy of this tactic depends on the rationale for changing any distribution model to direct delivery. Courts are likely to ask why. If direct distribution has been adopted to reduce parallel trade, it will probably be disallowed in markets where parallel trade is legitimate. However, if the supply chain is part of a coherent commercial framework that obviates resellers, then the courts are likely to be sympathetic to the manufacturers' position. An example of such items would be radioactive pharmaceuticals, some cold-chain items and others that require special handling under strictly controlled conditions.

The decision-making process that leads to the establishment of a particular distribution model is very complex, with a wide range of variable parameters (see Figure 8.5). Developing the strategy for a new product coming to market is essential to ensure projected value is preserved post-launch. Every product, every market and trading situation will lead to the generation of a different model. For simplicity most organisations adopt the standard route options: direct using a third-party logistics (3PL) provider, wholesale or preferred distributor.

Figure 8.5   Some considerations necessary when bringing a new product profitably to market

Use of such a model may not lead to the use of a different distribution model, yet it will help to identify risks and potential areas of weakness. Pricing, product design and regulations can then be used in a co-ordinated effort to reduce any diversion that might otherwise have occurred.

Product Design, Technology and Branding

The reasons for pursuing any of the strategies below are twofold: to build consumer awareness and loyalty and to increase the barriers for traders who wish to divert product, from one channel or market to another. Again, the margins available to both traders and primary manufacturers are considerable, yet the complexity and cost of producing, managing and distributing different brands in different markets may be prohibitive.

BRAND NAMES

If a different branding is used in each market, life is harder for parallel traders. Local users will have some loyalty to 'their' brand, and some resistance to a product that is named and looks completely different from their local product. There is a trade-off and balance to be found here. The cost of establishing and managing a brand is substantial, so having many brands for one product will not allow benefits of scale and standardisation to be generated either in marketing or production. In pharmaceuticals the costs associated with marketing are by far the larger of these two functions.

PACKAGING DIFFERENCES

Differences in packaging will pose problems and incur costs for traders. These costs or barriers are not as great as those reformulations referred to above with HIV drugs to Africa. Using design and invention they can become awkward, costly and cause the repacker issues with regulations, Good Manufacturing Practice (GMP), trademarks or copyright.

If a product with expected monthly prescription is dispensed in units of 28 in Germany, the manufacturer could supply lower-priced markets with blisters of 30. If the trader repackages the product, it will be obvious if two tablets have been removed, thereby raising concern over product quality and integrity. More radical repackaging, such as putting the tablets in a completely new pack, may be allowed under certain conditions so long as the drug itself is not exposed (which would infringe GMP). These barriers represent a cost and the need to develop regulated facilities and infrastructure. The motive for a trader is the margin available from the arbitrage. The more this can be reduced through imposition of such barriers, the more this diversion will be reduced.

PACKAGE DESIGN TO PREVENT REPACKAGING

A variant on the preceding tactic is to design packaging in such a way as to make repackaging particularly hard. For example, if a tamper-evident box is used, then taking out a Greek leaflet and putting in a German one destroys the box, leaving the trader with the costs of reboxing. This tactic has been successfully employed by Pfizer: it provides a low-cost glue to provide this tamper evidence on its Lipitor product in Europe. Pfizer, in common with other manufacturers affected by this trade, regularly audits wholesale and pharmacy facilities to identify the number and type of packaging provided by traders. In one audit period they discovered some major faults:

- different dose of medicine inside the pack from that stated on the outside;

- medicine pack containing capsules but the box stating tablets;

- expiry date and batch number on the medicine box not matching the expiry date and batch number on the medicines inside;

- patient information leaflets in the wrong language.

Complex designs of blister packs can also make it hard to comply with regulations without damaging the product. The use of a standard dispenser (for tablets), injection devices or inhalers can effectively prevent substitution of the consumable drug item by using the consumer's loyalty and facility with the device.

A design to counter the repackers

Figure 8.6 shows a neat blister pack of tablets contained within a folded wallet package for easy carrying in handbags and pockets. The pack would be opened initially by tearing the perforations around the edge, similar to opening secure documents such as monthly salary notices or personal identification numbers (PINs) for bank debit and credit cards. This provides a tamper-evident seal which will guarantee the integrity of the contents to the dispensing pharmacist and patient.

This in turn provides a barrier to the trader, who must repack the item when transferring it across markets by adding their own licence number and registered address while obscuring that of the original manufacturer, removing the patient information leaflet (PIL) in the original language and replacing it with one in the language of the importing market.

The pack cannot be opened without exposing one of the tablets within the blister. This is contrary to the repacker's licence and would prove expensive if that tablet were discarded. Such pack designs merely apply technologies and design techniques from other industry sectors to that of diversion within the regulatory framework for pharmaceuticals. The important thing is that the issue and threat of diversion is taken into account while designing the packaging and labelling for the new product. Historically this occurs too late in the process. Tablet or dose form design is an early, patient-related issue. Packaging design relies on the low-cost conservative bottle, blister or vial being differentiated.

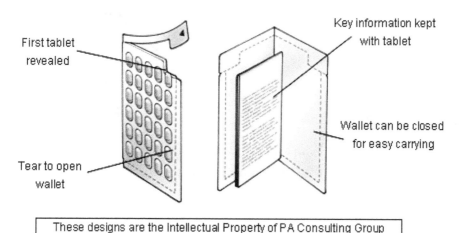

An example...

A robust and easy to carry pack which ensures product information stays with the medicine

First tablet revealed

Key information kept with tablet

Wallet can be closed for easy carrying

Tear to open wallet

These designs are the Intellectual Property of PA Consulting Group

Figure 8.6   An example – how to define the business case?
Reprinted with kind permission of PA Consulting Group.

In addition to packaging there are whole arrays of tablet designs that can be protected through patents and trademarks. These measures identify forensically the authenticity of the tablet versus a counterfeit; they do little to prevent the erosion of revenue and profit through diversion. An example of the complexity of designs is shown in Figure 8.7. Each complex design creates costs through patents and trademarks, procurement of specialised tooling and problems in production, yet build little if any patient loyalty. Patients take a product because they are prescribed it by a doctor, not because it is a fancy shape.

I would suggest that specialisation would be better placed in packaging design to build barriers against repackaging and the effects of diversion.

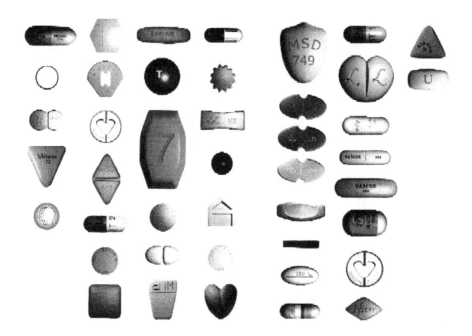

Figure 8.7   **A few examples of the complexity of tablet design – do they enhance the brand or just add cost?**

Commercial

INTERNAL MANAGEMENT REMUNERATION

Where national managers are given incentives that are largely based on local sales revenue, they have little or no motivation to support corporate objectives and limit the opportunity for products moving between markets. That may result in a manager in Greece benefiting at the expense of a UK manager. The resultant intra-company tensions are common, and do nothing to enhance shareholder value.

Larger, more sophisticated organisations have therefore implemented regional (as opposed to local) pricing, together with incentives for managers that are based on overall regional profit rather than local sales revenue. A case study is discussed in later chapters. This makes managers more likely to legally restrict sales to wholesalers that they know will export, particularly if they know that they have already sold enough packs to meet local requirements.

DISCOUNT STRUCTURES

Discounts and other commercial incentives offered to wholesalers can be co-ordinated in order to structure the business more effectively. It makes little sense to discount a product in Greece when the manufacturer knows that it will immediately be resold into the UK. Such activities only increase the traders' margin.

This type of situation presents the opportunity for what is known as equalisation deals. For example, if you know a UK wholesaler is buying a product imported from Greece, you can offer a product in the UK at a comparable price. The wholesaler and pharmacy will generally prefer to take the original UK pack, if at comparable cost, as the integrity and quality of the product is more appealing to the consumer.

At one meeting on this topic with the UK general manager of a well-known, mid-sized pharmaceutical company, the decision was taken to discount on this basis to a local wholesaler and integrated retail pharmacy chain. Upon this decision the UK sales targets and bonuses were achieved, yet the regional company profit was adversely impacted by over €5 million.

OFFERS TO PATIENTS

A similar type of initiative – but directed at patients rather than wholesalers - is common in the US in the form of seniors' or veterans' packages. These typically combine a product with additional services such as enrolment in a patient information group in order to persuade customers to buy the US product instead of looking to Canada or Mexico. These schemes are not completely effective, partly because customers cannot always afford to pay extra, and the services tend to benefit the manufacturer through increased information rather than the patient directly. Many patients on low budgets need to buy the drug itself at as low a price as possible.

Conclusion: Stable the Horse Before It Bolts

As we have seen, there is a wide range of techniques and processes available for companies to combat diversion and parallel trade. In the medium to long term many tactics lose their effectiveness as they become countered through the incentives and inventiveness of the traders.

On a more positive note, diversion, parallel trade and other grey market activities are well known and well understood. Manufacturers therefore have plenty of opportunity to minimise arbitrage through management incentives, product design and innovation in their supply chain processes.

In all cases these measures are infinitely more effective if they are planned and put in place before the product is launched. Life is much harder if the horse has already bolted, as most companies already know to their cost. There is little benefit to be gained by manufacturers, and certainly none by healthcare providers or patients, from spending vast sums on lobbying against what are effectively self-imposed problems arising from lack of forethought.

In the case of established products, rather than engaging in futile attempts to block parallel trade, manufacturers would be better off resolving to live with it, and to find ways to limit and manage it in such a way that it does not harm patients. In addition, they need to find ways to address certain loopholes inherent in parallel trade so that patients are fully safeguarded. It is to this task we turn in subsequent chapters.

9

Managing Compliance

It is the responsibility of any sustainable business to observe and operate within the structure of financial, operational and moral imperatives that are appropriate to the country and culture in which they carry out their business. These can be defined either by legislation – such as taxation, employment law, health, safety and welfare, control of waste and emissions and so on – or described in the form of guidelines. Such guidelines are generally accepted principles or professional codes of conduct. Where such codes of conduct prove inadequate for whatever reason, more formal regulatory control or legislation can be enacted. The Sarbanes-Oxley Act of 2002 is one example. In Chapter 6 we saw the 'stuffing' of the supply chain by Bristol-Myers Squibb. Examples of similar practices in a variety of industry sectors caused the authorities in the USA to ensure that accounting practices in all companies could no longer be interpreted in such a manner.

In this chapter we will focus on the regulatory framework that pertains to the development, marketing, manufacturer and supply of pharmaceutical and other healthcare products because of their special nature, their mode of use and potential for abuse.

Background

In previous chapters I have referred to the duties of the governing authority of a country inasmuch as they relate to protection of the welfare of its citizens and the provision of education and employment opportunities. We have seen how the pharmaceutical, medical devices and other healthcare industry sectors offer excellent opportunities to satisfy these duties. We have also mentioned the massive costs associated with the research and development (R&D) of these products and suggested that such risky, commercial investments are not the business of government. Governments are best placed to provide the environment within which such business decisions can be taken that will eventually benefit everyone. Businesses that are prepared to operate within this environment will thereby provide high-quality employment and wealth, and eventually make healthcare products available to satisfy unmet needs. Such businesses will comply with the regulations that apply to any other private, profit-making concern that supplies products to consumers.

The products to which we are referring within the scope of this book differ from any other class of product that is developed for consumers in one fundamental aspect: these products are prescribed and administered by trusted professionals for a consumer who has limited understanding of their use, abuse and application. In many cases the first knowledge that the consumer will have of the product will be when it is defined by the physician recommending treatment for a particular condition. At this time the consumer may be in one of a whole variety of mental and physical states: stressed, in denial, delirious, unconscious, frightened. These are not conditions in which consumers are likely to make rational judgements, so they depend on the skill and training of the doctor or other healthcare professional (nurse, pharmacist) who becomes involved in the supply and administration of the product.

Fundamentally, then, the regulations that are enacted are designed to protect patients, the vulnerable consumers, from exploitation. It is critical to the interests of these patients that the regulator is independent of the industry. The initial demand for the product will be driven by the doctor's prescription and recommended treatment regimen. This treatment will have been licensed and approved by the relevant authorities after rigorous and extensive testing. In previous chapters we have identified the timescale and cost estimates associated with developing and marketing a new drug. The majority of these costs are associated with the later testing phases of the process. It is clear then that in order to make a commercial return on this huge investment the developing company will want to make all possible users of the product aware of its existence and of the benefits from its use. It is in this area that the authorities rely on the integrity of the ethical industry to ensure that they are influencing prescribers and users of the benefits of the product, and not to encourage its use for trivial, non-medicinal or unapproved medical indications (see 'Zyprexa – stretching the boundaries?', p. 164).

Given this situation, however, there is an inherent complication: we are asking the private, profit-making organisation deliberately to restrict activities that would necessarily limit the awareness and eventual sale of its products. Within any commercial organisation the marketing professionals will endeavour to build the market for their product by raising awareness and interest in their target audience. This will hopefully lead to demand for the product and a stream of sales invoices. This process can be referred to by the unfortunate, yet unforgettable, acronym AIDS (Awareness, Interest, Demand and Sale). Again we rely on the skill, integrity and ethics of the members of the promoting organisation to ensure they have in mind the welfare of the patient or consumer in every case, as well as faith in the independence of the regulator. In the vast majority of cases this trust is not abused and all associated professionals recognise and value the position they hold in caring for patients by providing and administering the prescribed treatment. The case of Harold Shipman, a general practitioner (GP) in the UK who was convicted of causing the deaths of 15 patients through overdoses of diamorphine, sadly demonstrates what can happen if this trust is abused or misplaced (see Panel).

HAROLD SHIPMAN – POSSIBLY THE MOST PROLIFIC SERIAL KILLER IN THE WORLD*

An audit by the Department of Health following his conviction for the murder of 15 patients estimated that Harold Shipman was directly responsible for the death of 236 victims over 24 years.

Dr Harold Shipman, working in the north of England since 1974, had been convicted in 1976 of prescription fraud and forgery, fined £600, yet still allowed to practise as a GP. He had been requesting supplies of pethidine, a morphine-like painkiller used in childbirth, in the names of patients who had not been prescribed this product.

Between 1974 and 1998 he killed with impunity. The fact that one GP appeared to have an unprecedented number of deaths among his patients did not go unnoticed or unchallenged by undertakers, pharmacists and other doctors. When challenged about the large number of deaths, Shipman's warm and considerate responses were sufficient to satisfy these interested, yet powerless, groups. At that time coroners did not have to be involved and post mortems were not required, as the deceased victims had recently seen a doctor or been in hospital. If the body was to be cremated, which would destroy any evidence of overdosing, a second doctor had to sign a form. A fellow GP in Hyde, Manchester, who countersigned 18 cremation forms for Shipman, said doctors rarely asked questions of each other and often had blind faith in their peers and that he thought the serial killer was just an 'old-fashioned GP'.

Shipman's mistake came when it was discovered that he had forged the signature on a new will of an 81-year-old patient, Mrs Grundy, which left £386,000 to none other than Dr Harold Shipman. The victim's daughter, Mrs Woodruff, a solicitor, was puzzled. Her mother had made a will in 1986, which was lodged at her own law firm. She naturally became extremely suspicious when it emerged that a new will had been made without her knowledge. It was inconceivable that her mother would not have left her a penny. Further investigation linked the doctor to the death of 14 other victims.

On 31 January 2000 Shipman was found guilty on all 15 counts of murder and also of a forgery charge. Sentencing him, Mr Justice Forbes said: 'You murdered each and every one of your victims by a calculated and cold-blooded perversion of your medical skills, for your own evil and wicked purposes. You took advantage of and grossly abused their trust. You were, after all, each victim's doctor. I have little doubt that each of your victims smiled and thanked you as she submitted to your deadly ministrations.'**

The judge handed out 15 life sentences and told Shipman he would be recommending to the Home Secretary that he never be released. With the trial over the Department of Health were able to begin the work that would estimate Dr Shipman's true death toll as 236!

The formal public inquiry into the activities of Dr Shipman began in 2002, chaired by Dame Janet Smith, who is quoted as saying 'the system was inadequate and must be changed to meet the needs of society in the 21st century'.***

On Tuesday 13 January 2004 Shipman died after being found hanging in his cell in Wakefield prison.

Conclusions

The report identified in detail over 100 specific recommendations for change. It had gathered statements from over 2,500 witnesses and scanned 100,000 pages of evidence into its database. A series of five reports were published between 19 July 2002 and 27 January 2005 describing:

– how he managed to kill his patients;

– the conduct of the police in their investigations into Shipman's activities;

– the investigation of deaths by the coroner;

– regulations regarding the supply of controlled substances;

– handling of complaints and performance of GPs by their ruling General Medical Council.

Dame Janet said: 'There is no easy way to prevent a doctor who determined to obtain illicit supplies of a controlled drug from doing so, nor is there any fool-proof way of detecting, after the event, that a doctor has diverted controlled drugs, to his or her own use.'

Shipman's ability to go undetected could be attributed to his cunning and plausibility, but also to the 'admiration, respect and deference with which doctors have been historically regarded in this country. It was unthinkable that a doctor might harm his patients deliberately.'

[*]   General source the trial of Dr Shipman.
[**]   'Harold Frederick Shipman – Multiple Murderer' (published online 7 July 2005) <http://www.bbc.co.uk/dna/h2g2/A4241099>.
[***] 'The Shipman Enquiry' (2005) for this and following quotes <http://www.the-shipman-inquiry.org.uk>.

Striking the Right Balance

So we can see that there is an assumption that companies within the healthcare industry will work in the interests of patients and within a framework of regulations or agreed codes of conduct when carrying out their business. There is also an assumption that this framework will be provided by regulators independently and with the interests of patients as their prime consideration. The commercial interests of the industry will be satisfied through its long-term interest in and commitment to patient care. If companies fall short of the generally accepted standards of care or regulations they can expect punishing costs and sanctions enforced against them: closure of poorly maintained production facilities, criminal or civil suits where they have been negligent, fines and penalties levied by their professional bodies if they transgress their rules regarding inducements to doctors or inappropriate advertising or promotion.

Andrew Hotchkiss, Association of British Pharmaceutical Industry (ABPI) board member and managing director of Lilly UK, stated in November 2005, on the release of the updated industry code of practice, 'Self-regulation is by far the most effective means of ensuring that the industry's relationship with the Health Service and others is conducted in a responsible and ethical manner. Given that branded medicines can make the difference between life and death, it is incumbent on all of us who work in the pharmaceutical industry to ensure the highest standards when dealing with healthcare professionals and other stakeholders. The revised code is a strong message of intent but, ultimately, society will judge us on our actions and behaviour.'[1]

The need for such codes of conduct and regulations is generally accepted, yet there is a danger that too rigid a regulatory framework will stifle innovation and opportunity, perhaps working against the longer-term interest of patients. Where then is the balance to be struck? How will that balance change with developments in communication technology, manufacturing process capability, local budget constraints for healthcare provision and increasing understanding and awareness of new treatments? In exploring the answers to these questions I postulate the following assertion:

> *It is the role of the regulator to create the environment within which the private industry can develop products and services to achieve mutually desired outcomes. It will therefore establish guidelines and regulations to frame that environment and monitor standards and performance in each area. Working closely with, yet remaining independent from the industry representatives, the data provided by this monitoring activity will provide input to ensure the environment develops effectively and efficiently to achieve better the desired outcomes.*

With regard to the desired outcomes, there are four areas worthy of focus and more detailed consideration:

- unmet need;

- product development and supply;

- effective promotion, education and availability;

- value for money.

UNMET NEED

The pharmaceutical industry has been the primary source of new medicines and treatments for hitherto incurable diseases; polio, smallpox, tuberculosis (TB) and syphilis are but a few notable examples. The benefits to patients are clear, and the benefits to the economy come through reducing the number of lost days of employment, cutting the cost of extended treatment in hospital

---

1   'The Shipman Enquiry' (2005).

as well as the revenue earned from exports and so on. It is, therefore, in the interest of the regulators to assist and direct R&D towards the major diseases of the time. Currently cardiovascular diseases and cancers gain major focus in the developed world, alongside conditions related to increased longevity, such as Alzheimer's and Parkinson's diseases.

In the developing world the picture is quite different. Here we have major endemic plagues of AIDS, malaria and TB, together with the ever-present dangers of acute infections from poor sanitation and malnutrition. Although treatments are available for these conditions, the drugs by themselves are insufficient. Treatment must be provided together with improvements in living conditions, education and governance. This is another story altogether and we will not be distracted by it here.

In order to ensure that the industry develops products that will meet perceived and known unmet needs now and into the future, government institutions provide leadership through provision of research grants and other financial incentives for university and research-based companies to work in a given area. These could be direct grants provided by a relevant government department; the establishment of centres of excellence within universities and hospitals; or regional industry centres such as biotech institutes or science parks. These have been discussed in more detail in earlier chapters and are identified here as the means by which the regulators can steer the activities of the industry towards unmet needs.

Evaluation by the industry of R&D projects is necessarily draconian: they must kill off projects with little promise quickly so as to focus all available resources on developing those assets that will have greater chances of success. This evaluation has three main parameters: cost, risk and commercial potential. It is the area of commercial potential that is tricky when we consider unmet need because the patient population for, say, late-stage Parkinson's disease may be too small to generate sensible commercial returns at sensible prices. This has been discussed in previous chapters and remains a tool at the disposal of the regulator to encourage cures for patients with such conditions.

PRODUCT DEVELOPMENT AND SUPPLY

Product development

The desired outcome of the product development process is a continual flow of safe, effective, innovative medicines that will better treat existing conditions and potentially cure or eradicate diseases where no viable treatment exists. Excellent examples of this are seen in the number of treatments being approved and the launch in 2006/7 of treatments for human papillomavirus (HPV), the cause of certain cervical cancers. There had been no treatment for the type of HPV that causes cervix cell changes. Antibiotics or other medicines do not treat HPV.

As we have postulated, the regulator is responsible for identifying the framework within which the development process should operate to achieve its goals. In response it is the practitioners' responsibility to create their preferred set of operational guidelines, Good Clinical Practice (GCP), in conjunction with the regulator. These guidelines are refined as and when experience or technology identifies deficiencies. Here we discuss some of the complexities associated with the process.

As discussed above, the product development process is extremely costly and 'unproductive'. By unproductive we do not mean that people and processes are not working hard, but that the process is inherently risky and only one in every 8,000–10,000 products identified eventually finds approval as a new drug. An overview of the process, showing where arbitrage can occur within the supply chain, can be seen in Figure 9.1.

The schematic identifies a number of key areas in which the regulator has some control – the pre-clinical processes in which the drug is tested in silico (computer simulations) and in vivo (on living animals) and the clinical processes where the product is tested on humans to prove the concept – and that demonstrate the drug to be of sound quality, safe and efficacious: it works.

Finally the regulator has approval over whether the testing has conclusively demonstrated that the product works safely in a wide population group. These Phase III trials represent a major financial outlay for the organisation, and such trials are only sanctioned when there is strong evidence that the product will be viable. Trials involving over 10,000 patients in up to 40 countries are typical and necessary at this stage to gather the level of data required to satisfy the

Schematic view of the Drug Development process

The regulatory authorities control the testing in animals and man, and give final approval to market the product based upon the results of extensive trials. These trials are designed to demonstrate the quality, safety and efficacious nature of the product.

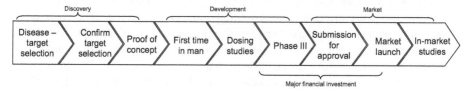

Figure 9.1   Schematic view of the drug development process

Monitoring of side effects of the product in-market enables close control. In rare instances the products are withdrawn from the market due to possible adverse side effects (for example, Vioxx Sept. 2004)

regulator. This is discussed further in the section 'Deontology – Constraint or Obligation' relating to the products Seroxat and Vioxx.

Increasingly there is pressure from regulators to show that the intended new product is sufficiently differentiated from existing drugs for it to be supported by both marketing approval and reimbursement pricing. Once the product has come to market there are stringent monitoring processes that identify any adverse reactions and hitherto unknown side effects from the drug in widespread use. Vioxx in 2004 and thalidomide in 1961 are two drugs that have been withdrawn from sale due to direct links to adverse side effects (see Panel).

THALIDOMIDE – THE CASE FOR THOROUGH TESTING

Chemie Grünenthal GmbH first introduced thalidomide in West Germany as a potent tranquilliser and sleeping pill. It was used extensively by pregnant women suffering from morning sickness. There are around 3,000 surviving thalidomide-deformed children, while an equal number have died. In addition, some 5,000 adult users of the drug are believed to have suffered permanent injury through its side effects.

The product was also launched in Great Britain, where there were over 1,000 victims; yet in the USA the authorities believed that more thorough and extensive testing was needed before they would give marketing approval. As a result the product was never approved and so only around 20 babies became victims.

Dr Widukind Lenz was a paediatrician in Hamburg when he began to study the effects of the drug. He was the man who assembled the evidence later used in court against thalidomide. Until 1960 phocomelia (seal limbs) had been one of the rarest of congenital defects. In 1961 thalidomide went on the market and the incidence of this extraordinary condition increased substantially – in line with thalidomide sales, but with an eight-month time lag. Lenz was able to dismiss other possible causes of the condition such as exposure to X-rays, TV radiation, fallout and so on. As a cautious clinical scientist he eventually rejected them all. 'There is no doubt that thalidomide caused the malformations,' he said in 1968 at the trial of Grünenthal executives.[*]

Thalidomide did initially pass safety tests in animals. However, it was not tested on pregnant animals. If a thorough protocol of tests had been performed on animals, the teratogenic (birth defect) effects would have been identified. After its withdrawal from the market, thalidomide was tested on pregnant animals and found to induce birth defects in mice, rats, hamsters, marmosets and baboons. If these tests on animals had been carried out earlier, the disaster would have been averted.

This case has been cited by anti-vivisectionists to illustrate the cruelty of animal testing. Clearly this is a prime example of an argument in favour of more animal testing, not less -- which is why it is now a legal requirement to test all drugs on pregnant animals.

At the trial in 1968 Dr Lenz confirmed that thalidomide had been shown to cause phocomelia in rhesus and other monkey species in which the condition does not occur naturally.

If doctors were to seek comparable proof in humans it would be at least unethical and in most countries illegal. It was the absence of rigorous animal testing and the failure of regulators in Europe to insist on the protocol that led to this human tragedy. Banning animal testing would create similar disasters on a staggeringly frequent basis.

* 'Thalidomide on Trial', Time (published online 6 September 1968) <http://www.time.com/time/magazine/article/0,9171,900340,00.html>.

Product supply

During the product development process there will be a parallel pharmaceutical development process. This means that the active pharmaceutical ingredient (API) will need to be formulated into appropriate dosage forms that will enable exact qualities to be applied. These doses must also be in a form that will ensure most effective bio-availability. For many APIs the pharmaceutical form is straightforward: solid dose tablet to be swallowed. In other cases the product may be ineffective if ingested and so may be made available to the body through inhalation, subcutaneously or intravenously using specifically designed devices such as injectors, patches or inhalers. The same API may be formulated in a range of dose forms to treat different conditions. An example of the range of dose forms is shown in the following panel.

A LARGE, BUT NOT EXHAUSTIVE LIST OF DOSE FORMATS

The list of formulations, devices or pack combinations is endless. The specific format chosen will depend on the product's general characteristics as well as the need for specific application methods and other patented devices in force.

Solid doses

Tablets: plain, film-coated in a range of shapes and sizes (see Chapter 8). Certain products can be made into rapidly disintegrating wafers that dissolve on the tongue.

Capsules which may contain API alone or API coated onto a substrate to enable slow release of the drug.

Powders, particularly micronised, or very finely ground APIs, are common in inhalation devices. There are a wide variety of these devices designed specifically for each drug and its particular mode of application. Examples include dry powder devices and others that propel the drug either via carrier solvent or by mechanically generated turbo.

Liquids, creams and ointments

Liquids can be aqueous or mildly alcoholic solutions.

Creams are formulated using water or hydrophilic materials. Ointments are formulated using oils or hydrophobic substances. Depending on the site of application (for example, eyes) these may need to be formulated and packed under sterile conditions.

Each may be packed into simple containers, such as tubes, or loaded into dispensing devices that apply fixed doses: pumps or sprays.

(Sterile) injectables

The API may be manufactured as a liquid and packed under sterile conditions. This is common for vaccines and other complex bio-pharmaceuticals that will be denatured by high temperatures.

Other, more stable, ingredients may be formulated and packed in ambient conditions and then sterilised by autoclave. In either case the formulation will be sealed.

Lyophilisation or freeze drying is common for sterile products that would be unstable as a liquid. They will be constituted into injectable form at the time of application by solution in a suitable sterile diluent.

Anyone with any experience of manufacturing will understand the complexity of cost and control problems that a wide range of formulations will present. It is the manufacturer's responsibility to produce the product according to the specifications submitted in the appropriate pharmacopoeia accurately and consistently. As we have seen above pharmaceutical products are potentially very dangerous; therefore their dose and application must be exactly as specified and tested through the pre-approval trial process.

The desired outcome for the regulator is that the products will be of agreed high quality. To achieve this outcome the manufacturers have developed a code of conduct in consultation with the regulators, Good Manufacturing Practice (GMP). This involves validation of every step of the production and packaging process, together with approved ways of working that define best current practice. This validation involves machinery, personnel training, documentation and supporting computer systems. It may have the impact of preventing improvements within the processes, since any changes would need to go through a rigorous and costly revalidation exercise. To overcome this possibility the regulators have introduced Process Analytical Technologies (PATs), which enable improvements to be made to a process while maintaining the validity and reproducibility of that process.

To ensure accuracy and reliability of the analysis the relevant guide is the code of Good Laboratory Practice (GLP). Similarly when the product is stored, handled and distributed the best current practice is defined in the guide to Good Distribution Practice (GDP). These GxP codes of conduct are developed by the industry in association with the regulatory authorities. Audits of facilities or processes are made by inspectors to ensure compliance and guide improvements in processes or facilities.

Regulators reserve the right to inspect the premises, production facilities, documentation and any other aspect of the business systems that support the manufacture and storage of the approved product. They have the power to close down a facility that is either knowingly operating outside the agreed code of conduct or that fails to implement improvement notices given from time to time.

Such action would be taken by the regulator to ensure that the product will be consistently manufactured and supplied as agreed, especially where patient safety may be compromised: non-sterile conditions; inaccurate formulation leading to inconsistent dosing; poor manufacturing batch documentation; untrained or unskilled personnel involved at critical steps. The impact of such a sanction harms everyone and is not in the long-term interest of the manufacturing organisations. It is in their best interest to understand the needs of the regulator and to help develop and apply the industry-wide codes of conduct. Manufacturers must always be able to demonstrate full compliance; this is the licence to operate in this important field of healthcare. Failure to show willingness to comply, or seeking to evade compliance, would do nothing but damage the industry as a whole.

Which of us would knowingly fly in an aeroplane piloted by an unqualified pilot, or eat in a restaurant that has poor kitchen hygiene or unsavoury eating conditions? In the aerospace and food sectors regulators set the guidelines, police them intermittently and rely on the professionalism of the practitioners to safeguard their customers and their own reputation.

Effective Promotion, Education and Availability

The desired outcome here is that patients and relevant healthcare professionals are aware of and fully understand the product and its use and application. In achieving this outcome the regulator will gain the therapeutic, economic and social benefits envisaged by the approval to market, and the developing company will optimise its revenue potential.

We identified above how this may restrict the opportunities for marketing organisations to get their message across; yet it is critical to both the industry and regulators that these potentially dangerous pharmaceutical products are prescribed on the basis of their efficacy, not on the basis of any inducements to the doctor by the company.

Historically these inducements have been hidden in the conferences, training courses and other educational meetings that have been held in faraway exotic locations with five-star accommodation and relaxation activities such as skiing or scuba diving. No more. Codes of conduct in this area dictated by regulators and agreed and policed by the industry professional associations in each market have gone a long way towards improving both the conduct and the image of the industry in this matter.

DEONTOLOGY – CONSTRAINT OR OBLIGATION

These codes of conduct are based on the philosophical, moral and ethical considerations of deontology. This word is derived from the Greek word *deon*, meaning obligation or duty. The principle holds not that the end justifies the means, but just the opposite; it is how those ends are achieved that is more important. The following case studies show how this principle is very exacting and one in which the pharmaceutical industry is regularly tested to demonstrate its adherence. The outcome which both regulator and industry agree upon is the availability of high-quality, safe and efficacious drugs to fight disease. The test is that both regulator and industry representatives must, in all cases, demonstrate that the availability of these products has been made in the interest of patients and not just in the commercial interests of the private companies.

Seroxat – non-disclosure of test results?

The chemical paroxetine, marketed under the brand name Seroxat (Paxil in the USA) is in the class of selective serotonin reuptake inhibitors (SSRIs) used to treat patients suffering from depression. In June 2003 the Medicines and Healthcare products Regulatory Agency (MHRA), the regulators in UK, advised doctors that the drug should not be prescribed for paediatric use because of an increased risk of suicide. This action was followed closely by regulators in the USA, France, Ireland and Canada. At that time Seroxat's annual sales were almost $5 billion worldwide.

This would seem to be the just role of the regulator as previously determined: monitoring and evaluating the performance of a new drug and acting on emerging information. It was revealed, however, that the company that developed and marketed the product, then SmithKline Beecham, later GlaxoSmithKline (GSK), had withheld data from one clinical trial – Study 329, conducted in the US from 1993 to 1996. The results indicated that paroxetine was no more effective than a placebo. This had been the largest trial to that date on using an SSRI in a paediatric population. In another trial, Study 377, carried out in Europe, South America and elsewhere, a placebo was actually more effective than the antidepressant. Regulatory approval had been provided without a full review of all the clinical data.

The study was published in 2001, after the product had received marketing approval. It showed that five of the 93 adolescents given Seroxat developed increased suicidal tendencies – compared with only one in the 95 given the comparator product, Tofranil, and one in the 89 given a placebo. GSK did not decide to publish this clinical trial data of its own volition; it was forced into doing this as a result of legal action by the Attorney General of New York, Eliot Spitzer.

Vioxx – misrepresenting the safety of a drug?

On 30 September 2004 the US Food and Drug Administration (FDA) confirmed that manufacturer Merck voluntarily withdrew Vioxx from the market after the data safety monitoring board recommended that the study be halted because of an increased risk of serious cardiovascular events, including heart attacks and strokes. They had been overseeing a long-term study in patients at risk of developing recurrent colon polyps.

Vioxx is a non-steroidal anti inflammatory drug used in the treatment of chronic pain. It was given approval in 1999 and was the only drug of its type that showed reduced gastrointestinal side effects associated with the existing treatments. A study published in 2000, however, showed not only the reduced gastrointestinal problems, but also an increased risk of cardiovascular diseases such as heart attacks and strokes. This prompted the regulator, the FDA, to investigate over 1.4 million medical records of patients prescribed Vioxx over a long period. This study indeed showed increased heart attacks and strokes in Vioxx patients compared with those using alternatives. This evidence, together with the earlier study, led to the voluntary withdrawal of Vioxx in late 2004.

Immediately there were lawsuits aimed at the company on the basis of harm caused to patients who were not informed about the risks of the drug. At the time of writing there are over 27,000 cases, and the company has decided to treat each one separately and set aside over $1 billion for legal expenses to defend them. A number of these cases have been tried by juries who have found that the company misrepresented the safety of the drug.

As a supply chain aside, Vioxx was launched only four months after the first product in its class, Celebrex, and was stocked in over 40,000 pharmacies only 11 days after receipt of approval – a remarkable feat. The product was certainly made available, but not all the relevant data that could help doctors and patients decide on the risks they were taking. On a personal note I can testify to the benefits of the pain relief from the drug. My mother was a Vioxx patient before she died in December 2003. Her pain through gout brought on as an effect of chemotherapy was debilitating. Once prescribed Vioxx the relief from pain remarkably improved her quality of life in her last few months. This illustrates the dilemma faced by companies and regulators given the nature of any pharmaceutical preparation: how to assess the balance of risk and benefit.

Zyprexa – stretching the boundaries?

An analysis of Florida Medicaid data from September 2002 to September 2003, by the Florida Department of Children and Family Services, found that 41,993 children aged 12 and under were given 190,210 off-label prescriptions for psychiatric drugs by doctors in fields that included anaesthetics, dermatology, geriatrics, allergies, nutrition, ophthalmology, obstetrics, pathology, otolaryngology, haematology, diabetes, plastic surgery, radiology, rheumatology and hand surgery.

In California the highest Medicaid expense was for Zyprexa, at a cost nearing $250 million in the year ending June 2005. Similar drugs – Paxil/Seroxat (by GSK); Zoloft and Geodon (Pfizer); Prozac (Eli Lilly); Celexa and Lexapro (Forest Laboratories); Luvox (Solvay); Seroquel (AstraZeneca); Abilify (Bristol-Myers Squibb); Risperdal (Johnson & Johnson) – had combined sales of $20.7 billion in 2004 (*Wall Street Journal*, 27 June 2005).

The off-label marketing of these medications includes prescribing a drug for a different illness, or at a different dose, or with a different combination of other drugs, or for a different patient population than that approved by the FDA. Both Lilly and AstraZeneca received subpoenas from the Attorney

General in California regarding the promotion of Zyprexa and Seroquel. In December 2006 the FDA was urged by a senior politician to investigate Lilly's activities with regard to its promotion of Zyprexa to doctors.

It is alleged that the company has been encouraging doctors since 2002 to use the drug – which is approved only for the treatment of schizophrenia and bipolar disorder – on older patients who had neither condition but were suffering from dementia. These allegations were brought to light when internal confidential documents were sequestrated by a lawyer acting for patients suing Lilly since they allege that use of Zyprexa caused their diabetes. These documents then came into the hands of the *New York Times*, which took up the case in a series of high-profile articles.

In June 2006 the state of Mississippi filed a suit alleging that representatives of Eli Lilly convinced Mississippi doctors to prescribe Zyprexa to patients suffering from anxiety, mood swings and disturbed sleep. The suit also alleged that the pharmaceutical company did not properly emphasise the dangers of the drug, such as an increased risk of diabetes. Mississippi estimates damages at $30 million incurred as they paid for drugs that were provided for conditions outside the licence, and as they suffered greater costs from patients who became ill from its use.

It would therefore appear that the escalating cost to state medical insurance schemes (see Chapter 5) is causing a review of the practice of 'off-label' promotion. This practice – the promotion of drugs for uses that have not been approved – is illegal for drug companies, but it is common knowledge that they do it and had hitherto suffered few, if any, sanctions.

The complexity of the products, their use and the interpretation of the regulations provide many trips and traps for marketing professionals aiming to ensure that their products are promoted as widely as possible to build brand value. Any action taken against their company for non-compliance or misrepresentation can be very costly indeed. The following examples demonstrate this clearly:

- In 2004 Pfizer/Warner Lambert were fined $430 million when they pleaded guilty to charges related to illegal promotion of Neurontin by Warner Lambert from activities in 1996.

- Serono were charged $704 million in 2005 in fines and civil payments for promoting Serostim in a similar manner.

- Bristol-Myers Squibb agreed with the Department of Justice a figure of $499 million to settle several investigations involving the company's drug pricing and sales and marketing activities.

- InterMune paid $30.2 million to the US federal Medicare and Medicaid programmes, the Veterans Health Administration, Department of Defense and Federal Employees Health Benefits programme. This settled charges of off-label promotion of Actimmune in treating lung scarring, an unapproved use of the drug, through June 2003. Actimmune had been approved for treating immune system disorders. The company also paid about $6.7 million to state Medicaid programmes because the off-label promotional activities led to Medicaid fraud, bringing the company's total penalty for promoting an off-label use of Actimmune to $36.9 million.

- Schering-Plough agreed to pay $180 million in criminal fines plus $255 million in civil penalties to the US Department of Justice and state of Massachusetts. This settled an investigation into the company's sales and marketing practices and Medicaid fraud for a portfolio of products: Temodar, Intron A, Claritin RediTabs and K-Dur. Charges included off-label promotion and violating the anti-kickback statute, where doctors were paid to prescribe Schering-Plough's drugs in the 1990s.

In each of the above cases the companies signed corporate integrity agreements (CIAs) with the Office of Inspector General (OIG) of the US Department of Health and Human Services (HHS), the department that controls the FDA. These agreements would govern their promotion activities for five years. The Schering-Plough settlement came soon after a previous settlement in 2004 of $300 million with the state of Pennsylvania regarding insurance pricing violations around Claritin, with the ink hardly dry on its original CIA.

Given the scale and complexity of policing the regulations, regulators turn more towards voluntary codes agreed by the companies and their professional bodies. In Belgium the Code of Deontology is managed by the industry association Pharma.be, and all of its members agree to abide by the code. In the UK the ABPI, as mentioned above, produces and polices its own code of conduct in this field. It is called The Prescription Medicines Code of Practice Authority (PMCPA) and regulates the advertising of prescription medicines to health professionals and administrative staff; it also covers information about such medicines made available to the general public. Compliance with the code is obligatory for ABPI member companies and, in addition, around 60 non-member companies have voluntarily agreed to comply with the code and to accept the PMCPA's jurisdiction.

To assist the industry in understanding and developing strategies to ensure compliance there have been a range of conferences and other events. In October 2006 the American Conference Institute ran its fifth national forum on fraud and abuse in the sales and marketing of drugs. This forum sought to share experiences and lessons from recent court cases and develop best current practice among pharmaceutical companies.

In concluding this section I can cite a conversation I had with a very senior member of a major pharmaceutical company while facilitating a confidential review with them into the possible impact of pharmacogenetics on the revenues of the future patient-specific, lower-volume pharmaceuticals that would inevitably be developed using this branch of science. He said emphatically 'if this is good for patients then it is good for my company'.

Value for Money

The outcome here might, at first sight, be a reduction in the cost of medicines; yet this would be short-sighted. It will certainly be the role of government providers of healthcare services to continually monitor costs and seek constantly to reduce them. However, taking a wider view, we know that spending money on drugs to treat chronic conditions such as high cholesterol or asthma can have major benefits through reduced costs of acute care in hospital, loss of patient contribution to the economy and other effects caused by the failure to treat these diseases.

In markets where the major provider of healthcare is effectively the government, marketing approval for a new drug on the grounds of quality, safety and efficacy may follow a separate process from that of price negotiations. Upon receiving marketing approval the product can be made available to the private market, those who are prepared to pay the published price. It will not be adopted by national or local formularies until their bodies decide that they will adopt the product and reimburse pharmacists at an agreed price to dispense it. In markets where the product is purchased by private or state insurance funds similar second-stage negotiations will take place.

This effectively means that the marketing companies must show that their product provides a clinical benefit over any existing products or treatments before it can be made widely available through prescription. This should not represent a serious issue to the industry; if it cannot show clinical and economic benefit, how can it expect public funds to pay? There has also been ample opportunity during the large-scale, expensive Stage III trials to demonstrate the drug's performance against both placebo and other existing treatments. The design of these trials has become more critical since this pricing hurdle has become more prominent with regulators in advance of approval to fund the product.

Conclusion

The USA's current regulatory framework was born in response to a medical tragedy. The FDA's original function with respect to drugs was primarily concerned with matters like the removal from the market of contaminated drugs; new drugs did not need its approval before launch. In 1937, however, over 100 people died after taking a 'wonder drug', Elixir Sulfanilamide, containing the substance better known as antifreeze. Physicians had prescribed the drug in good faith. However, it had not undergone any toxicity testing or pharmacological studies.

A new piece of legislation, the Federal Food, Drug, and Cosmetic Act, was already in the pipeline when this tragedy occurred. It was passed in 1938 and featured an additional New Drug section, designed to prevent a recurrence of this tragic situation by requiring new drugs to gain FDA approval before being launched onto the market. It is arguably thanks to this Act that the USA did not suffer from the effects of thalidomide seen in Europe.

It is in this example that the reason for the existence of the regulator is apparent: to protect public health. The examples in this chapter illustrate that shared outcome will inevitably become confused in commercial opportunity if the regulator is not strong, independent of the industry, yet working alongside it. The regulator faces four major challenges in maintaining this position and being assertively vigilant on behalf of patients:

- The ever-increasing sophistication of science and its application in the field of medicine. New techniques and products will be made available. How can the regulator ensure that new treatments will be safe?

- The products themselves, and their associated production techniques, are becoming increasingly complicated. The imminent expiry of patents on many complex biopharmaceuticals will lead to a range of generic products becoming available. How can the regulator ensure that these alternatives can be produced with the same quality and pharmacological effectiveness as the patented product, given their variability and the experience needed to validate and control the production process?

- As price control becomes an increasing issue there will be greater and greater pressure to enable cross-border trade and encourage generic prescribing.

- Ensuring the quality of these products will become ever more challenging, and this will be compounded by the opportunities of supply via mail order and the Internet.

These challenges will place increasing emphasis upon the integrity of the industry. The cost and complexity of the regulatory process on the public purse will increase substantially to accommodate the challenges set out above. The industry players must be scrupulously fair, open and seen to be continually protecting patients' interests.

It is critical to the long-term future of the industry that it positions itself, through its thoughts, words and actions, on the side of protecting patients and improving quality of life, and is not perceived merely to be protecting short-term commercial interests that could cause untold damage to patients and the industry.

From the supply chain management perspective, compliance with the regulatory framework creates the access to the demand for the product. If the supply chain manager or manufacturing manager focuses on cost efficiency and customer service criteria without an appropriate, strategic underpinning focus on compliance, they unnecessarily risk everything.

10

The Case for Enhanced Patient Protection

The exceptional complexity of the pharmaceutical supply chain creates a variety of threats to patient safety. Some of these arise from criminal activity, notably counterfeiting of drugs, and others from human error. Wherever manufacturing or distribution passes outside the direct control of the manufacturer, there is potential opportunity for something to go wrong. While such events may be beyond a manufacturer's control, that manufacturer may still find itself liable for the consequences.

Business Models for Supply, Distribution and Dispensing to Patients

The pharmaceutical supply chain is long and complex (Figure 10.1). To bring a new drug to market currently takes over 10 years and costs $800 million. In addition, overall supply chain activities can take around two years to complete, since the manufacturing process typically involves many steps in many different facilities – often located in several different countries. The typical supply chain for a pharmaceutical product has a number of distinctive characteristics, discussed below.

MANUFACTURE OF PRECURSORS

The intermediary products or chemical precursors to the Active Pharmaceutical Ingredient (API) are often made in low-cost manufacturing countries such as India, China and Korea. These countries tend not to place the same emphasis on protection of intellectual property (IP) laws or values as more developed, western economies. The importance of this fact will become clear in the course of this chapter.

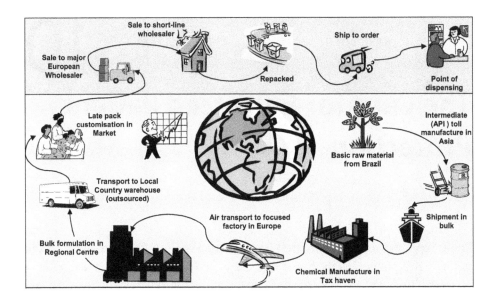

Figure 10.1   The complexity of the global pharmaceutical supply chain

MANUFACTURE OF API

The API itself is usually manufactured in a country that provides significant incentives through tax, capital relief programmes or low cost of labour. The main environments for this activity have been Singapore and Puerto Rico.

The active production of this ingredient may technically be commissioned by a subsidiary company of the holding group on a toll basis. Toll manufacture is the process by which a manufacturing facility is commissioned to perform a specific manufacturing step or steps, for which it receives a fee (toll); however, the title to the goods does not pass to that manufacturer. The subsidiary is likely to be incorporated within a region that has advantageous tax regulations, such as Switzerland. This arrangement is a highly effective technique for ensuring that taxes paid on profit gained through transfer pricing are optimised. It may never be necessary for the physical product to be stored in, travel through or be processed within the region in question, provided that all relevant administration and documentation is carried out there. This then becomes a supply chain of documentation overlying that of the physical product.

PRODUCTION OF BULK PRODUCT

Similarly, the production of the formulated bulk product may take place in one or two focused (that is specialised) factories. These factories will have invested significantly in a particular technology, and will have the capacity to fulfil a significant proportion of the global demand for the product.

Lyophilisation, or freeze drying, is an example of a process that is likely to be handled in this way. The investment, running costs, expertise and regulatory controls associated with freeze drying facilities are considerable; the facilities therefore require high utilisation to minimise the unit cost of production. Such facilities can readily carry out product formulation on a subcontract basis for other companies whose product volumes do not justify investment in an in-house capability.

SUBCONTRACTING ISSUES

Although subcontracting offers great advantages from a cost point of view, control of subcontracted work presents challenges. Contracts for manufacturing activities are often managed or overseen by the subcontractor's own technical specialists, who are tasked with ensuring regulatory compliance and technical competence. Once the technology inherent in the manufacturer of a product is transferred to a third party, however, it becomes difficult to control the manufacturing quantity, yield and quality other than through direct and active management. It is my direct experience that the level of supervision required within such subcontracted manufacturing arrangements is difficult to achieve; inadequate supervision can place product supply, brand quality and values in jeopardy. I have also observed that any corrective actions required have been practically unenforceable by the IP owners. The contract suppliers have their own priorities, which will take precedence whenever pressure is applied. Securing quality and supply in these cases dictates that there are always other options available.

FULL-LINE WHOLESALERS

The majority of packed goods supplied to the dispensing pharmacist are controlled through a few major full-line wholesalers who are licensed and regulated. These wholesalers accept a range of obligations to supply any approved medicine, and not just to 'cherry-pick' profitable high-volume items. Whether they are private and commercial or government directed, wholesale organisations need an infrastructure that enables them to procure finished packs in pallet quantities from tens of suppliers, and to receive, pick, handle and distribute single-pack volumes to thousands of pharmacy outlets. In Europe wholesalers may have to make deliveries throughout the day. Typically there are two delivery slots per day, with the ability to place 'urgent' requirements with a two-hour turnaround. Two factors serve to perpetuate this situation: the large number of stock-keeping units (SKUs) that can be dispensed (>20,000) and the high inventory holding cost of these products for the pharmacy. Why hold any stock when I can get it within two hours?

Alternatives to full-line wholesalers

There are, however, a number of other routes through which the packs can reach their eventual destination. These include 'short-line' wholesalers, Internet or mail-order supplies. Such routes may or may not involve the transfer of product from one country to another; international routes allow the supplier to take advantage of differential pricing arrangements, some of the savings from which can then be passed on to the customer.

As we have learned, in Europe this cross-border activity is called parallel trade. It represents an opportunity to procure legitimately supplied, low-priced product in one market and sell it in another market at a higher price. Some, but of course not all, of the price advantage is passed on to the pharmacist and then the healthcare provider (government, sick fund or insurance organisation). There may be a requirement to repackage or relabel the product to ensure that it complies with the regulations in the country of final consumption. In each case there is an obligation to inform the trademark owner (generally the original manufacturer) of the reimportation and repackaging so that they can ensure the trademark is preserved through the process.

Threats to the Security of the Supply Chain

Each link of the supply chain is subject to regulatory control and process validation, which might seem to imply that the supply chain is secure, and that patients will inevitably receive a medicine that is approved, authorised and authentic. Sadly, however, the pharmaceutical supply chain is not nearly as secure as it appears. The World Health Organization (WHO) believes that around 10 per cent of the pharmaceuticals supplied around the world are counterfeit or substandard. The US Food and Drug Administration (FDA) reported that during 2004 it 'initiated 58 counterfeit drug investigations involving hundreds of thousands of fake dosage units'.

It is not surprising that the supply chain is subject to attack, intrusion, fraudulent activity, diversion and counterfeiting, given the amounts of money involved. The pharmaceutical market as a whole is currently worth around $550 billion per year. Major blockbusters such as Pfizer's Lipitor (atorvastatin) generate enormous revenues while protected by patent. In 2006, Lipitor generated global revenues of $13.6 billion, making it the bestselling drug in pharmaceutical history.

In addition, the margins to be made on counterfeit pharmaceutical products are enormous. The material costs (excluding those of the active ingredients, which a counterfeiter may omit) will be fractions of dollars, while the branded product can be priced at tens, hundreds or even thousands of dollars.

The pharmaceutical company itself will be reaping gross margins in excess of 90 per cent from legitimate manufacture of the drug. That is despite the fact that, unlike the counterfeiter, it has to supply the active ingredient, undergo major regulatory control processes and amortise the costs of research and development over the patent-protected life of the product. Imagine what counterfeiters can realise, even if they do include a counterfeit version of the high-cost active ingredient.

Pharmaceutical fraud, then, is potentially very profitable. What is more, the fraudster will probably incur few penalties if caught; there is little chance of conviction given the pall of secrecy that covers this whole area. Manufacturers are reluctant to raise the issue of counterfeit drugs as patients may become concerned about taking their medicines. In reality, compliance with a prescribed regimen for most chronic medicines is already poor.

It is easy to see why pharmaceutical companies are not keen to publicise the frauds perpetrated against them. A poll of financial analysts in 2003 identified that a major counterfeiting or other brand-damaging event could wipe 10 per cent off a company's share price; recovery could take months. Figure 10.2 charts one such incident, showing a striking correlation between the drop in the share price of Eli Lilly and the announcement of the discovery of counterfeit Zyprexa. Recent research has shown that this pattern is consistent across other similar revelations (Figures 10.2 and 10.3).

Figure 10.2   Share prices dip following the discovery of a counterfeit drug

Since the impact on a share price is a major issue for any public company, 'leakage' of sensitive fraud-related information will be discouraged. It could also be argued that disclosure of the existence of counterfeits to warn the public runs contrary to the fiduciary duty of a company director (to maximise the current value of future cash flows) since such an alert will inevitably damage sales and share prices.

The reader will note that here we have a conflict between public safety and corporate interest. From the point of view of the patient, it is desirable for the discovery of counterfeits to be disclosed as soon as possible. As yet, however, even sophisticated markets place no compulsion on manufacturers to do so, though some have a voluntary code of practice. However, knowingly failing to alert the public could be considered negligent in any legal case that might be brought with respect to damage caused through a counterfeit product.

How Fraud Puts Patients at Risk

Pharmaceutical manufacturing companies go to considerable lengths to ensure that they adhere to the best manufacturing and distribution practices available.

All their efforts may, however, count for nothing if their products pass outside their control before they have reached their intended destination. Patients are then at risk either from receiving the wrong product or from receiving a version of the right product that, in some sense, has been made non-compliant as a result of the way it has been distributed or repackaged.

Even something as simple as inappropriate transportation or storage conditions can impact on the patient. Consider, for example, a vaccine which is being transported from one country to another. It is often critical that vaccines are kept within predefined temperature limits throughout their journey. Monitoring and control of temperature are unlikely to be a priority in the case of a drug that is being fraudulently supplied. In any case the more times the product is handled and transported the more risk there is that the product will be damaged and thereby become non-compliant beyond its approved conditions of storage. Blood products are an example of products requiring special transportation and storage, and where it would be hard to tell if the correct conditions had not been maintained.

Repackaging poses other threats to the integrity of the supply chain. Under some circumstances, bona fide suppliers are obliged to repackage goods to meet local regulations, for example removing a Greek-language leaflet and replacing it with an English one. At the repackaging point it is possible to replace the good product inside the outer carton with a counterfeit and place the good product in a counterfeit carton, thereby making it even more difficult for an untrained observer to detect what is a fake and what is not. Much of this could be avoided with the widespread use of tamper-evident packs carrying a rubric such as: *'If the seal is broken on purchase, do NOT use.'*

This practice is ubiquitous in food packaging, but sadly not in pharmaceuticals, even though packaging costs here are generally much smaller in relation to the value of the product. However, the benefits of this type of security became evident to the healthcare industry following a case of contaminated Tylenol in the USA (see Figure 10.3).

Pfizer has recently announced the use of tamper-proof packaging for Lipitor, a product that is subject to extensive parallel trade in Europe and to counterfeiting in the USA. AstraZeneca are trialling the application of a unique serial code to every pack of Nexium. This will enable them quickly to identify authentic and non-authentic packages that they might find in the marketplace.

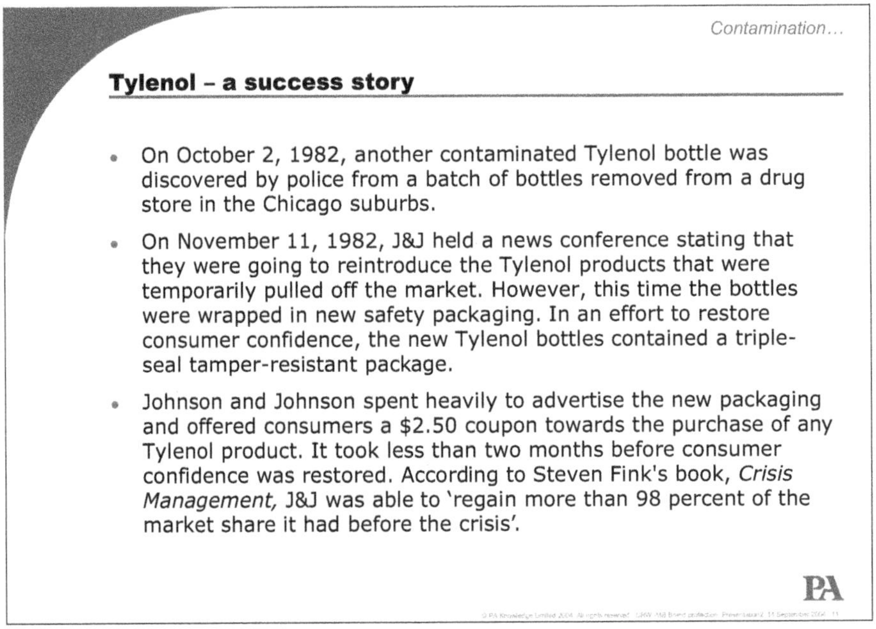

Contamination...

Tylenol – a success story

- On October 2, 1982, another contaminated Tylenol bottle was discovered by police from a batch of bottles removed from a drug store in the Chicago suburbs.

- On November 11, 1982, J&J held a news conference stating that they were going to reintroduce the Tylenol products that were temporarily pulled off the market. However, this time the bottles were wrapped in new safety packaging. In an effort to restore consumer confidence, the new Tylenol bottles contained a triple-seal tamper-resistant package.

- Johnson and Johnson spent heavily to advertise the new packaging and offered consumers a $2.50 coupon towards the purchase of any Tylenol product. It took less than two months before consumer confidence was restored. According to Steven Fink's book, *Crisis Management,* J&J was able to 'regain more than 98 percent of the market share it had before the crisis'.

PA

Figure 10.3   Tylenol – a success story

Reprinted with kind permission of PA Consulting Group.

The main point to note here is that once the product passes outside the manufacturer's direct control, after having been sold, that manufacturer has no rights over what happens to the product, yet can be held liable for any injury caused by non-compliant products reaching the patient. Therefore, manufacturers are rightly concerned about all repackaging activities and product changes that take place once the product has left the factory.

Risks to Patients Arising from Human Error

In addition to the risk that a distributor will mishandle a product, or that a fraudster will alter or substitute it, patients are also at risk from dispensing and administration errors. A patient picking up a prescription from a pharmacy may accidentally receive the wrong substance or dose; a nurse might inject an intra-muscular drug into a vein by mistake, and a surgeon might even remove the wrong kidney. All of these represent human error, where the controlling systems are not working effectively. As a manufacturer we might consider that these errors are out of our control: how far does supply chain control need to be extended? In response it is clear that the manufacturer certainly has a duty to ensure that all users and consumers understand the nature of the product and its correct use.

As a result of human error, patients may need to be hospitalised; at worst, they may die or suffer a permanent impairment, leaving the health organisation liable. In the UK it has been estimated that 11 per cent of hospital admissions are due to adverse medication-related events, some, but not all, of which are dispensing errors. Avoidable medical errors are estimated to be responsible for between 44,000 and 98,000 deaths in the United States each year, and are estimated to cost between $17 billion and $29 billion per year.

The costs of such errors are well documented. In addition to the harm caused to the patient, the health service will incur costs in helping the patient to recover from an adverse reaction, to say nothing of possible legal penalties or damages claims.

Conclusion

The key conclusion is the question of control over the supply chain processes: who has responsibility and who will be accountable if things go wrong? Here I offer a point of view. Accountability lies with the regulator to ensure that procedures and codes of conduct are appropriate and operational at every point. Responsibility lies with the individuals within the organisations that operate each aspect of the supply chain to ensure that they provide training, information, supervision and resources to be compliant at all times. Operatives on production lines, delivery drivers, warehouse and other order picking staff, pharmacists, prescribing doctors and nurses who administer to the patient – all must know their role and carry it out diligently to ensure that the patient is protected.

This chapter has pointed to some of the loopholes that are inevitably present in a process as complex as the pharmaceutical industry supply chain. In the next chapter we shall discuss how technology can counter all of these threats.

11

Applying Technology to Secure the Supply Chain to Patients

A number of technological approaches have been proposed for enhancing the control provided by regulatory systems, processes and guidelines. We describe the use of IT, focusing on product identification provided by two technology groups: firstly product 'barcoding' and secondly mass serialisation through Radio Frequency Identification (RFID) and more complex symbologies. Barcoding allows product and patient identity to be confirmed, avoiding errors in the dispensing of drugs by pharmacists and their administration by trained health service professionals. Mass serialisation technologies can be used for both patient protection (detecting counterfeiting, diversion and so on) and for promoting efficiency in the supply chain, particularly with respect to the 'reverse supply chain' (for example, recalls or returns).

Coding Systems in Common Use

The main technology types that are of interest in the context of mass serialisation of pharmaceutical products are barcodes and RFID tags. Essentially, these are both methods of storing data in a form that is machine-readable.

The first practical use of barcodes is generally accepted as dating back to 1974, when Wrigley's chewing gum was sold via a packaging process that used a barcode reader. The value of barcoding in a retail context lies in being able to identify a product and track it through the supply chain. This brings huge benefits for everyone associated with the distribution channel: manufacturer, wholesaler and retailer. The barcode identifies what the product is and, when barcode readers are integrated with other systems, makes it possible to track where it is.

As printing and scanning technology became more advanced – through the use, for example of thermal transfer and laser-jet printing – it was possible to print more lines in a smaller space, and hence to store more information in a barcode. This led to the emergence of '2D' or 'data matrix' barcodes, which are more data-rich and hence of potentially greater benefit than their predecessors.

Radio Frequency Identification entails the use of a silicon chip into which a number or code is etched at the time of manufacture. Unlike a barcode, this number can be read remotely and out of the line of sight. This technology was first used at the end of World War II to distinguish friendly aircraft from those of the enemy but again, thanks to technological advances, it has recently become much more affordable.

A Solution to Dispensing and Administration Errors: Coding of Drugs and Patients

Product coding systems provide a way to combat threats to patients arising from error. The systems can confirm the identity of prescription, product and patient, and link the right product to the prescription and that prescription to the right patient. A variety of technologies, including barcodes and RFID tags, are available for uniquely identifying products (see Figure 11.1). In fact, most pharmaceutical products already carry barcodes. Very little use of these codes is made at present, however, other than by the manufacturer.

We can see that coding technologies come in a variety of shapes, sizes, formats and materials. In Europe the ubiquitous European Article Number (EAN) 13 code structure provides excellent item identification opportunities. As the structure of the code changes more information can be encrypted, for example batch number, expiry date, unique or mass serialised identity. Printing and scanning technologies have now advanced to the level that this information can be contained within a Reduced Space Symbology (RSS), or data matrix. By inspection we can see that the physical size and material of the product to be coded limit the number of choices available. If small cylindrical ampoules or vials of product incorporated linear 128 barcodes it is unlikely that they could be read by camera scanning equipment effectively, yet a smaller data matrix code may be applied and be more easily readable. Given the range of technologies currently available it is inconceivable that there is no coding

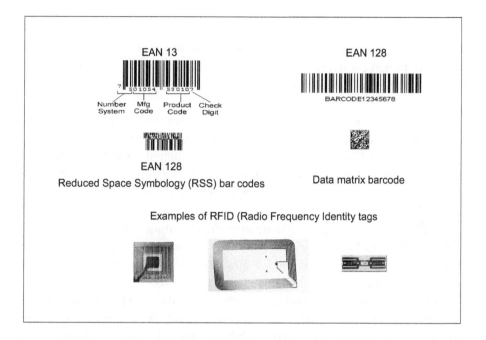

Figure 11.1   Examples of coding technologies

system that allows mass serialisation of any pack format. RFID has three main benefits over printed barcodes:

- copying is practically impossible at a reasonable cost, thus reducing the incentive for counterfeiters;

- it does not require 'line of sight' to be read;

- the wide variety of formats allow local, distant, read and write capabilities and detection of the ambient conditions such as temperature.

However, there is a significant amount of discussion about RFID as the panacea for all ills in the supply chain. 'Never before in the field of human communication has so much been discussed by so many who have such little understanding.'[1]

---

1   Anon, IQPC PharmaSecure Conference, Philadelphia, July 2005.

In reality RFID is a highly technical subject. Effective application of this technology requires business insight and vision, together with the desire and capability to make it happen in spite of the Luddites, lunatics and the myriad technical challenges that stand in the way.

RFID tags are, however, significantly more expensive than printed barcodes and so their use may be limited, on commercial grounds, to high-value products that are at risk of fraud or changes in environmental conditions. Marginal costs are estimated as greater by factors of >100, and almost equivalent to the manufacturing cost of some of the cheaper generic pharmaceutical products.

If patients as well as products are identified by unique codes there are even more possibilities for protecting their safety. Patients in hospitals commonly wear wristbands that carry barcodes, and patients already carry healthcare or social security insurance cards which identify them specifically. It is, therefore, possible to see how the two coding systems for verification and authentication can come together to help prevent dispensing or administration errors. When a doctor prescribes an item, the prescription is recorded on a local dispensing computer. When the nurse dispenses that item, both the product and the patient are scanned, after which a 'lookup' confirms that the combination is correct. Moreover, an electronic record of any 'near misses' is captured, which can then be used to improve training and procedures.

To what extent are these technologies already in use within health services? Localised pilot implementations have occurred within some forward-thinking institutions, yet we are a long way from formalising or mandating this as a compulsory process as the cost of scanning equipment and IT hardware and software are often prohibitive. It is this cost and complexity of developing and implementing such systems for both the institutions and the manufacturers that provides such a large barrier and prevents these practices becoming more widespread.

Tagging Alone Does Not Prevent Fraud

Tagging, as we have seen, can be used to prevent dispensing errors and administration errors: codes on packs and on patients, along with patient record systems, can be used to cross-check that the right drug is given to the right patient.

Tags do not in themselves protect patients from fraud. A barcode can easily be counterfeited or copied, so is not sufficient to authenticate a product. Equally, a counterfeiter can place an RFID tag on a product, just as they can apply a hologram or use special colour-shifting ink (as seen on US $50 bills and other banknotes); the dispenser is in no position to spot the fraud unless they know what to look for or whether it is authentic.

To secure the supply chain and thereby protect patients from fraud, the pharmaceutical industry will need to move a step further in its delivery. To understand the type of systems architecture that will be necessary, it may be helpful to consider an example from the finance industry: the use of 'chip and PIN' credit and debit cards. Here, the card itself can be counterfeited, but both card and PIN (personal identification number) are required. The PIN is encrypted and embedded within the chip. Referring to a central, secure database then authenticates the transaction.

To authenticate pharmaceutical items in a similar way, three elements are needed. The first element is mass serialisation, that is, the identification of individual product packs with a code that can be used to authenticate the item against a secure database. The second element, therefore, is a safe, confidential database listing all authentic drug packs against which the pack code can be compared. The third necessary element is a network infrastructure to 'close the loop' between manufacturer and dispenser (see Figure 11.2).

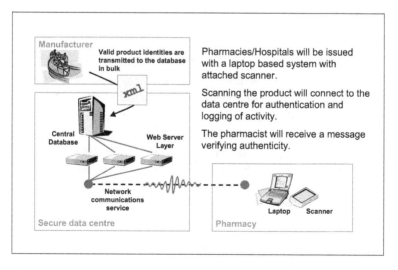

Figure 11.2   Technical overview – structure of a secure supply chain

Each of these elements will be explained in the following sections. To complete the chip and PIN analogy, the mass serialisation code will function very much like a PIN, enabling a database lookup to be performed remotely via a network. In the case of cards, the lookup ensures, at the very moment of the transaction, that the card has not been identified as stolen, that the account is in credit and that the card is within its validity period. Similarly, a lookup authentication for a pharmaceutical product at the time of dispensing or administration will confirm that it is authentic, not subject to recall and within its shelf life.

MASS SERIALISATION TO IDENTIFY INDIVIDUAL PRODUCTS

Mass serialisation is simply the identification of individual items with a unique number. In the case of pharmaceutical products in Europe, an item is likely to be the 'unit of use' item – the pack as dispensed to patients. In the USA and other markets the habit is to dispense from bulk manufacturers' packs into local, patient-specific packages with dispenser or pharmacy branding.

Unique referencing is not of course a new notion, but until recently it has been administratively impossible for all but high-value consumer items (such as cars or personal computers) because of the costs and the immense volumes of data involved. Until recently, even manufacturing operations that emphasised the importance of traceability were used to trace items only at batch level. Improved tagging and database technology is now putting mass serialisation within reach of more and more industries.

There are, of course, costs associated with mass serialisation – the cost of printing a barcode or creating an RFID tag, the cost of applying it to the packaging and the cost of acquiring electronic equipment to read the tags. While printing a barcode costs only hundredths of a cent, RFID tags cost 10 or 20 cents – a non-trivial amount that is a significant barrier to adoption in the case of very low-cost generic items. However, the potential costs of poor security may make the proposition appealing even in those cases, and RFID has the important advantage that it cannot be copied without access to a silicon chip factory.

This last consideration highlights the importance of thinking through the entire business process before making decisions about mass serialisation. Unless it is possible to read and use the codes at each appropriate point, applying those codes could be a waste of money. But with a well-designed process in place, the benefits may be surprising (see Figure 11.3).

Where mass serialisation is being used to enhance security, special consideration must be given to applying the serial number in a secure way. It is important in the pharmaceutical context to make packaging 'tamper evident' to guard both against removal or substitution of the medication and against altering of tags.

A CENTRAL DATABASE FOR AUTHENTICATION OF ITEMS

Mass serialisation alone provides a range of benefits within the supply chain. Because more complete information can be made available via mass serialisation than via conventional coding systems, there are advantages in terms of stock management, asset tracking and the electronic reconciliation of orders, delivery notes and invoices. (To see the importance of this type of reconciliation, consider that as many as 25 per cent of orders involve errors serious enough to require rework.) The organisation EPCglobal (Electronic Product Code) is working to create standards for tags, databases and scanning technology to support the use of RFID in trading networks.

Positive engagement…

- The tags are being trialled to test their ability to enable Marks & Spencer to check stock deliveries, and count stock more quickly in stores and depots. The scanned information is transmitted to the central stock database where an automatic comparison with the stock profile for the store triggers a replenishment order.

  Marks and Spencer

- We will work with our suppliers to educate them regarding RFID and to help them move to deployment at whatever speed they are comfortable with, says Greg Sage, a spokesman for the company. We don't have an exact date for having all suppliers on board, but it is likely to be sometime in 2007.

  Tesco

- RFID-Chip-Embedded Passports Nearing Reality

  - The plan is to introduce an electronic version of the traditional passport, using an embedded 64-Kb RFID chip to store the cardholder's personal information, such as name, birth date, and place of birth. The passports will include security technology to prevent digital data from being altered or removed, according to the government.

  InformationWeek **March 31st 2005**

Figure 11.3   Mass serialisation is working and its use is increasing within logistics systems

However, mass serialisation on its own does not allow us to safeguard a product against fraud, or the consumer against a substandard item that has expired or been subject to recall by the manufacturer. This security can only be achieved when we are in a position to have the dispenser or administrator check – at the point of dispensing – that the product is what it purports to be. For this purpose, we need a way to verify that the product's serial number is appropriate to the drug, formulation and packaging, and also that the item is not subject to recall, whether because of a defect or because counterfeit batches have been detected.

The necessary checking can be performed if the dispenser can access a central database of product information, or use the public/private key encryption mechanism.

- This database must identify every item that has been manufactured, and also flag expired items and those that are subject to recall (for example because counterfeit items have been discovered in the supply chain). It must be constantly managed to ensure that the information is fully up to date. Only by giving dispensers access to this database at the precise point of dispensing does it becomes possible to prevent fraudulent products reaching – and potentially harming – patients.

- The public/private key mechanism will identify that the product is that which left the factory, yet will not provide 'updated' information such as stolen product warnings, subsequent recall of substandard items, expiration date issues and so on.

We should note that the existence of a database could potentially guard against fraud in other ways. Around 2 per cent of products supplied by wholesalers to pharmacists get returned, and this reverse supply chain presents an opportunity for counterfeit products to be fed into the supply chain. There is evidence that counterfeiting via the returns process is already taking place in the US. With mass serialised identities used within their local inventory and order management systems, wholesalers would be able to identify whether the packs that are being returned are the same ones that they supplied.

An additional possibility is for patients themselves to be given access to the database. In the US, particularly given the use and costs of drugs, some patients are likely to be willing to equip themselves with scanners so that they can check that the drugs they are receiving, via mail order or the Internet, are authentic.

NETWORK TECHNOLOGIES TO 'CLOSE THE LOOP'

The authentication approach we are describing will work only if dispensers are able to scan products, and receive authenticating information, in real time. If there is a delay in receiving information back, dispensers will quickly become disillusioned with the system and will stop using it.

To authenticate scanned tags in real time, users must operate in a networked environment – one that provides instant access to the central database. This is a challenging requirement given the size of the community likely to be using it. In the UK alone there are around 20,000 dispensing points; across Europe there are 250,000 and in the USA over 100,000. All will require a near-instant response. Fortunately today's technology, including broadband, wireless and satellite communications, is coming together to make this aim achievable and affordable. Examples such as credit card clearing systems show that the problem can be solved, and with the requisite level of security.

Another enabling factor is that some health services are already rolling out national networks for other purposes. Under the UK's National Programme for IT, being delivered by a government agency called NHS Connecting for Health, every pharmacist and doctor will have a broadband connection, primarily intended for transmission of patient medical records, electronic transfer of prescriptions and the like. These networks are also likely to be available for other appropriate uses, including drug authentication. With telecommunications infrastructures already available, the incremental cost of connecting pharmacists to a central database will no longer be prohibitive.

How Mass Serialisation Can Protect Patients

If supported by the right infrastructure of database and network, mass serialisation can protect patients in a number of ways. At the point of dispensing, the pharmacist can scan an item's code, initiating a lookup process in which the code is used to retrieve all relevant information about the item. With the information instantly displayed on a screen, the pharmacist can verify that the pack is authentic, and is on record as containing the right type of drug in the right formulation and packaging. If there has been a dispensing error, the pharmacist will notice a discrepancy between the retrieved product information and the prescription. If the drug is counterfeit, there will be no item to match its ID on the central file.

Local computer systems within pharmacies contain warnings about potentially hazardous drug interactions. The scanner, integrated with this system, could provide additional warning prompts to protect patients against such dangers. This Authentication at the Point of Dispensing (APOD) approach has been initiated by Aegate.

Aegate: The potential of mass serialisation to improve patient safety

Aegate, a PA Group Company, was set up in 2004 to investigate Authentication at the Point Of Dispensing as a method of improving patient safety. The approach uses mass serialisation technologies such as RFID and barcodes. These are applied to medicines by the manufacturers and then scanned by pharmacists as they are about to be dispensed.

The scanned information is supplied in a visual display to pharmacists, through communication with a secure central database. APOD can validate that the products are being used in accordance with the intentions of manufacturer or regulators, have not been subject to recall and have not been supplied fraudulently. These products are normally hard for pharmacists to spot, since the human eye cannot easily detect minor differences in holograms or pack sizes. With a unique, machine-readable identifier on each pack it becomes simple to verify authenticity against a central database (Figure 11.4).

Starting in October 2004, Aegate conducted a three-month qualitative observational study that set out to demonstrate how the scanning process could work in the dispensary without significantly disrupting workflow, and whether the use of unique serial numbers to identify individual packs (mass serialisation) was technically feasible.

In total 44 pharmacies across England and Wales took part, representing community pharmacies, hospital pharmacies and dispensing doctors' practices. Each pharmacy was equipped with one or more custom-built scanners designed to simultaneously read both RFID tags and barcodes (including 2D) and to display information on a laptop. The scanners were connected to a secure central information database via broadband telecommunications links.

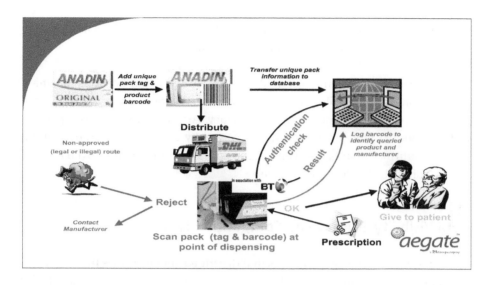

Figure 11.4   The use of mass serialisation to uniquely identify all drug products is the single most powerful tool available to secure the US drug supply (FDA)

Six pharmaceutical companies also took part in the pilot, allowing RFID tags to be added to the packaging of eight of their products. In addition, dummy packs using both barcodes and RFID tested conditions that were considered unlikely to occur during the trial, such as the presence of counterfeit drugs or recalls. The pilot showed that, with scanning, staff can be effectively warned at the point of dispensing if they have selected the wrong medicine. Some 70 per cent of participating pharmacists found the information displayed after scanning to be the most useful aspect of the authentication process.

Through the use of dummy packs, it was also shown that the scanning process was 100 per cent reliable in identifying illegal products, including counterfeits and illegally reimported products, both of which may pose a danger to patients since their quality cannot be guaranteed. Expired and short-life products were similarly highlighted, eliminating time-consuming manual checks.

Even though use of scanners in pharmacies is uncommon in the UK, the task of scanning items integrated smoothly into a pharmacy's normal processes, with nine out of ten pharmacists reporting that they 'got on well' with scanning. The associated delay was minimal, the average time taken to retrieve and display data from the central database being less than one second.

Concerns have been voiced about the privacy implications of mass serialisation, but the pilot demonstrated that the technology can enhance patient safety without compromising privacy. Aegate implemented a privacy code of conduct which has been well received by civil liberties groups, and a survey confirmed that 95 per cent of consumers who recognised RFID found this use of the technology acceptable.

Data Visibility, Privacy and Competition Law

A mass serialisation process such as that described above implies the extraction and storage of vast amounts of data that can be made visible very quickly for the benefit of patients. The other side of the visibility coin, however, is privacy. It is important to be selective about what data is made available to whom. Privacy is as important in a pharmaceutical context as it is in, say, a banking context, where online clients must be shown their own data but no one else's, or in the case of a mobile phone account, where only the customer wishes to be able to see their itemised bill. There are two separate angles to the privacy issue: patient privacy and commercial privacy.

PATIENT PRIVACY

In order to address concerns about the privacy implications of mass serialisation it will be important to implement a code of conduct of the type proposed by the Aegate pilot. Privacy can be further safeguarded through the use of a system that allocates serial numbers to packs randomly rather than according to a hierarchy of product numbers. Random numbering means that there is no way to interpret a serial number as identifying a particular type of drug. This ensures that, even if an unauthorised person manages to scan an RFID tag on a drug packet in someone else's pocket, they have no means of identifying the drug type.

The importance of this aspect of privacy can be understood by considering, for example, the case of someone attending a job interview; the prospective employer should not be able to detect that the interviewee has medication in their pocket for, say, depression. In some countries, confidentiality of health information is legally a grey area. In others, the law requires health information to be treated with extreme confidentiality: an example is the US's complex Health Insurance Portability and Accountability Act (HIPAA) Privacy Rule.

The selection of numbering systems is, however, a controversial area, demonstrating a possible conflict between efficiency and privacy. From the supply chain point of view, particularly in Fast Moving Consumer Goods (FMCG), there are some advantages to allocating meaningful numbers. However, not only privacy, but also counterfeiting considerations militate against this idea. With a hierarchical system it becomes possible for counterfeiters to 'crack' the system and generate plausible codes themselves.

COMMERCIAL PRIVACY

Data created at any point in the supply chain is owned by the creator. They are able to sell this data, without exclusivity, to anyone who will buy it. Access to this data by a third party cannot form part of a binding arrangement between the parties. Marketeers in pharmaceutical companies pay millions of dollars per year to data providers to attempt to gain insight into activities within the supply chain and the behaviour of the prescribers. They all seek to understand what is happening in those areas of the distribution channel over which they have no control, only influence.

In Europe competition law encourages free movement of goods and services. Under the 'exhaustion of intellectual property rights' the supplier of a product has limited rights, after that product has been sold, to control either what customers do with it, or where or to whom they sell it – provided the original trademarking is not destroyed or diminished. That means that, with certain provisos, it is legal for a wholesaler to buy a drug in Greece for 50p and sell it in the UK for £1, exploiting the fact that pricing within the European 'free market' is controlled by local governments.

The situation in the USA is quite different from that in Europe. There, on grounds of quality and safety impacted by the dramatic rise in cases of counterfeiting, in 2004 the US Food and Drug Administration (FDA) launched 58 drug counterfeiting investigations – a significant increase from the 30 cases in 2003 and a dramatic increase when compared to the handful of drug counterfeit investigations launched annually in the late 1990s. The FDA considers fakes, diluted drugs or drugs that have been stolen or diverted from the legitimate supply chain to be counterfeit. As a result manufacturers may legally refuse to sell to a wholesaler who also buys their product from another source. Indeed, a number of manufacturers have invoked this right, and do business only with wholesalers who have agreed to deal with them exclusively.

Competition law, and the attitude to parallel trade, varies considerably internationally. New Zealand and the Philippines, for example, are actively encouraging the importation of products from other countries in order to reduce healthcare costs. An APOD system would therefore have to be able to adjust to different legal environments in different parts of the world.

This whole issue is far from straightforward because of the sensitivities and tensions that exist in the industry. In general, manufacturers would like to have more information than wholesalers are willing to provide. For example, European manufacturers sometimes offer incentives to compete with and reduce incentives to buy parallel-traded goods, but are unable to discover whether wholesalers are abiding by their agreements.

In future, European manufacturers may be able to justify access to greater information about wholesalers' activities in the interests of patient safety. The European Union (EU) may allow this access, provided that it does not restrict freedom of use of goods and services; if manufacturers tried to impose quotas or prevent sales, however, they could be in breach of competition law.

For obvious reasons, wholesalers are likely to be resistant to this idea, and the freer flow of product information has a potential negative impact for manufacturers themselves, as some have already identified. Once there is a way of reliably authenticating an item in a parallel market, it becomes hard to justify suppression of that parallel market and prevent the sale of, say, an authentic Canadian product in the US market. That means that the current industry model would have to change, since the system of differential pricing in different markets would break down. Yet manufacturers view this model as essential to the viability of their businesses and the funding of research and development (R&D).

We shall discuss possible future developments with respect to the legal environment and the overall shape of the industry in more depth in the final chapter of this book.

Who Benefits, and Who Should Pay?

Mass serialisation offers clear benefits to patients in terms of protection from fraud and error. Manufacturers, health service organisations and anyone else along the supply chain who can read the codes also stand to benefit in terms of supply chain and marketing efficiencies. Dispensers (both pharmacists and dispensing doctors) stand to gain, especially by reducing their liability for dispensing errors. (Currently in the UK it can be determined that an individual community pharmacy has a 3–4 per cent chance of an error-related claim against it in any given year.)

There are benefits too for whoever pays for healthcare, whether government, insurance company or citizen. These organisations will know the price at which a wholesaler has purchased a product and ensure that reimbursement takes place at the appropriate level. At present, wholesalers sometimes gain discounts through parallel trade, which they do not pass on to the payer. Healthcare organisations also stand to benefit by reducing the cost of dispensing errors. In the UK, work carried out by the Department of Health suggests that 11 per cent of hospital admissions are due to medication errors (including dispensing errors), and that serious errors in dispensing prescribed medicines account for 20 per cent of all clinical negligence litigation.

As for who should pay the costs of mass serialisation, the question is currently up for debate. The fact that so many parties can benefit from mass serialisation suggests that the costs should be spread, with all those who benefit (with the probable exception of the patient) expected to contribute. The question of who actually will pay looks slightly different, and depends in part on how the system is implemented. Since they will be applying the tags, manufacturers are likely to pay the lion's share of the costs, but in practice will only be willing to do so when they perceive a clear benefit.

The supply chain efficiencies mentioned above will not be enough for the manufacturers. For them, the most important potential attraction is access to the end user – the pharmacist – to whom they would like to pass authentication and other product-related messages directly via the system to ensure that pharmacist and patient understand best use of the product. They will also want to send marketing messages, pointing the pharmacist in the direction of a new or improved product perhaps. For the manufacturer, these messages are ways to increase the amount or value of product that they sell. The more of these messages they are able to convey, the more attractive the proposition will become to the manufacturers.

In addition, manufacturers stand to gain by receiving sales information back from the system, depending on how it is implemented. At the moment manufacturers pay millions of dollars annually to receive this information from intermediaries, and do not get it in the form, or at the time, they would like. Subject to agreement of other participants, and of regulators, there is the potential for manufacturers to receive the information they need much faster, –and in a much more convenient form – from an APOD system. Manufacturers will then be much more willing to fund such a system.

A health service may also be willing to contribute to the costs since, as we have seen, it stands to benefit from the use of serial numbers in the supply chain, from the ability to see the acquisition cost and from a reduction in the cost of errors. Pharmacists can be expected to contribute at a relatively modest level, perhaps paying towards the cost of scanning equipment and broadband links.

To sum up, patients and dispensers *want* APOD, while health service regulators and payers may *demand* it. Wholesalers and manufacturers need it to do business effectively, but some are currently sceptical given the far-reaching impact that a freer flow of information may have on their business model. In the author's view, the advent of APOD is inevitable, but the question is who is going to take the first step. Manufacturers are likely to pay in the short run, both for mass serialisation and for infrastructure costs; but in the longer run the health service will probably take over as these costs will inevitably be passed on to the payer.

SWOT Analysis for Mass Serialisation

Here we will sum up the strengths, weaknesses, opportunities and threats (SWOT) inherent in the adoption of mass serialisation technologies.

STRENGTHS

- The technology works and is gradually becoming more affordable.

- Successful applications have already been proven in other areas.

- Pilot studies have shown that it can add enhance patient safety and add value for all participants in the pharmaceutical supply chain.

WEAKNESSES

- There are significant risks, both in terms of expenditure and in terms of disrupting current business models and arrangements.

- There is no one clearly defined standard for mass serialisation, so a choice will have to be made.

- The business case is currently unclear; in particular, we do not know exact costs (of hardware, ongoing data management, business processes, training and so on).

- Implementation of such wide-ranging business process initiatives is daunting for managers. The author remembers with affection a conversation with a technical operations director of a renowned medical devices company who proclaimed with candour 'I've never done a supply chain project, and I don't want to start now. They are so complex that once you have started you have to stick with it, and they won't promote you until you've finished it.'

OPPORTUNITIES

- APOD makes it possible to secure patient safety and eliminate counterfeits from supply chain.

- APOD may reduce overall drug bills by effective use of the 'pharmacy cost of acquisition' – the health service or other payer can reimburse what the pharmacist paid and no more. The incentive to purchase cheaper, traded product would be reduced.

- Manufacturers can build relationships with pharmacies and patient groups to which they do not currently have access.

THREATS

- Current business practices could stand in the way of adoption – because of vested interests, the industry could simply refuse to accept the technology.

- Some regulators may not have sufficient independence from the industry to impose APOD.

However, the benefit in terms of patient safety is obvious. No one can make a case for failure to protect patients when the technology is available – and it is.

Current Usage of Coding

Barcodes are ubiquitous today, and there is now a one-to-one relationship between a product and a barcode. Typically there is a range of barcode technologies from which to choose. The application will vary for different purposes at different points in the supply chain. For example, wholesalers use Pharmaceutical Interface Product (PIP) codes, while manufacturers have their own product codes. This means that at different points in the supply chain the same product will have different codes associated with it.

In part because of the proliferation of numbering systems, barcodes are not yet being used to their full potential. The barcodes applied by drug manufacturers are available for everyone else in the supply chain to use, but in the vast majority of cases no one other than the manufacturer actually does use them.

ALLOCATION OF CODE NUMBERS

Consistency in the allocation of barcodes is vital to the effective use of product codes. Unless use is intended to be purely local, either a given barcode must always be used to identify the same product or, if usage is allowed to change, all the relevant records need to be updated. If this does not happen, then errors can easily occur. For example, if a hospital reuses wristbands with barcodes to denote more than one patient, unless great care is taken to update central records, mistaken identity is an obvious possibility.

In the pharmaceutical industry, barcode usage is not yet foolproof. We have seen examples of barcodes being reused to denote more than one product. Clearly there are safety implications here. When the UK's National Health Service (NHS) rolls out its system for electronic transmission of prescriptions, consistent use of machine-readable tags will be critical.

Indeed, reliable numbering systems are essential to any system that depends on automatic identification of products with barcodes. Major retailers are aware that if the level of damaged or unknown barcodes on stock items that prevent easy reading rises, then inventory management and order replenishment systems become chaotic and costs rise due to delays at the checkout.

Standardisation: Coding Systems and their Importance

A standardised method of coding drugs is essential if, for example, a health service wants to establish which product is being administered to a patient. However, the taxonomy of coding structures for different products and purposes can become hugely complex.

It is not sufficient to use a code that identifies a particular product: the same product can exist in multiple formulations and pack types, which also need to be identified. In addition, it is often the case that more than one supplier offers the same product. To understand who is receiving what, and who should be paid how much for it, health services need coding structures that let them cope with this situation too, identifying that two products from different manufacturers may be effectively the same medicine, formulation and pack type.

The UK's National Programme for IT in the NHS is developing a coding hierarchy designed to fulfil these needs. Acceptance of this system is vital to creating a fully electronic service. Different countries, however, may adopt different hierarchies.

STANDARDISATION OF NUMBERING SYSTEMS

Barcode allocation in the retail sector is under the control of various EAN bodies and the Uniform Code Council (UCC). The EAN systems predominate in Europe (although they are used worldwide), while the UCC predominates in the US. In the UK, number allocation is the responsibility of GS1 UK, formerly the e.centre.

While some attempt is being made to unify the various numbering systems into single EAN/UCC architecture, in practice a range of different allocation processes exist in parallel, which means that a European barcode may mean nothing in the US and vice versa. The political and governance issues of aligning the various standards are daunting.

STANDARDISATION OF TECHNOLOGY

As RFID technology becomes more popular, there are initiatives in progress to develop universal standards for RFID tagging, covering the information to be stored, the choice of tagging and scanning technology and so forth.

Should we wait for standardisation? As is so often the case with advancing technology, there is a question as to how far tagging and scanning technology needs to be standardised before it can be used. Must everything be universal before it can usefully be taken up, or can we gain benefits even as the technology and standards continue to evolve?

12

The Importance of Information

Those who have any practical experience with supply chain management operations will know that timely and accurate information is critical to the planning and positioning of capacity, resources and inventory in order to meet customer service and utilisation objectives. Those who have experience in marketing or sales will know how important it is to understand the market by researching, questioning and testing assumptions. In this chapter we will explore, in a structured manner, the need for information, ways of accessing it and its value, as well as the use of that information for advantage in the management and control of the business.

Introduction

For five years I observed a long-running disagreement between two senior managers in the manufacturing and commercial operations of a global pharmaceutical company. The commercial operations manager had responsibility for the receipt and management of forecasts and orders from local operating companies and third-party customers around the world, as well as the management of supply against those demands. The manufacturing manager had the responsibility for managing the resources and processes necessary to execute the supply against those demands. Generally the on time in full (OTIF) delivery of goods against orders was steady at around 90 per cent, fluctuating between 75 and 95 per cent.

The disagreement centred on the manufacturing manager's request that the commercial operations manager provide him with inventory levels of the local operating companies' in-market, for all the local operating companies. He felt that with this data he would be able to control costs and service more effectively. The commercial operations manager simply responded by saying 'Tell me how you will use that data to improve our customer service levels and

I will discuss it with the local operating company managers.' The disagreement occurred because the manufacturing manager could not explain how access to that data could be used to manage the major, jointly agreed performance indicator – customer service. Apart from amusing onlookers, the disagreement ate into productive management time.

As this anecdote illustrates, there is a huge demand for data within all supply chains, especially within the marketing operations of pharmaceutical and medical devices companies, but a lack of understanding of how to use it to improve the business by driving changes in key business parameters: sales, cost and service. To make appropriate use of data we must first understand how it can create value.

Getting Value from Data

To understand how data can deliver value to a business, it is helpful to understand that there is a hierarchy of data, information, knowledge and understanding. A massive amount of data can be collected about anything. In the pharmaceuticals business we could gather data about prescriptions, doctors, pharmacies, prices, competitors, time (day, week, month), patients, pack format, location, first sale to, movements between and so on and so on. Some of this data we may not be able to access, yet we might feel that if only we could get it we could achieve all sorts of things. A focus on data that is unavailable is, I believe, the start of frustration and distraction within this field and can be used as a reason for not making progress, as in my anecdote above.

We must instead learn how the mass of data that is available can generate understanding and hence value. By developing some questions, by postulating a few hypotheses to test or by interrogating and reconfiguring the data elements this raw data can be developed into a powerful weapon. For example, in order to understand how we might sell more products we could start with the question:

'How many of the doctors in our market are writing prescriptions for our product?'

Let us say that we discover the answer is 23 doctors. This data element in itself may be of little value; it does not help us move towards our ultimate goal of selling more at lower cost. If, however, we could identify that 85 per cent of doctors in region A are prescribing our product, compared with only 10 per cent of doctors in region B, or that 23 represents only 5 per cent of the doctors in that market, then we have the start of an action plan that could help us improve the company performance based on useful information. Given this information we might then ask:

Why do doctors choose to prescribe, or not prescribe, our product?

Among the many possible reasons are these:

- they do not know about it;

- they do not like or trust it;

- they are not allowed to prescribe it as it is not on their health authority or patient's insurance formulary;

- they are better persuaded by the merits of the competitor product;

- the particular patient has side effects from it.

Some of these reasons reflect deficiencies in the product or process, while others are extraneous, for example adverse reactions on the part of a specific patient. To find out which of these reasons apply, we can conduct a survey, asking a sample of doctors directly why they either prescribe the product in question or not. The answers to the questions will represent knowledge. After the survey we will know why doctors prescribe and we will know more about why doctors may not currently prescribe our product.

If we identify a deficiency, we are presented with an opportunity. As responsible managers, we have an obligation to exploit the opportunity (and correct the deficiency) by taking action. For example, we could take steps to bring a poorly performing area up to par, or spread good practice across the wider organisation.

Knowledge is of no use for its own sake. It becomes valuable when it is applied to new and unfamiliar situations, or to new problems and circumstances. It is in these situations that a real understanding is developed. This understanding is demonstrated by a change in behaviour: 'We will do things differently in the future now that we understand ...' In this case we might include our knowledge in marketing and promotional materials such as sales detailing aids to ensure that positive messages are communicated to doctors.

This change in behaviour is commonly called learning. If the new knowledge is directly transferred to a new situation en masse, with little interpretation or alteration to reflect the new circumstances or nuances of the new, unknown situation, it may or may not work. Addressing new situations effectively and efficiently is a risky business and requires careful analysis. Actions or behaviour must be based on as much knowledge and understanding of other analogous occurrences from the past. These situations or circumstances may not always be available or accessible; the data may not be sufficiently clear to make extrapolations confidently, yet action may well be required urgently. It is in these situations that managers demonstrate their skill, knowledge, experience through learning and real understanding of their business. When we seek to implement a major new IT system we want someone in charge who has some experience; when appointing a national manager for a large and important market we would choose someone who has had some success in that capacity in smaller markets or in the same market for another company. Application of learning reduces risk and increases confidence in success.

We now have many tools available to us to assist in the acquisition of understanding. Computer models can be built to simulate the performance of almost any system under a whole range of conditions. These models can replace many years of practical experience and provide the opportunity to gain a real understanding of the overall environment at little risk. It is fortunate for air passengers that pilots train, and make their inevitable mistakes, in flight simulators. These simulators are at the more sophisticated end of the spectrum of tools available to managers, but there are many more simple and easy-to-use examples: from dice games, spreadsheets and Monte Carlo simulations through to more complex systems dynamics models. In the example described above relating to doctors prescribing our product we could construct a relationship model such as that described in Figure 12.1.

Here we can see that the increase in sales over a period will be driven by underlying increase in patient population, patient preference for the medication and also switching of the medication prescribed, by the doctor, both to and from our product.

What then makes patients not use a medication? Why do doctors prefer another available treatment, and how can we influence patients with a disease

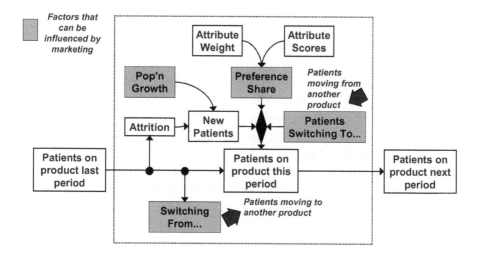

Figure 12.1   Using a preference share model to understand how to influence sales

to visit their doctor? This is the information we need to manage a business proactively. We then need to devise a plan of influencing, and use the raw sales data to measure performance against planned interventions. Then we can measure the return on investment of our marketing, improving the good interventions and discarding less profitable activities. Tools like these have been used very effectively to solve many problems in a wide variety of circumstances:

- Reducing the procurement price of the largest single raw material by half. This item was albumen. It is affected seasonally by the number of chickens hatched before Easter, and the pasta season in Europe. Through developing an understanding of the possible interactions between key parameters in the system (suppliers, market supply and demand characteristics, currency fluctuations, timing of purchase, and length of commitment) I was able to dramatically impact the raw material costs of a developing food company in which I was employed to establish their supply chain operations.

- Providing an opportunity for a major credit card company to evaluate possible new marketing scenarios that can reverse a decline in market share.

- Creating better drug development processes through a better understanding of the human immune system.

- Preference share model of a rapidly changing market with complex interactions between disease status and patient/physician preferences. One company has modelled market expectations for a family of products (injection needles) based on physical product attributes and price.

- Proving that it is possible to introduce, effectively, a new car into an existing production line. This resulted in a huge saving in the avoidance of capital investment, significant reduction in time to market, and the development of the most efficient car assembly plant in Europe.

- Simulating dramatic changes in the environment and possible responses. One major oil company had built simulation models to help it develop an understanding of what might happen in a range of disaster scenarios. When the oil price rose steeply during the early 1970s it was able to respond more effectively than its competitors as it had a greater understanding of the situation.

It is my aim to ensure that use of these tools is more widely considered and applied within the pharmaceutical supply chain. One example of the major positive impact that they can have on operations is reviewed in the following case study.

Case Study – Opening up the Market in China in 1994

The situation that we were exploring was, and still is, characterised by a huge demand for intravenous antibiotics in China. The market was dominated by one supplier and my company made similar products. We were experiencing difficulty penetrating the market because of a poorly configured and therefore unresponsive supply chain.

Complication: The market was serviced by trade partners (third-party distributors) who were unable and unwilling to forecast accurately their future requirements. Weekly requirements could fluctuate between zero and 1 million units.

- Owing to our inability to supply reliably the trade partners were losing patience and moving their business away.
- Prices were discounted to provide some compensation for the lack of competitive delivery service.

Question: How could we, as the manufacturing facility, provide a better service to the local operating company to help them compete with the established supplier?

Answer: Develop a responsive supply chain that could assist the local operating company to compete effectively.

Actions: Build a simulation model to represent the supply chain using our knowledge of the relationships and experience of demand and supply fluctuations.

- Vary the parameters (data elements) examining how the supply chain responds to different situations, and develop some options for changing the supply chain.
- Pilot the process, gain learning and then implement the most effective option.

Results: The construction of a supply chain from the UK to Hong Kong that reduced order to delivery lead time from 12 weeks to 1 week

- Massive increase in sales from ~20,000 units per month to ~100,000 per month within three months; consequent increase in market share and the ability to increase average selling price by avoiding discounts.
- The ability of customer service staff to say 'yes' immediately to demands of any order size from their trade partners without reference to the supply factory.
- Promotion for the author!

The rest of this chapter will focus on the different categories or characteristics of the supply chain: demand, supply, money, understanding and controlling the market. The categories, although adapted through my experience, were first suggested by Alan Braithwaite at Logistic Consulting Partners in the 1980s. I am indebted to Alan and his colleague, Rod Inger, who coached and inspired me in the wonders and opportunities that a thorough understanding of the supply chain could present to the operation of any business. These gentlemen had true understanding, in the sense referred to early in this chapter. They were able to apply this to a number of situations within my companies and help me to produce some dramatic results. I trust that I have demonstrated my understanding of their model appropriately, as it is applied here, specifically to the pharmaceutical industry sector.

Demand

Demand is perhaps the critical piece of information required within the business. It represents all that the business can be, and changes in demand represent the future threats or opportunities for the business. Managing demand is therefore crucial to the success of any business and is most often, in my experience, misinterpreted. I hope here to identify ways in which this can be better understood and more effectively managed.

'Demand manager' is a job title often held within a pharmaceutical company's technical or commercial operations department by the people who collect forecasts from their local operating company affiliates or third-party customers. Demand managers do an important job in providing factories with a forward plan that will allow them to install the necessary resources, line capacity and component inventory to manufacture effectively and efficiently.

Let us not delude ourselves, however, that demand managers manage demand. What they do is manipulate a set of numbers that are derived through the application of a sales projection upon a set of inventory, reorder policies and parameters. A term that better describes the numbers they manage would be 'net demand projected forwards', one of those definitions that were designed by the task force of a global supply chain design project in 1993! Table 12.1 illustrates the type of data that demand managers work with. A graphic representation highlights the immediate problem that this approach creates (Figure 12.2).

In the near term, wide fluctuations are created by the policies embedded within the system that automatically calculate the necessary replenishment order to bring the in-market inventory back to the agreed policy. All would appear to be well after three months, as the replenishment order then tracks the sales projection directly. Unfortunately this picture tends to remain constant over time. Every month there is a problem with supply in the first periods which appears to correct itself in the medium term.

Table 12.1   A typical master production schedule

Period	1	2	3	4	5	6	7	8	9	10
Sales forecast within the period	1000	1000	1000	1200	1200	1200	1400	1400	1400	1500
Inventory on hand at start of period	**900**	500	1500	1800	1800	1800	2100	2100	2100	2250
Projected inventory at end	500	1500	1800	1800	1800	2100	2100	2100	2250	2250
Target inventory level at period start	1500	1500	1500	1800	1800	1800	2100	2100	2100	2250
Net replenishment order due in period	600	3000	1000	1200	1200	1200	1400	1400	1400	1500

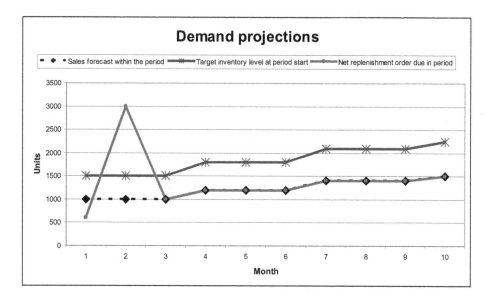

Figure 12.2   Demand projections

How many times have I seen such charts and suffered the wrath of production managers whose resources are under capacity one month and over capacity the next? The more enlightened demand managers within a branded, research-based company will override their system and provide a smooth projection onto the factory. They will not take a risk with inventory and possible lost sales, so they inevitably add more inventory into the plan for 'safety' in a misguided attempt to stabilise the situation.

By contrast the demand manager within a generic manufacturing or over-the-counter (OTC)-based business, where margins are smaller, will review the overall cost of production and inventory holding against the risk of being short of supply to the wholesaler. Their final decision will be taken with a detailed knowledge of the amount of inventory in the total supply chain and the risk of their wholesalers being unable to supply against a pharmacy demand.

An actual sales pattern, as life, is not like the smooth projection of net demand projected forwards. It does not generally go to plan and there will be wide fluctuations about the mean, expected or forecast level. We must not forget that in most cases the sale we are recording is a transfer of stock from the local affiliate warehouse to a wholesaler or distributor – another stock replenishment that no doubt has been projected forwards using similar logic to that above – so the problem of excess stock is multiplied throughout the supply chain.

A Basic Supply Chain Model

Figure 12.3 represents the key elements within a simulation of a simple supply chain. In this model a sales forecast is provided monthly to a manufacturing organisation by a 'direct to consumer' facility. This means that customer demands are placed directly on that facility. A demand is only equivalent to a sale if the stock is available. If not, the demand still exists but the sale is not possible.

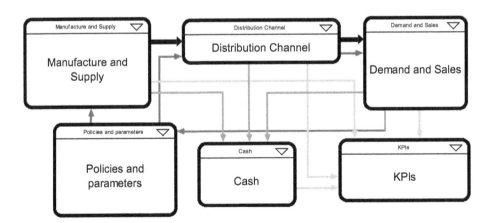

Figure 12.3   A supply chain model to show the flows of product, information and money

This simple model helps to show how sales can be lost without really being aware of the lost opportunity. A 'lost sale' occurs when there is an opportunity to supply a product because the customer is there demanding it, but the supplier cannot provide it owing to lack of inventory or availability of inventory in an acceptable timeframe. Lost sales are not recorded in any pharmaceutical operating company affiliate that I know, but in practice they are a frequent occurrence.

The forecast daily sale appears quite realistic and stable. The fluctuations around that forecast which represent the actual daily demand will represent the sales on any one day. Should there be lower inventory at the sales point than the level of demand on that day, then some orders will be unfulfilled and the difference will represent lost sales. These are shown accumulating in the output chart (Figure 12.4).

In many situations we will accumulate back orders and not actually lose a sale, yet in the urgency of the healthcare environment, and given the margins available on the products, we do not want the customer to go away without satisfaction. Only when we really understand variability on demand can we set appropriate inventory and resupply policies to ensure that demand can be fulfilled directly.

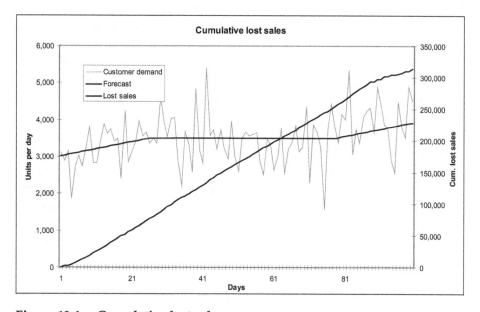

Figure 12.4   Cumulative lost sales

Lost sales result from inertia that is inherent in system policies and parameters that define the replenishment quantities and lead times. In one major retail pharmacy chain in the UK, while working with them to understand their inability to improve sales performance at store level, I discovered that if a particular product sold twice its estimated sales per day for two consecutive days that store could be out of stock of that item for over 10 days. This was clearly demonstrated to the relevant supply chain managers of that company, who confirmed the system policies of inventory, lead time offsets, reorder levels and so on interacted as shown. This was the first time that they had had a opportunity to review these policies interacting with one another rather than as separate, local management, efficiency levers.

I have used this simple simulation model with three different global clients separately during interactive, competitive workshop sessions with key supply chain managers (including their demand managers). Not one group managed to understand the interactions sufficiently to arrange the policies and parameters so as to achieve 100 per cent customer service within the workshop environment. These functional managers deal with lots of data and are well informed about situations that exist at any given time. Also they have much knowledge of their own products and their specific supply mechanisms. But their difficulty with the simulation exercise shows that there is not enough general or broad understanding to enable this knowledge and experience to be applied effectively to similar, unknown situations and achieve the same results. As a result the contribution that the supply chain function can make to the overall business is discredited and undervalued. It is not therefore too surprising that the supply chains for new products with new characteristics are stuffed with inventory by the real business decision-makers – marketing – and prior to launch, to insulate themselves against the risks posed by their supply chain colleagues.

Figure 12.5, entitled 'Create the demand', shows that in the ethical pharmaceutical industry it is the prescribing doctor, and only the prescribing doctor, who creates the demand. The real demand manager is the person who can influence this doctor to write prescriptions for the product in question when a patient presents with a suitable condition. Everyone else in the supply chain has a role of ensuring that the pharmacist can dispense that product against the prescription that the doctor has written.

Marketing departments attempt to influence doctors through the presentation of their message. The sales teams who contact the doctors directly

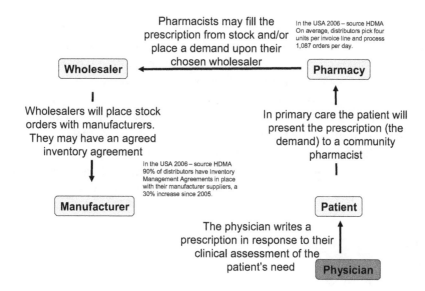

Figure 12.5 Create the demand

to deliver that message in an effective manner are in reality the people who manage the demand. They can help create it and they can help destroy it through inappropriate presentation and delivery. These are the people who are fired if they are unable to meet their sales or related targets; not the person designated 'demand manager', who manipulates computer parameters and graphs before presenting their monthly plan to the sales and operations planning meeting. I can say these things as I have been involved at both ends. Both roles are complex and demanding; only one carries real risk associated with failure, and the rewards are generally balanced appropriately.

Figure 12.5 confirms the distribution channel structure, or framework, and refers to data from the USA. Other markets are similar in that there are more manufacturers than wholesalers, and that as we move down towards the patient, the wholesaler : pharmacist and pharmacist : patient ratios decrease substantially, showing that the distribution chain fragments rapidly. All patient consultations with doctors are assumed to be independent of one another. In this case we can simulate demand (doctors prescribing and patients presenting at a pharmacy with that prescription), modelling the corresponding supply capability (given the supply chain policies and parameters) to determine the essential outputs: customer service level and cost.

The overall conclusion, from any perspective, is that demand is not deterministic, subject to strict algebraic relationships and formulae like those necessary in spreadsheets or materials requirement planning (MRP) systems. Demand is stochastic, subject to probability and uncertainty in both quantity and time. As long as we plan to manage supply against inevitably fluctuating demand using deterministic planning tools, and assess the performance of managers on independent variables such as stock levels, labour or plant utilisation, then we are doomed to lose sales and suffer higher than necessary costs to provide those sales. In short, we are condemned to a working life of frustration and conflict within the channel. There is hope in the next section.

Supply

In this section we examine the options available to ensure that supply can be matched to demand (see Figure 12.6). Supply is possibly the area to which most attention is drawn when something goes wrong. Indeed, when things do go wrong it is often because the established supply chain structure or framework is incapable of managing the demands placed upon it. That is, the fixed element of the infrastructure and system has not been designed based on an understanding of the likely range of variable parameters that could reasonably impact it.

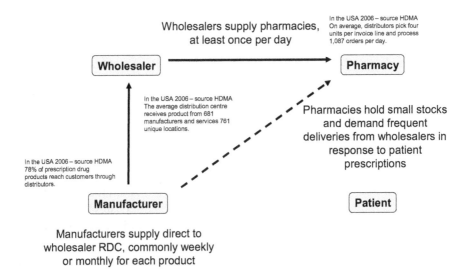

Figure 12.6   Execute the supply

In my experience, two types of supply chain structure or framework are effective, or can be made to be effective in most situations by the application of appropriate variable parameters such as order quantity and replenishment frequency. Firstly we have those supply chains that are structured according to rules of Fixed Order Timing (FOT) or schedule templates; and secondly that type of supply chain configuration governed by Fixed Order Quantity (FOQ) or Kanban rules. When one of these structures or governing frameworks is established at a high level and its rules of operation established, the overall costs, inventories and service levels are largely determined. The structure will come under stress (measured by the levels of inventory, service or cost outputs becoming out of control) only when the rules are broken or the parameters vary outside the planned limits.

We may all have experienced such stress in these systems. During late summer in the USA when stormy weather disrupts flight schedules, many passengers experience poor levels of service and costs increase as aircraft are not in the right places at the right times. Similarly, we may have encountered the inflexibility of a supplier who will not manufacture or deliver less than a large minimum order when our requirement is for a significantly smaller quantity; print runs of labels, leaflets or cartons are among the most frequent examples. Only three things are required to establish an efficient supply chain:

- forecasts, so that capacity, labour and materials can be positioned correctly;

- orders, which are the triggers to move, make or buy;

- rules by which the supply chain will operate.

It is the rules that take the most time to agree and establish, and they must be applied with zero tolerance if the supply chain is to operate as planned, delivering customer service outputs at agreed costs.

FIXED ORDER TIMING OR SCHEDULE TEMPLATES

These structures are used when there is a close relationship between the capacity calculated to meet the demand and the productive capacity available. In reality there will be one bottleneck facility or constraint, and it is this facility that must be managed within a fixed order timing or template schedule.

Given that this bottleneck constrains the throughput available from the entire supply chain, it is this resource which should be nursed, managed and supported. All other facilities are to be aligned with this schedule, both upstream and downstream, so that it is as productive as possible. In scheduling this bottleneck facility we must be guided by the technical teams who installed and manage the plant. They must set the template, the fixed cycle of products that will be produced by the plant in quantities and frequency that will achieve customer service targets. The schedule will be arranged to maximise production time and minimise changeover time.

In a paint factory, for example, the sequence can easily and intuitively be arranged – white, yellow, orange, red, green, blue and black paint – then a thorough clean-down allowing the production of white paint again at the beginning of the cycle. The quantities of any one colour produced in a cycle will relate to the level of demand expected between runs, adjusted for correction to the planned inventory policy. Similarly, in a paper mill or a steel rolling mill the cycle would start with the thickest items first, the thickness of product gradually decreasing; the fact that each adjustment is minor means that the heavy rolling equipment can be rapidly reset. This approach has worked for me in a variety of settings:

- vehicle scheduling in a chemical distribution company;

- pharmaceutical production of blister packs for a whole variety of markets, where even the smallest change between packs required a major line adjustment;

- tablet manufacture of cytotoxic products where batch sizes were small and clean-down processes long;

- supply of antibiotics to China mentioned previously;

- the manufacturer of food products using a major ingredient whose supply was constrained.

As the relationship between available and required capacity improves as a result of other management actions, opportunities will arise to improve the efficiency of the supply chain. For example, reducing cycle times will enable a reduction of overall inventory and hence greater responsiveness to changes in demand.

FIXED ORDER QUANTITY OR KANBAN

There have been all kinds of discussions about the philosophies of 'just in time' continuous improvement associated with Japanese manufacturing methods. Kanban is part of that debate and relates to the fact that quantities of components and manufactured items are defined and constant, whether these quantities are batch size, reorder quantity, minimum purchase quantity or truckload.

This technique is used where the available capacity is significantly greater than the capacity required by the forecast demand. To be cost-effective each procurement, production unit or distribution load (buy, make or move) must be operating at its most efficient. The lorry will not leave half full as distribution costs per tonne are an important parameter. The machine will only make in a batch size of 1,000 if this has been calculated to be the most cost-effective quantity, taking into account set-up costs, waste incurred and cost of carrying inventory over and above the immediate requirement.

As production, procurement and distribution processes are gradually improved through continuous improvement techniques and other management activity, the supply chain can be made more efficient by reducing the number of Kanban quantities circulating within the system. Just like a game of musical chairs, taking away a Kanban reduces the amount of inventory within the supply chain, lowering overall cost and improving the opportunity to respond to changes in demand. Suppose the customer suddenly changes their demand from blue units to red units; the smaller the number of blue units and associated components left in circulation, the quicker the change can be implemented and the smaller amount of obsolete inventory exists in the chain.

I have operated this supply chain structure to good effect on only one occasion. This is because most of the supply chains that I have operated have been capacity constrained and more suited to FOT described above. The instance where I did apply FOQ related to a major, and politically sensitive, pharmaceutical product, available as either 100-mg or 250-mg formulations, whose dosing regimen was changing as doctors began to understand its effect on patients. The initial batch size of each capsule formulation was six granulating mixer loads, producing around 3 million 100-mg capsules and just over 1 million 250-mg capsules. As demand fluctuated between the two formulations, inevitably the scarce active ingredient was consumed to make what turned out to be the wrong formulation at the wrong time.

Developing an interactive model of this supply chain, which involved 52 variable parameters, made it clear that this secondary manufacturing (the formulation stage of the production process) batch size was the key determinant of responsiveness and overall inventory levels. By reducing the capsule manufacturing batch size to a single mixer load, we were able to ensure rapid response to the changing demand, and also reduce overall inventory levels by £15 million in a 12-month period. This example confirms that the way to reduce inventory within the supply chain is to replenish more and more frequently in smaller and smaller quantities.

My experiences in executing demand and operating supply chains lead me to conclude that there needs to be a clearly defined framework structure and set of rules (algorithms) determining how the parameters are allowed to vary and operators to behave. Any such structure will need to be planned and tested against a whole range of scenarios. With dynamic modelling tools, the proposed structure, its parameters and governing rules can be tested to identify the limits of its effective operation and also the range of expected outputs: cost, quality and service.

Managing Money

In this section we will describe the ways in which money flows through the supply chain and how this can be managed to ensure that the profit of the organisation is maximised (Figure 12.7). There would seem to be three high-level routes to managing money:

- sell more at the highest price possible (revenue);

- spend as little as possible (procurement);

- ensure that the flow of money within the organisation is as profitable as possible (transfer pricing).

REVENUE

As discussed elsewhere, the healthcare industry is characterised by the fact that the consumer is not, in general, the ultimate payer. The services are provided and managed by insurance or healthcare funds, be they private or public. In order to sell pharmaceuticals or other healthcare services it is necessary

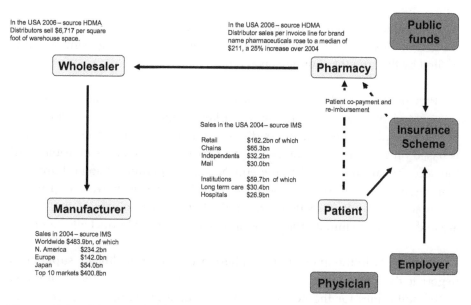

In the USA 2006 – source HDMA
Distributors sell $6,717 per square
foot of warehouse space.

In the USA 2006 – source HDMA
Distributor sales per invoice line for brand
name pharmaceuticals rose to a median of
$211, a 25% increase over 2004

Public funds

Wholesaler

Pharmacy

Patient co-payment and
re-imbursement

Sales in the USA 2004 – source IMS

Retail	$162.2bn of which
Chains	$65.3bn
Independents	$32.2bn
Mail	$30.0bn
Institutions	$59.7bn of which
Long term care	$30.4bn
Hospitals	$26.9bn

Insurance Scheme

Manufacturer

Sales in 2004 – source IMS
Worldwide $483.9bn, of which

N. America	$234.2bn
Europe	$142.0bn
Japan	$54.0bn
Top 10 markets	$400.8bn

Patient

Employer

Physician

Figure 12.7   Manage the money

to influence these providers, as they are the buyers. Where the services are provided by public bodies, it is important to be aware that, in spite of complex bureaucratic structures, these departments are ultimately members of the same organisation – the government – which also provides and controls the regulatory approval to sell and market the product in the first place. Regulatory approval is important because this is required before the product can be sold in a market, and therefore is the determinant of any money flow.

In order to achieve regulatory approval to market a new drug it must be shown that the drug meets all necessary standards of safety and efficacy. Latterly we have also seen an additional criterion being placed in the way of gaining reimbursement status (that is to say the criterion must be met before the authorities will agree to pay for the product). This additional hurdle is that bodies such as the National Institute for Health and Clinical Excellence (NICE) in the UK must review whether or not the new product offers value for money over existing treatments before it can be reimbursed.

Once the product is approved by regulators and bodies such as NICE, the agreed reimbursement price will then dictate the volumes that can be sold. The formula (volume × price) gives the level of tax revenue that the authorities must budget for. It is this total revenue parameter that becomes the limiting element in the equation: the volume sold is the dependent variable. This means that we cannot effectively forecast or project volume without recognising that it is limited by the amount of budget available.

Part of the complexity of this system lies in the fact that doctors are encouraged by the sales force and marketing messages to prescribe their products, creating the demand as discussed above. This prescribing decision is based on clinical need. The consequent spend of revenue is invisible until the accounts are reconciled at the end of a given period. In some European markets, notably France, the authorities will claim retrospective rebates from the manufacturers, and subsequent price reductions, if the volumes actually sold are in excess of the initial projections and expectations of budget allocation.

It is clearly in the interest of the pharmaceutical or healthcare supplier to negotiate the highest possible price for reimbursement. Part of the submission to the authorities for the negotiation will involve the long-term overall cost reduction or benefits to the healthcare provider based on reduced hospitalisation or expensive long-term care, increased quality of life or increased productive life of the patients; these benefits and reductions are used to justify a higher price.

Pricing is negotiated by healthcare providers, sick funds or insurance companies. The scope of negotiations will be limited to the members of the insurance group and the region governed by the sick fund or local health authority; it is always confined to one national market. National government sick funds will carefully compare the prices of the products in their and other markets, using this as a negotiating tactic to gradually reduce prices in their market in the medium term.

Where products are unable to move across borders between markets because of regulatory controls, it is desirable for this negotiation to occur at a local market level. As we have seen, products approved for sale outside the USA cannot currently be imported into that market. Together with the fact that federal tax dollars represent only a small proportion of the revenue (as discussed in the previous chapter), this means that the prices are maintained at a high level. Similarly in Europe product for sale outside the European Union (EU) cannot be imported.

The situation is quite different for products approved for sale within the European Union; in general these products can be moved freely between member nations. As discussed in Chapter 11, the price differentials between particular markets make this parallel trade a very lucrative undertaking for traders and a source of revenue and profit erosion for manufacturers. Any consideration of revenue must therefore consider the impact of this trade before finalising prices in any states where parallel trade is allowed or even encouraged. One major pharmaceutical company routinely uses simulation and optimisation techniques (made possible by the use of computer models) to ensure that the regional impact of an apparently local pricing decision can be foreseen and managed at a regional level.

The information that is being used here is available in the wider political sphere where prices are negotiated; the consequences and implications of those prices on the broader business perspective can be analysed. By knowing the pricing differentials (data) and observing their effect on the level of parallel trade (information), we can develop models to gain an understanding of the impacts of this on the business (knowledge), and then adapt this to new situations such as the sequence in which we launch new products onto the market (understanding). Again, the interrelationships are so complex that the possible outcomes can best be predicted by use of simulation tools to model the interactions and most appropriate values of each of the variable parameters.

PROCUREMENT

In this section we highlight the need to understand the information available about products, their ingredients and process technologies – information that can be leveraged to gain a competitive advantage. This information exists in the world outside the company, and it is therefore necessary to ensure that someone within the procurement function has expertise in, and understands the strategic importance of, these facts. With this expertise in place, the procurement function can play a major role in the development of the supply chain strategy alongside the market development team.

An entire book could be dedicated to the management of the procurement function within an organisation. Here it will suffice to say that the control of spending is self-evidently a major contributor to managing money. Procurement can play a strategic role in maintaining a high market price for the end products by reducing overall capacity available to competitors and raising their barriers to entry. This may be applicable to all products, yet is most effectively used where the product in question has a specific characteristic which limits the number of facilities in which it can be manufactured.

Examples of such products could be those that have a limited raw material supply, perhaps exotic plant species such as foxgloves (digitalis, an early treatment for congestive heart disease, was originally extracted from the foxglove plant *Digitalis digitalis*). Other examples would be those whose production involves a unique, capacity- or technology-restricted step. These include cytotoxic products (poisonous products that will kill any cell that can replicate), the freeze drying of sterile injectable items, vaccines using animals as incubators and the fermentation of biological products (whose many process variables and possible outcomes make them difficult to validate and transfer between production plants).

In these circumstances the procurement and management of adequate capacity, technology or skilled resources to meet the projected demand is often a problem in itself; yet this very problem can provide the opportunity to maintain high prices in the market and simultaneously limit the opportunities for competitors to enter.

In recent years there has been a trend to move the production of pharmaceutical intermediate products, and some active ingredients, to areas of low labour cost such as India or China. The production facilities may be wholly or partly owned, representing a joint venture for the buyer, or the procurement simply governed by contract. In either case there is a need to exercise and ensure a level of control over the quality, scheduling, yield and final delivery of product to safeguard the supply to market. The supplier must conform to all the rigorous demands for quality required by the regulatory authorities within the procuring markets, such as the US Food and Drug Administration (FDA), and be open to audits by representatives or agents acting on behalf of the buyer.

The procurement of a five-year contract for the entire output from a specialist plant would be a strategic investment. It may seem overcautious, yet if it secured the supply of that product over the foreseeable future and simultaneously made it difficult or expensive for competitors to enter the market, it could be a very positive step. It would be wise first to model all the possible parameters and assumptions as to the future values of the product and behaviour of competitors in order to evaluate the advantage of making that decision. It also needs to be borne in mind that the higher the market price and opportunity, the greater will be the attraction to competitors to enter the market, or for buyers to find alternative products (see Panel).

INDIGO

An example not related to the pharmaceuticals or healthcare industries, yet illustrating the point well, is the history of the dye indigo. In the nineteenth century there was great demand for indigo in the industrialising world to satisfy increasingly prosperous consumers. The dyestuff was extracted from a range of species of the indigo plant, particularly *Indigo sumatrana* and *Indigo arrecta*. The cultivation of indigo plants and the extraction of the dyestuff were important to the industry and economy of India, where supplies and prices were managed by the European colonial powers, notably the British East India Company.

As indigo was a costly ingredient with controlled supply and increasing demand, there was much interest in developing synthetic indigo or finding alternatives at lower prices. The chemical structure of indigo was announced in 1883 by Adolf von Baeyer and a commercially feasible manufacturing process became available by the late 1890s. This development revolutionised the textile industry and devastated the plantations and the local economy in the areas of northern India that depended on the crop.

The lesson that can be learned here is that if the supply of an important product with strong demand becomes constrained, especially deliberately and commercially as shown, then substitute products will be developed to remove that constraint and satisfy the demand. Current examples of this can be seen in the supply of low-priced HIV treatments to Africa and the provision of strategic bird flu or swine flu vaccines and other treatments in advance of any threatened pandemic.

Currently the development of biopharmaceutical products is restricted to major research-based companies with resources to invest in the installation, commissioning and manufacturing of specialist plant and equipment. The resulting biopharmaceuticals, protected by both patents and cost barriers to entry, have very high prices. As the patent protection expires over the coming years and the technology improves so that costs are reduced, we may see a corresponding change in the cost and availability of such 'biosimilar' or 'biogeneric' products.

TRANSFER PRICING

Transfer pricing is a mechanism for maximising overall profit to an organisation by effectively utilising the differential in taxation policies across the globe as product is produced in one country and sold as finished product or as unfinished intermediary in another. It is this financial overlay that often causes confusion and concern to those logistics managers who focus on optimising transport costs, lead times and risk. Only when the flow of money is aligned against the flow of goods can the overall profitability of any two supply chain options be evaluated.

Singapore, Puerto Rico and Ireland offer tax benefits to encourage companies to provide high-value jobs and a boost to the local economy. Many companies have taken advantage of these generous opportunities to develop their manufacturing operations in these markets. The goods can be exported to countries where prices are high, yet the profits can mostly be booked in the countries where the tax incentives are available. Through this mechanism a company can achieve high profit margins in low tax areas and low profits in high tax areas. However, the advantages only become clear when the situation is examined strategically rather than functionally.

When the patent on one major drug expired, it was licensed for over-the-counter (OTC) sale in Europe, and its supply chain was redeveloped as follows. Initially the active ingredient was:

- title owned by an affiliate in Switzerland;

- manufactured under contract at a plant in Scotland;

- transferred to a site in southern England, where it was formulated into tablets, packed and distributed across Europe from the same facility.

At the time of patent protection the cost of goods sold (COGS) as a proportion of the selling price was around 10–15 per cent. As the price fell dramatically after patent expiry, and even further as it was priced for the consumer market, COGS represented a much higher proportion of the selling price and would have been unsustainable, leading eventually to the withdrawal of the product. Instead the company strategically reviewed and redeveloped its supply chain. To support and enable a profitable OTC launch its configuration became:

- owned in Switzerland;

- active ingredient manufactured under contract in Scotland;

- transferred to Spain to be formulated into tablets;

- shipped to Germany to be packed for the OTC markets;

- shipped again to a UK affiliate for distribution to local customers.

Accepting the additional costs of these extra operations would seem to be counterproductive, yet the ability to have ownership in Switzerland and manufacture under toll contract with affiliates in Spain and Germany provided the opportunity to take advantage of the transfer prices and tax differentials, as well as minimising value added tax (VAT) liabilities. Overall, this case is a magnificent example of creativity and invention, enabling a product to be available to millions of consumers while still generating valuable contributions for its owner.

We should focus not on the data available about different national taxation regimes that apparently have no direct relevance to operational supply chain professionals, but rather on the use of these data and the possible opportunities or risks that might emerge from them. The sequence of learning is clear: I have data about different tax regimes across the world; I know that this results in reduced profits available in my current supply chain configuration; I understand its impact and what I need to do to reduce that impact. Finally, when I launch a new product I can configure the supply chain and manage local costs and transfer prices to provide the optimum profit for the organisation as a whole.

We are now aware of the wider perspective and what we as strategic supply chain and business managers need to understand to generate the best contribution to our business overall. The next section will outline a way in which we can gain a voice at the highest decision-making levels within the organisation.

Understand the Market, Control the Environment

Many aspects of the environment, both local and global, will ultimately impact on the supply chain. It would be inappropriate to suggest that the supply chain's function could control all of them. Within its functional remit are the ability to control some aspects, and the need to respond effectively and efficiently to changes in others. Strategic supply chain managers must at the same time seek to acquire understanding of the environment and gain advantage from that understanding. They must be constantly vigilant for signs that the environment is changing so that they might evaluate options for change, and must also make considered recommendations about future supply chain configurations.

With reference to Figures 12.8 and 12.9, the supply chain manager will optimise the operational activities that define the supply chain to wholesalers, pharmacies and patients in the knowledge that there exist supply contracts, partnerships, competing products, other importers of the company's own product, a sales force, as well as external pricing and reimbursement schemes and buyer formularies whose parameters define that framework.

As a strategist, the supply chain manager will be continually posing questions that both accept and challenge the current situation, such as:

- How can I operate within this framework more effectively (customer service) and efficiently (cost)?

- How can I reduce my dependency on my current contracted relationships with wholesalers to gain greater influence over the pharmacist and the patient?

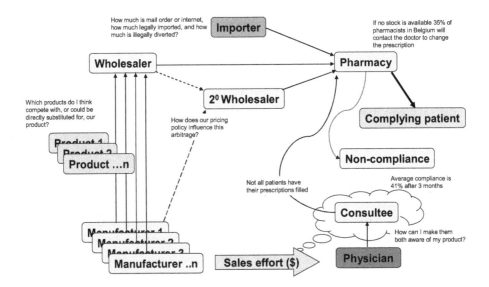

Figure 12.8   Understand the market

- How can I influence my regional colleagues to exercise greater control over their local supply operation, thereby limiting the amount of low-price product available to importers or secondary wholesalers?

- How do I convince my business colleagues that the sales force's discretion over discounting (while it may help them achieve their quarterly and annual bonuses) creates product diversion, organisational tension and forecasting confusion while simultaneously destroying shareholder value? What evidence do I need to gather, and how do I construct the argument?

- What contractual, service or pricing arrangements with my supply chain partners are needed to gain a substantial and long-term advantage over my competitors? What evidence is there of their effectiveness?

- How do we reconfigure our supply chain frameworks to gain substantial and sustainable advantage over our supply chain partners and competitors?

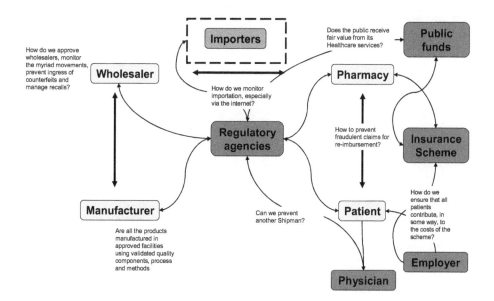

Figure 12.9   Control the environment

Questions like these – and their responses – define the future not only of the supply chain but also of the enterprise as a whole. The final chapter will address more of them.

13

The Future of Healthcare

Predictions of the future that later turn out to be incorrect are often used as points of ridicule by future presenters, so there is little point here in attempting to forecast the outcome of developments in the industry over the coming years. Instead we will discuss the ways in which the healthcare environment, with its many conflicting perspectives and agendas, can be more easily understood – hopefully enabling the process and outcomes to be managed more advantageously.

It is the role of every party within the supply chain to ensure that changes occur so that their own goals are achieved more efficiently. They will work to their own agendas: patients want to influence the politicians and local healthcare providers to improve their services; doctors want better conditions in which to operate, and improved technologies with which to work; regulatory bodies wish to make available new or improved products for practitioners to use to the benefit of their patients, while simultaneously controlling the costs of so doing. Similarly the manufacturers, wholesalers and retail or hospital pharmacies that order, make, move and use the products individually wish to maximise their positions in operating their businesses. Who then has the responsibility of managing the overall change and development of the sector, leading to improvements for patients?

Expressed in this way the answer is clear – it is the role of governments to provide healthcare services to their citizens and to ensure continuous improvement in the costs and nature of those services. As discussed earlier in the book, this is achieved by establishing a market and regulatory framework within which independent organisations operate to provide their services. For these operators to be able to provide sustainable services they must be able to generate adequate rewards for their shareholders.

The operational activities within this framework create a dynamic system within which many different forces and agendas are at play concurrently. This creates inherent tensions in the system. An example could be the desire for the development of new technologies and products versus the drive to control and reduce costs. Similarly the interests of the independent wholesaler in maximising profits for its business are diametrically opposed to the interests of their suppliers and customers, who seek to increase prices paid by customers. Also authorities wish to make medicines safely and more widely available to patients through retail outlets other than licensed pharmacies. This is clearly at odds with the commercial interests of independent retail pharmacists, who will seek to maintain their role. This role involves pharmaceutical care of patients, both with prescribed medicines and those available for self-medication, whether that role involves advising a parent in a retail pharmacy on how to treat a child with a bad throat or a physician in a hospital intensive care unit regarding the best combination of drugs for a critically ill patient. Medicines are a fundamental pillar of modern healthcare, yet they are no ordinary commodity. They can provide enormous benefit if treated correctly, and enormous harm if used or administered incorrectly. The need to ensure that patients have access to medicines as prescribed is paramount for manufacturing companies and is aligned with the professional and commercial intentions of every other party.

How the System Operates

As we saw in Chapter 5 the model of healthcare provision is complex and involves four main parties: the consumer, the supplier, the payer and the regulator. Each has their own role, yet only the consumer or patient has a fixed position. Suppliers will change as products and services change. The payer and regulator, as public funding provision varies with the political climate, will slowly increase the barriers and controls in the name of patient safety and in support of their public funding agenda.

Figure 13.1 shows that there are only a few issues that characterise an event or change within any system. Equilibrium will exist when there is a balance between normal market forces and a fair return for contribution. An effect or alteration in that equilibrium may be brought about by another action or change that is seen to be the direct cause. That action may or may not be predictable in time, in scale of impact, and it may result in some sudden, dramatic change brought about by a whole variety of previously dormant factors impacting at the same time.

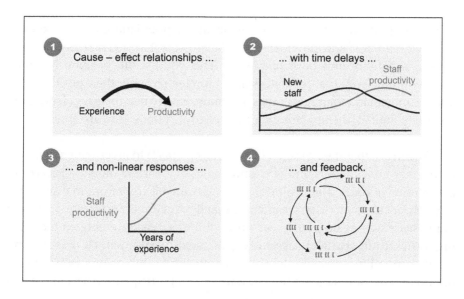

Figure 13.1   The characteristics of the real world make predictions difficult

There are some analogies in the physical sciences upon which we may draw to help us illustrate this. Firstly, Newton's First Law of Motion states that a body will remain at rest or continue to move at a constant velocity unless acted upon by a force. Secondly, Le Chatelier's principle of dynamic equilibrium forces describes the way in which a system which is currently at equilibrium or in balance will tend to react if a change in that position is imposed. If the system is acted upon in any way then the dynamic equilibrium position will change in such a way as to oppose this action. Can these principles be applied to our system which is composed of non-scientific, subjective and competing behaviours? Why not? At least by reference to where they demonstrate similar behaviours we can use them to enhance our understanding and then better predict outcomes.

By way of illustration we saw in Chapter 9 that a number of states in the USA were taking action to recover medical insurance costs from pharmaceutical companies who had been promoting the use of their medicines for conditions that were not approved. Everything was fine and dandy until such infringements were identified. This action, in this case legal action, is the effect of blatant promotion in the face of regulations at a time when state-funded insurance schemes are being forced to find a rapidly increasing level of cash to support healthcare provision to an ageing population. The relationship between regulator and provider could have been characterised as stable (in a state of equilibrium) until this event. This equilibrium position has now changed in the way that regulators are enforcing strongly their position. It is easy to understand their reaction as they must ensure that their regulations are not easily flouted, thereby bringing their control systems into disrepute.

We can see that it takes some time (delayed effect) to investigate where the money has gone, understand why and gather evidence to mount a successful prosecution in court. The first fines were high and clearly meant to discourage further transgressions. Can we imagine that if regulations are blatantly ignored in the same way again in the near future that the penalty will be in the same proportion to the costs? I suspect not: the next penalty will be massive and punitive (non-linear response) to demonstrate the regulators' authority and the importance of compliance to the standards by all participants. An example will be made.

If this behaviour were to continue – and considered alongside other transgressions such as the Seroxat clinical trial data admissions or continued and unreasonable delays in implementing secure supply chain management, as proposed by the Prescription Drugs Medication Act (PDMA) – that could be seen as a failure to co-operate. Taken up in that way by the popular media, whipped into some public outcry at an election time, then we could well envisage a dramatic reshaping of the entire regulatory system in the USA (feedback).

The system is complex and the law of unintended consequences will be applied if the relationships between supply chain partners, stakeholders and customers are not fully understood. How can we possibly understand the complexity and take into account every interaction throughout the network? Again, as we have discussed in previous chapters, it would be advisable to spend time and effort in modelling various relationships, testing their nature against experience and examining the impact of an alteration in each parameter, rather than to be left at the mercy of 'events'. How likely could any particular change occur in reality, and what would be the one change that would produce the most significant impacts?

Possible Futures

As the value of our parameters change and therefore alter the equilibrium position between the relationships, so there can be a range of possible outcomes. At its simplest there could be two possible extreme outcomes, but let us consider a few examples by way of illustration.

In co-payment there is either the opportunity for all costs incurred to be recovered through insurance schemes, or complete payment for delivered services at the point of use is expected from the consumer or patient. In either case the patient pays – directly for services received or indirectly through insurance premiums or tax contributions. There is an equilibrium position established and it tends to remain settled for long periods.

Suppose for a moment that a government or private insurance company suddenly proposed an increase in their premiums of over 100 per cent. Such an action could be in response to, and the effect of, the rising costs of new treatments and the expectation of an ageing, needy population in the near future. Consider the possible responses from the patients and consumers. How would they react? What new equilibrium position could be established after what period of disruption? What impact would this have on the established services and infrastructure required to deliver it? Everyone will have their own ideas, and contributors in an open brainstorming environment with knowledge of or ideas in the sector could identify many possible outcomes and finally reach a consensus on the most likely scenario.

In another example we could consider the need to deliver highly specialised care services to a wide range of patients across a broad geographic area. We could either have a few concentrated specialist clinics as centres of excellence, or we could spread the expertise more thinly to give faster access to centres of mediocrity. I use these emotive terms deliberately to stretch the imagination and provoke a response. Only when we explore the extremes of the ideas can we recognise the new equilibrium position towards which the probable outcomes will gravitate. This is, of course, a simulation. It is not reality and it is an opportunity to develop 'thought experiments'.

Now, how many such issues can we identify? Clinical diagnosis vs. personal diagnosis; patient well informed vs. largely ill-informed; face-to-face consultation by doctors vs. tele-diagnosis; obesity rising relentlessly vs.

exercise and healthy eating becoming the norm. The list is endless so we need a systematic methodology to tackle the problem.

A Systematic Approach to Understand the Likely Futures

In order to pick our way through this forecasting process we need firstly to identify the key questions currently presenting the biggest risks or threats to organisations from tensions within the system.

Secondly, we need to accumulate the range of issues, drivers and uncertainties that appear to impact on the decisions that could conceivably be made. These decisions could be anything that will affect the strategic direction of the organisation: reshaping entire research and development (R&D) departments into independent centres of excellence; selling the consumer healthcare division of the business to provide funds for R&D; changing the sales force focus from detailing doctors to account management with major healthcare providers; outsourcing all secondary manufacturing activities; acquiring smaller generic houses to leverage economies of scale. There are many examples of such major decisions taken by organisations every year.

Thirdly, it is necessary to explore the issues in a wide-ranging brainstorming forum bringing together a host of knowledgeable and erudite individuals. A number of such forums could act like focus groups to explore the whole range of opinions within the stakeholder community (see panel opposite). The groups will be empowered to recommend changes to processes and push the boundaries of accepted practices. Here, in a 'no risk' environment, we are encouraged to think the unthinkable!

Having opened out the range of ideas and possible outcomes, only then do we begin to bring a sense of realism to the debate and consider where, along the continuum for each alternative, is the most likely scenario that would represent the future equilibrium position within the timescale of our interest. The key point at this stage of the forecasting process is to identify which parameters are the most sensitive, that is with only a small change in value of the causal factor a major effect or impact will result.

This approach has helped a variety of organisations direct their strategies quite fundamentally, and they can then be managed in a more proactive way to 'be the change they wish to see in the world' (Mahatma Gandhi).

A TYPICAL BRAINSTORMING FORUM

Representatives from 17 pharmaceutical and healthcare organisations attended an event on 18 May 2004, hosted by PA Consulting Group in London, to consider the short-term future of the supply chain in Europe. Figure 13.2 illustrates the concerns, risks and issues identified.

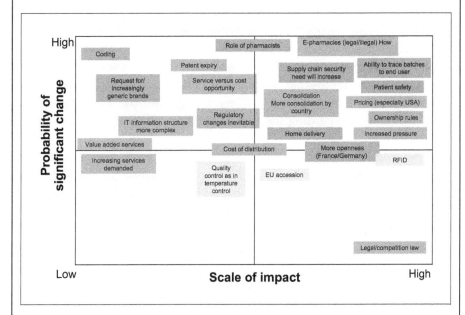

Figure 13.2   Priorities for risk and concern were identified

The security of the supply chain to the patient was considered by all attendees to be paramount, whether through the existing supply chain, via the Internet, mail order or indeed by direct delivery to the patient at home. The current regulatory framework in Europe, however, militates against supply chain control by manufacturers as the legal framework allows the repacking of product by licensed wholesalers and intermediaries, thus negating the effect of tamper evidence, unique coding as mass serialisation or anti-counterfeiting measures such as holograms or similar covert features.

Despite the frustrations of the group the consensus was that any change to improve the situation from the security perspective is unlikely as they considered a change in European competition law to be highly improbable, and the impact of any pan-European coding system adopted by the industry unilaterally to have a very low impact on the situation.

This systematic approach necessarily collects ideas and thoughts from stakeholders who have knowledge of and direct interest in the future. Within a group of stakeholders, or between different groups of stakeholders, there will inevitably be differences of opinion. We have here an inexact, subjective approach. It is very different from our considerations of science, technology and process validation that are necessary to the development of products and services used to support patients within the healthcare sector. We are, of course, not dealing with science; we are dealing with art, the art of the possible – politics. Here I mean both small-scale political manoeuvring between supply chain partners and large-scale politics involving local, regional, national and international governments. This is where our quote from Machiavelli's *The Prince* in Chapter 2 regarding the implementation of change applies directly and completely:

> *There is nothing so difficult to achieve, nor uncertain in its outcome than to initiate a new order of things, for there will be only lukewarm support from those who might profit, yet active resistance from those who may lose.*

Possible Futures for the Supply and Distribution of Healthcare Products

Given this complexity, there is still the need and drive to continue to improve the system and framework that governs healthcare provision as a whole, and also for each organisation operating within that system to improve its own position. This position will be determined by shareholders and investors and will invariably mean, for a publicly traded company, that it must endeavour to increase the present value of its future cash flow. Given the limited pot of cash available from either governmental sources or individuals via insurance schemes, this will mean that organisations will jockey for new products and services and an increasing share of the existing market (cash available). The inevitability of a significant shift in the equilibrium currently enjoyed by supply chain partners becomes evident when we consider some of the factors that are driving change across the sector:

- continued reduction in R&D productivity;

- ever-increasing costs of compliance with more and more regulations designed to protect both patients and public finances;

- pressure on cost of reimbursed products leading to demands for and protection of parallel trade and legal diversion;

- the demand for more patient-centred medicine – taking the care to the patient rather than a self-funded visit to a clinic, doctor or hospital;

- the need for patients to make increased contributions towards the cost of their treatment, which increases the desire for cheaper, generic medicines, the number of OTC licenses granted and the pressure to make products available more widely in retail outlets;

- consolidation of industry players through merger and acquisition;

- expiry of patent-protected life and the inevitable growth in generic and bio-equivalent products at a fraction of the original price;

- continuous media pressure to expose inappropriate 'fat-cat' management behaviours and decisions that adversely impact on the public perception of the industry;

- location and availability of skilled workforce becoming more limited;

- increasing capability of technology to enable greater control of the distribution of products from manufacturer to patient.

This looks like a pretty gloomy picture, leading to some dire predictions:

> *When all the different threats to the pharmaceutical industry are taken into account, the conditions are building for a 'perfect storm' which will change the industry so dramatically that it will no longer exist in its current form.*[1]

---

1 The Gingrich Group, a 21st Century Pharmaceutical Industry < http://www.gingrichgroup. com/home>.

Possible Futures for Supply Chain Control

As discussed throughout this book, reasserting greater control over the supply of products into the market will yield significant benefits. At the time of writing there is a major debate on how technology can enable this. Radio Frequency Identification (RFID) tags used as a carrier of unique, mass serialised codes are seen as potentially making a major contribution here. Current technology is seen as expensive and unproven in the environments in which it needs to operate. Figure 13.3 identifies possibilities that could exist, depending on the way technology changes with future developments.

The starting position is that the coding technology is emerging, scarce and cost prohibitive. What if 2D barcodes, significantly cheaper alternative code carriers, become more widely available? If the reading equipment becomes as common as the current linear barcode equipment in retail outlets, warehouses and so on then we do have a possible solution to controlling product distribution all the way to the patient. It may not be as secure, arguably, as RFID technology or enable the cost efficiencies that are dreamed of within wholesale operations, but it does go part way.

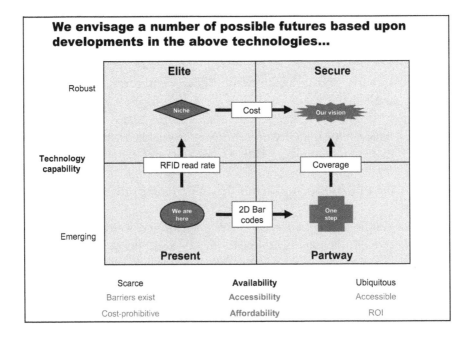

Figure 13.3   Possible futures based on developments in technologies

What if the technology associated with RFID becomes more robust, while the costs cannot be reduced to levels affordable for the majority of items to be distributed? Then we could see its use restricted to high-value items where the business case is acceptable or where the risks of losing control are too high. Finally, what if the technology becomes affordable, widely available and the security and control of the procedures surrounding its deployment enable implementation? We could envisage a different world altogether.

Here the focus has been on what are considered the two most sensitive parameters within this particular system, cost and technical capability, and we created four possible distinct environments. In order to ensure that the actual future is the environment in which our business operations will be most effective, we must be proactive and intervene to drive progress along the desired path. This requires a vision in order to drive the industry forwards along that chosen route (see Chapter 2).

Legislation and attempts to assert authority are not enough. This is evidenced by the inability to implement the provisions of the Prescription Drugs Medication Act in the USA. Despite the consultations, exhortations and protestations of the Food and Drug Administration (FDA) and the State Boards of Pharmacy the industry is no further forward. The legislation has only managed to highlight the contrasting positions that pharmacists, wholesalers and manufacturers take up, while simultaneously reconfirming their vows to support patient safety through a secure supply chain.

The USA is not alone in attempting to assert authority; in Belgium, Italy and Greece the authorities have mandated their own versions of mass serialisation to control and manage reimbursement fraud. In spite of driving increased costs in the manufacturer of the products supplied, the actual control that can be exercised is negligible and perhaps embarrassingly small. But this is not stopping Turkey, Spain and France moving ahead with their locally controlled versions of the same mechanism. In response the research-based manufacturers' association, the European Federation of Pharmaceutical Industries and Associations (EFPIA), the European Generics Association (EGA), wholesalers (GIRP), patient groups and the Pharmaceutical Group of the European Union (PGEU) are all retreating rapidly into their own corners and proposing alternative approaches to the problem.

My prediction is that the supply chain environment is so fragmented that nothing will happen to secure it unless a galvanising compelling event occurs. This event could be either a terrorist attack on the western democratic countries through wide-scale contamination of the healthcare supply chain or, more palatably, the development of a new service or technology that is able to provide some degree of measurable benefit to all parties.

I can predict that this will happen by looking at the development of point of sale authentication of credit cards in retail outlets. In the 1990s incidents of fraudulent transactions involving cheques and credit cards at retail outlets was becoming unacceptable. Not only was it possible for the odd rogue to pass a worthless cheque and make away with the goods, but organised criminal elements were able to exploit the weaknesses to great effect. Now, readers, chip and PIN credit cards and the necessary high-speed telecommunications are available everywhere. How did this come about? Banks, insurance companies, retailers and customers all had something to gain from the elimination of fraud; it was tangible and quantifiable. By imposing the technology on retailers and customers, the banks were able to reduce fraud significantly. By having the technology available, retailers were able to attract more customers to spend more, and thereby offset the charges for the technology. Customers benefited from having more convenient ways to pay for their goods, knowing that their transactions were secure.

Possible Futures for the Industry Sector

The supply is important, yet it is only one aspect of the healthcare environment. We can see how difficult it is to understand how the future might evolve for the sector as a whole, yet it is the role and duty of the governing authorities to ensure it develops for the benefit of its (voting) citizens. Here I identify possible futures that were developed by a group of my colleagues within PA Consulting in their Global Technology Group. Using the processes described in Figure 13.4 the team considered the myriad of drivers for change and key uncertainties within the sector, and developed four different visions or possible futures: Panacea World, Vanity World, Health-seeker World and www.health World. I shall describe them in turn.

PANACEA WORLD

This is a world in which there will be a medicinal cure for every illness. There would be an expectation in the mind of every citizen – no matter where in the world they lived, how rich or poor they were, how well educated or informed

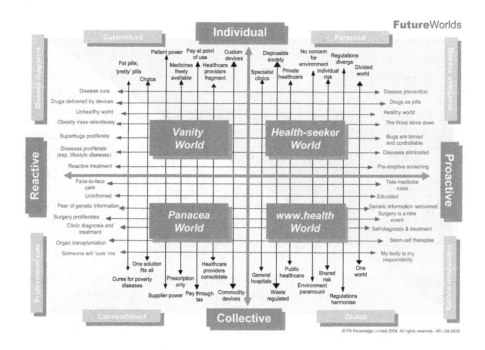

Figure 13.4   Possible future states in the healthcare industry

Reprinted with kind permission of PA Consulting Group.

or whatever lifestyle they pursued, a cure would be available, prescribed and delivered unto them. There would be no choice about the type of service provided, and it would be funded through the imposition of state taxation at the level necessary to cover the cost.

VANITY WORLD

Here we have a world inhabited by intelligent, well-informed individuals who believe it is their right to choose whatever treatments they wish to support their healthcare needs. They are prepared to pay whatever is necessary; they can afford it and they expect an appropriate treatment will be available for them to purchase as they need it.

Should they wish to stuff themselves with unhealthy food and drink, sleep as little as possible, bathe under strong sunlight for days on end while 'exercising' via a sedentary, battery-operated device attached to their bed, they will do so as they have the right to abuse their own bodies, and they believe they have the right to have others standing in line ready to support them when they fall.

HEALTH-SEEKER WORLD

Here we have a divided world. There will be those who have no power, education or means to support themselves and their needs; and those who feel that they can isolate themselves within their space, excluding others and sharing only with those who share the same means, education or attitudes. In this case the technology will be developed to diagnose and identify problems, and cures or treatments will be made available for the diseases that affect this group.

In this world those who are able will take responsibility for their own welfare, act responsibly in this respect, yet care little about healthcare provision for the underprivileged, the less able or the poor and needy.

WWW.HEALTH WORLD

In this final possible future world we have inhabitants who have a sense of responsibility for themselves and for others. They care about their health and their environment and are sufficiently educated and wealthy to use every technology available to improve both.

There would be no moralistic imposition on the use of stem-cells, information technology or genetic coding. These would be considered tools that can be made available to cure and support all citizens, and should therefore be freely available and their use safeguarded.

Conclusion

Despite my very best endeavours, I have come to no firm conclusion as to the way the future will develop. I recognise and accept that our current world is imperfect, incomplete and that it offers fantastic opportunities for everyone to make an impact on their own health through their lifestyle, and on the welfare of others through their education, invention and enterprise.

Nothing will move forward without a sense of vision or purpose. With this sense of purpose the means to deliver will be found. This may mean the development of new technology, new application of existing technology, the creation of a regulatory framework that encourages invention and enterprise or just money and resources.

I wish to foresee a world in which pioneers such as Edward Jenner are encouraged to experiment and there are volunteers who are happy to participate under careful supervision; a world where the naivety of well-meaning practitioners such as Alexander Fleming, in failing to patent penicillin, is not exploited but applauded.

I hope to see that the future world will continue to be inhabited by brilliant minds like Bill Gates, who can create so much and gain in similar proportion, who will then seek ways in which they can benefit those less fortunate and less able to contribute.

Within the supply chain arena I fear that the conflicts between partners will continue as long as parochial interests prevent each party from remembering why they joined such an environment – to improve the availability of products and service to support people who have a disease or other disability. This battle is big enough.

This hankering after a Utopia that never existed, nor is likely to exist, was expressed by Thomas, Lord Macaulay in his *Lay of Ancient Rome – Horatius*:

> *As we wax hot in faction, in battle we wax cold:*
> *Wherefore men fight not as they fought in the brave days of old.*

Let us each determine our own vision of the future and make every effort to manage the technology, the processes, the regulatory environment and human resources needed to deliver it.

Glossary of Terms

Acute   Severe short-term impact of a disease or symptoms.

Antisepsis   The use of products that prevent the growth of micro-
                         organisms which cause disease.

API   Active pharmaceutical ingredient.

Arthrotomy   A surgical operation on the interior of a skeletal joint,
                         often facilitated by the use of an arthroscope.

BCG   A vaccination shown to give 70–80 per cent protection
                         against tuberculosis (TB). It is given in a single dose
                         following a negative Mantoux skin test to assess an
                         individual's suitability for the vaccine.

Bioavailability   The proportion of a drug that reaches the body's
                         circulation system and is ready at the site of action.

Biopharmaceutical   A biological macromolecule, cell component or blood
                         product that is prepared for medical use.

Carbolic   Pertaining to carbolic acid (phenol) used as a
                         disinfectant.

CAT scanner   Computerized axial tomography – a scanner that takes
                         images of slices through the body.

Chronic   An illness persisting for a long term or recurring
                         constantly.

Deontology   The study of duty and obligation, morals and ethics.

Diagnostics   A tool, product or investigative process used to identify
                               the presence of an illness or specific medical condition.

Diversion   The unauthorised and unwarranted movement of
                               products between these channels initiated by supply
                               chain participants.

Fluoridation   The addition of fluoride minerals to a public water
                               supply with the purpose of improving the health of
                               consumers, who may or may not consent to this form of
                               mass medication.

Generic products   Goods produced and distributed without patent
                               protection at generally lower prices than branded
                               products.

Intellectual property   Intangible property that is the result of creativity
                               and protected by patents, copyrights and trademark
                               legislation.

Laminectomy   A surgical operation to remove one or more discs from
                               the back to relieve pressure on nerves or gain access to
                               the spinal cord.

Magnetic resonance   MRI, or nuclear magnetic resonance imaging (NMRI), is
imaging (MRI)   primarily a medical imaging technique most commonly
                               used in radiology to visualize the structure and
                               function of the body.

Mass serialisation   Individually coding each separate unit of sale within a
                               given stock-keeping unit using different technologies
                               (for example, barcoding).

Medical devices   Particular tools used to aid diagnosis of a specific
                               medical condition or therapeutic problem.

Meniscectomy	The surgical removal of a meniscus – a crescent-shaped film of cartilage within a skeletal joint, especially the knee.
MHRA	The Medicines and Healthcare products Regulatory Agency – the UK government agency responsible for ensuring that medicines and medical devices work and are acceptably safe.
Pandemic	The occurrence of an infectious disease that spreads across a wide geographic region.
Parallel trade	The importation of a non-counterfeit product from another country without the permission of the intellectual property owner.
Pharmaceutical	A product manufactured or prepared specifically for medical use.
Radiography	The taking and study of X-rays in medical examinations.
Technology	The branch of knowledge that deals with engineering and the practical application of science.
Tropin	A hormone secreted by an endocrine gland, the presence of which can indicate damage to the heart muscle.
Vaccination	An antigenic agent (vaccine) prepared to provide immunity against disease.
Vision	The articulation of a future state that facilitates debate and consensus among the stakeholders and enables the formulation and implementation of plans to create that desired position.
WACC	Weighted average cost of capital – the minimum return a company must earn on an existing asset base to satisfy its creditors, owners,and other providers of capital.

Index

References to illustrations are in **bold**